UNDER THE HAMMER

UNDER THE HAMMER

PROPERTY IN IRELAND —
A HISTORY OF THE IRISH AUCTIONEERS
& VALUERS INSTITUTE, 1922-97

Con Power

Oak Tree Press
Dublin
in association with
The Irish Auctioneers & Valuers Institute

Oak Tree Press
Merrion Building
Lower Merrion Street
Dublin 2, Ireland.

A catalogue record of this book is available from the
British Library.

ISBN 1-86076-043-0

Printed in Ireland by ColourBooks, Ltd.

CONTENTS

Foreword vii

Acknowledgements ix

CHAPTER 1
New Beginnings — The Twenties 1

CHAPTER 2
Going, Going, Gone — The Thirties 29

CHAPTER 3
War And Peace — The Forties 55

CHAPTER 4
Back To The Future — The Fifties 79

CHAPTER 5
Modern Times — The Sixties 97

CHAPTER 6
Brave New World — The Seventies 123

CHAPTER 7
Highs And Lows — The Eighties 161

CHAPTER 8
Fin de Siècle — The Nineties 193

CHAPTER 9
Towards The Millennium 223

Bibliography 235
List of IAVI Presidents 239
About the Author 241
Index 243

FOREWORD

The year 1922 saw the foundation of the Irish state. That year was also a historic one for Irish property, as it was in 1922 that the Irish Auctioneers' and Estate Agents' Association, subsequently to be renamed Irish Auctioneers and Valuers Institute, came into formal existence.

The IAVI has played a key role, throughout its 75-year history, in shaping legislation which affects the property profession and the property-dealing public in Ireland, and in advancing the cause of education for property professionals. The Institute has been to the fore in representing Ireland's property sector abroad, evidenced by the IAVI's co-hosting with FIABCI-Ireland the Bank of Ireland sponsored 1997 World Congress of the International Real Estate Federation (FIABCI) in Dublin in May 1997, the second occasion for Ireland and the Institute to be so honoured.

In approaching our 75th Diamond Jubilee celebrations in 1997, the FIABCI World Congress was always likely to hold centre-stage, being the most important property event to take place in Ireland in the 1990s. It is pleasing, however, that this landmark year in the Institute's history should be so fittingly marked by the publication of this excellent account of IAVI successes, excesses, foibles and occasional failures, over the past 75 years.

Con Power, one of Ireland's most renowned property journalists, has accomplished most successfully the gargantuan task of assembling a wealth of relevant material into a cogent, enjoyable and very readable history which will be of immense interest to all those engaged in, or wishing to engage in, the Irish property arena.

Cormac J. Meehan
IAVI President, 1996-1997

Paul McDowell
IAVI President, 1997-1998

ACKNOWLEDGEMENTS

Writing is a solitary task, particularly when the work is uninterrupted by the daily demands and disturbances of journalistic deadlines. The burden in this instance was eased/exacerbated by my simultaneous efforts to re-invent myself and my career from the ashes of *The Irish Press*. Nothing concentrates the mind quite like a hanging. . . .

As a property journalist, I have always had a somewhat fraught relationship with auctioneers — frustrated when rival newspapers were favoured before mine and elated when rewarded by an exclusive story, constantly running the gauntlet between the estate agent's desire to promote their property and my primary obligation to the consumer/reader. I would, however, like to avail of this opportunity to publicly record my sincere thanks for the genuine concern and generosity towards my plight in auctioneering circles following the closure of my newspaper group. I was quite simply unprepared for the groundswell of goodwill — in some instances in what I would previously have imagined to be the unlikeliest of places/agencies. It has been an altogether re-affirmative experience.

Regarding this book, there are a number of individuals to whom I would like to express my particular gratitude: thanks to Cliodhna O'Donoghue, *Irish Independent* Property Editor for mentioning the IAVI project to me in the first place (and not writing the book herself!); to IAVI chief executive, Alan Cooke for rewarding me with the commission to commemorate the 75th anniversary of the Institute; to Patrick Leahy, for his help with residential price details; and, last, but by no means least, to my long-suffering family — Arlene, Karina (even though she escaped to Paris), David and Alan.

By a sad quirk of fate, my mother passed away on the very day I submitted the final draft of this book. Her life exactly spanned the IAVI years. May she and my father rest in peace. I dedicate this publication to them both, with great love and gratitude.

C.P., January 1997.

CHAPTER ONE

NEW BEGINNINGS — THE TWENTIES

*"Got up wrong side of the bed. Must begin again those Sandow's
exercises. On the hands down. Blotchy brown brick houses.
Number eight still unlet. Why is that? Valuation is only twenty
eight. Towers, Battersby, North, MacArthur: Parlour windows
plastered with bills."* — James Joyce, *Ulysses.*

The War of Independence in Ireland came to a close with the
signing of the Anglo-Irish Treaty in January 1922. Michael Collins took formal control of Dublin Castle, ending a millennium of
colonial domination, while Leinster House was purchased from the
Royal Dublin Society to accommodate the new Saorstát Éireann parliament of the fledgling Irish Free State. The political turmoil took a
heavy toll on the building fabric of the capital city. Architect James
Gandon's two riverside glories were destroyed in anger during these
violent times: in 1921, the Custom House was gutted by fire, while
the Four Courts was occupied the following year by anti-Treaty
forces and bombarded by Government troops using borrowed British army field guns. The old order was fading away, but an internec-
ine Civil War had to be endured before the new regime could fully
assert itself. Turbulence and hostilities continued through 1923. By
the end of the year, however, the new "status quo" was in the ascen-
dant and the country was settling uneasily into its new identity as an
independent state.

The emerging Irish Free State shared in the uncertainty that prevailed throughout Europe and beyond in the wake of the Great War.
Political tensions confronting the new regime were compounded by
economic depression at home and abroad. There was widespread
criticism that the first Irish Government was "honeycombed with
jobbery and corruption," while allegations were rife that "thousands
of Irish civil servants had been dismissed and their places filled with

. . . friends and relatives". The destruction/dislocation caused by the conflict spawned a range of fresh social and economic problems — falling prices, high rates of interest, unemployment, emigration and poverty. Irish farming compared favourably with England and elsewhere in many respects, but a prolonged decline in agricultural prices was aggravated by poor domestic harvests — ensuring a traumatic birth for the new State even without the attendant political upheaval.

Everything is relative, of course. A twenty-minute journey by horse-drawn cab through the city of Dublin cost a shilling in those pre-inflationary days, while the first mile in a new-fangled taxi cab involved an outlay of the same princely sum. Only the more affluent members of society could afford to splash out £145 for a four-bedroom Morris Oxford Saloon. A set of head phones, 10 feet of aerial wire, earthclip, lead and insulators, sold at £1. House values were a fraction of today's levels too. A double-fronted cottage (semi-detached, eight rooms, large garden, side entrance, let to yearly tenant, near links) in Kingstown was on the market at £450 in January 1920. A terrace of five houses in Rathmines was put up for sale the same year at £2,400. Even at the very top of the market, prices appear bargain basement by today's standards: in fashionable Monkstown, £4,000 would have secured a "handsome well-built residence; four reception; fine billiard room in panelled walnut and bathrooms; seven bedrooms" — all on one acre. Values remained much the same throughout the decade. A seven-roomed house (hot bath, garden, garage, electric light) was available in Clontarf for £950 in 1929. Prices outside the capital were even lower: in Bray, the price tag on a seven-room house (bath, electric light and gas) was £525. Wages, of course, were proportionately less: a housekeeper earned £30 a year and residential prices in the best locations were beyond the reach of most workers then as now.

The Free State Census of 1926 records a 5 per cent decrease in the population of the 26 counties to 3,139,668 (4,390,219 all-Ireland) compared with fifteen years earlier. The political changes in the last intercensal period — in particular, the withdrawal of British forces and the deaths of Irish soldiers in World War II — were now becoming evident. In Dublin, as in other cities, the female population exceeded the male, while in the country districts and small towns, there was a male excess. A feature highlighted by the census was a consistent movement of population out of the countryside to the towns, where just over a million people now lived. The population of Dublin City stood at 316,471 in 1926 compared to 245,826 on the eve of the Great Famine in 1841 and less than Dr Johnson's London. The total number living in Dublin and the four adjoining urban districts at the latest census date was recorded at 419,156 — Rathmines/Rathgar 40,367; Pembroke 3,395; Blackrock 9,931; and Kingstown 18,992. Cork had a population of 78,468, Limerick 39,690, Waterford 26,646 and Galway 14,223.

The Dublin Artisan Dwelling Company had left Dublin with "a heritage of singularly fine design and detailing" dating from its inception in 1876. But the local authorities did not finally assume responsibility for providing housing until towards the turn of the century, with the first Dublin scheme designed by city architect D. Freeman constructed at Benburb Street in 1887. The expansion of the Irish housing industry was a top priority after 1921, with the Provisional Government making £1 million available for urban housing schemes. The Housing (Building Facilities) Act 1924 and the Housing Act 1925 enabled the government and the local authorities to make grants to private individuals or groups wishing to erect new dwellings or to reconstruct dwellings in town areas. The Dublin Reconstruction (Emergency Provisions) Act 1924 enabled the Corporation to develop derelict sites, while the first house improvement grants were introduced in 1924. The influence of the new "garden city" approach to house design coincided with the birth of the new State. The layout for Marino was developed in 1922 by city architect Horace T. O'Rourke together with F. G. Hicks in accordance with the new concept. Other schemes followed off Clonliffe Road, Crumlin, Drumcondra, Donnybrook, Bath Avenue and elsewhere. But little headway was made in resolving the abiding problem of overcrowding and decaying tenements housing large sections of the working class. With the national question preoccupying politics in the early 1920s, accommodation problems could easily take a back seat.

Notwithstanding the exodus into the cities, Ireland remained a predominantly agricultural nation, with the Free State dependent almost entirely on the production of livestock and livestock products. Almost nine-tenths of Irish trade was with Britain and there was an established movement of capital and labour across the Channel. Total Irish exports amounted to £43 million in 1925 — of which £32 million represented the value of agricultural products of one kind or another. The Agricultural Credit Corporation was established by the State in 1927 as a statutory corporation to provide credit for persons engaged in agriculture and businesses ancillary to agriculture.

Whatever the plight of the nation's poor, change was the order of the day for the business community. On September 28, 1921, 40 auctioneers representing leading firms from all over Ireland met at a historic gathering at the Gresham Hotel in Dublin (with apologies for unavoidable absence received from 27 more who were unable to attend). Issues of major importance to the profession were debated, notably the ease with which unqualified persons could obtain an auctioneer's licence by merely paying a fee to the Inland Revenue. It was unanimously decided that the formation of an association was a necessity in order to deal with such matters with any degree of effectiveness. The Auctioneers' & Estate Agents' Association of Ireland was accordingly formed with the following officers:

- President Mr George H. Lennon

- Vice-President Mr Patrick Leonard

- Committee: Messrs George B. Garvey (Garvey & Good); James Ganly (Ganly Sons & Co.); George W. Greene (P O'Connor & Son); Gavin Low (Gavin Low Ltd.); P. MacArthur (MacArthur & Co.); James S. McMahon (Thomas Dockrell Ltd.); S. W. Mackie (Joyce Mackie & Co.); T. F. Toole, Edenderry; W. H. Wilkinson (R&J Wilkinson).

The first secretary of the Association was Frank Warner and its bankers were the Bank of Ireland. Auditors were N. Peterson & Son of Foster Place, Dublin. One of the earliest documents of the new body states:

> For a number of years, leading men in the Auctioneering & Estate Agency profession have felt the want of a thoroughly representative Association for Ireland which would bind them together for mutual assistance, support and protection, keep up the proper tone of the membership, and by

examination, lectures, &c., help to maintain the body in its highest interests. A very influential Association has existed for years in Great Britain, but a purely Irish Association was greatly needed to further the best interests of its members and safeguard their rights. Again, in consequence of grave difficulties having arisen in connection with the holding of auctions, and in some cases of unlawful means having been adopted to prevent Auctioneers from conducting Sales; also in consequence of certain irregularities being prevalent amongst a certain class of persons holding Auctioneers' licences. Accordingly, steps were taken to form such an Association on similar lines to the organisation on the other side of the Channel.

Various attempts had indeed been made on earlier occasions to form such a body, but these had all proven unsuccessful. The Irish Auctioneers' & Estate Agents' Association was incorporated on May 24, 1922 under the Companies Acts 1908 to 1917 by solicitor Frank Fottrell (no explanation has been ascertained for the Association's name change) and the certificate of registration was in the possession of the Association's secretary on December 22, 1922. The stated aim of the Association was to obtain a charter like other professional bodies as soon as membership levels justified the application. The new association was the first and only Irish body of its kind representing the auctioneering profession. All licensed auctioneers, estate agents and valuers bona fide practising in Ireland were, on election, eligible for membership. "The advantages of membership are manifold, and it will be realised that a courteous hearing from other public bodies, Government Departments &c., is always obtainable by the Association when individual applications might not always have the desired results," the Association declared.

The first registered offices of the new association were located at No. 23 Lower Ormond Quay, Dublin, a Liffeyside city centre address shared with G. F. Healy & Co. Ltd., who printed the yearbook of the auctioneering association and specialised in auctioneer's catalogues. A telephone was installed and a room for use by members was made available for interviews. The registration fee for membership of the Association was £5 5s 0d, subsequently reduced to £3 3s 0d in 1924. The objects for which the new association was established were:

a) To provide a central organisation for Licensed Auctioneers, Estate Agents and Valuers in Ireland, to promote and protect the
general interests of the profession, and to maintain and extend
its usefulness for the public advantage.

b) To provide for the better definition and protection of the profession and the education of its members by a system of examination, and the issue of certificates of the results of such
examinations.

c) To provide opportunities for mutual intercourses amongst the
members, and facilities for the delivery of lectures and the exchange and communication of information connected with the
profession.

d) To establish, undertake, or manage any charitable or benevolent fund from which donations may be made to necessitous
persons who are or have been members of the Association,
their widows, children and immediate relatives dependent
upon them, or other deserving persons who, though not members of the Association, may be or have been connected with
the profession, and . . . to make any contribution out of the
surplus property or income of the Association to any such
fund.

e) To purchase, take on lease or fee farm grant, or otherwise acquire, hold, and dispose of any real and personal estate which
may be deemed necessary or convenient for any of the purposes of the Association, provided that in case the Association
shall desire to hold more land than the law for the time being
shall permit it to hold without the licence of the Ministry of
Industry and Commerce, such licence shall be obtained.

f) To erect, purchase, or hire and furnish any buildings to be used
by the Members of the Association as an institute, club, meeting, exchange, sale or lecture rooms for the advancement of the
foregoing objects or any of them.

g) To apply, petition for or promote any Act of Parliament, Royal
Charter, or other authority with the view of attaining any of
the objects of the Association.

h) To promote, form, establish and incorporate any Association or Society not being an Association or Society for the purpose of trade or profit, having objects similar to or advantageous to those of the Association.

i) To pay the costs and expenses of and incidental to the promotion, formation, establishment, incorporation and registration of the Association or of any such other Association or Society as above mentioned.

j) To join with any other person or corporation in doing any of the aforesaid things, or for the attainment of any of the above objects.

k) To do all such other lawful things as are incidental or conducive to the attainment of the above objects or any of them. Etc. Etc.

A series of meetings of the new association were held around the country and an important branch was formed in Tipperary with a membership of 76 by the end of 1922. The first general meeting of the Association took place at the Shelbourne Hotel in Dublin on March 14. Two hundred rubber stamps were purchased by order of the council bearing the wording "Member of the Irish Auctioneers' & Estate Agents' Association". One of these stamps was sent to each member upon election and members were asked to adopt the letters "MIAA" after their names in all advertisements and other promotional literature. In the event, some members proved slow to adopt the new designation and had to be urged to do so as a matter of priority by the Association. Instances of unauthorised persons adopting the letters MIAA were reported and "suitably dealt with" (in one case, the matter was placed in the hands of a solicitor who demanded an apology, together with a fine of £15). The first IAA Yearbook, Diary and Calendar was published in April 1926. A copy of the new yearbook was sent to all Government departments, solicitors offices and banks. The new publication was well received (despite an unfortunate error by the printers in omitting the diary section in the first edition!). Containing increasingly comprehensive professional information, the diary/yearbook has been published and steadily embellished on a regular basis — apart from a two-year gap in 1932–33 — right down to the present day.

A striking aspect of the auctioneering business in Ireland has been its continuity, with family-run businesses passing down over the years from father to son. The IAA yearbook provides annual membership listings, chronicling the steady growth of the Association. Some of the names featuring prominently in the earliest IAA lists persist right up to the present day — names like Craigie and Ganly in Dublin; Coonan, Kildare; Marsh, Cork; Palmer, Waterford; Armstrong, Kells; McMahon, Ennis; Quirke, Clonmel; Smith, Navan; and others. Auctioneering firms had indeed been operating in Ireland for well over a century prior to the launch of the national auctioneering body. Battersby & Co., one of the early member firms operating out of 39 Westmoreland Street in Dublin, was established in 1815, while James H. North & Co. dates from 1829; Ganly & Sons was founded in 1847 and James Adam & Sons was established in 1887.

But there can be no denying the significance of the formation of the Association, the only body of its kind to represent the interests of the profession on a national basis. After just five years, the institute could already lay claim to 164 members in 28 counties, both north and south. The Association was conceived as a 32-county body from the outset. The list of officers elected at the inaugural general meeting included five representatives from each of the provinces of Ireland, including Ulster — Robert Griffin, Ballymena; F. J. Harkin, Londonderry; G. A. Knight, Clones; F. J. MacCartney, Ballymena; and Thomas McGuinness, Cavan. The City of Belfast was represented by W. P. Gray of W. P. Gray & MacDowell. The holder of a licence to practice in Northern Ireland had, however, to obtain another licence before practising in the Free State and vice versa — a matter which caused understandable annoyance to those affected. The geographic spread of the new body was written into its "modus operandi" from the very beginning — a council meeting on July 19, 1923 passed a resolution that members of the IAA council from outside Dublin would be paid travelling expenses at the rate of £2 2s 0d for over 50 miles and £1 1s 0d under this distance.

Auctioneering has always been a hard-nosed business, with little quarter either given or asked by vendors, clients or their agents. This was decidedly the case in those pioneering days. Writing about the auctioneering profession in the mid-1920s, an unnamed IAA scribe displayed the kind of caustic wit that would not go amiss today. He prefaced his comments with a quote from Cowper that "estates are landscapes gazed upon awhile, then advertised and auctioneered away," but observed that the method of conducting an auction at this time differed in many respects from the less sophisticated times of some 50 years before. The scribe instanced as an example a case in which the auctioneer remained silent throughout an entire auction:

> It is only right to mention he was not a Dublin auctioneer — but when anyone bid he gave him a glass of brandy and the person who got the last glass of brandy was declared the purchaser of the lot offered for sale. A glance at earlier reports shows that in one case the owner put up a slip of paper with the reserve price on it underneath a candle and it was agreed that no bidding should avail if not equal to that. There was also "Candlestick Biddings", as they were called, where the various competitors did not know what the other had offered. A bidding of so much per cent more than any other person had offered would be binding on the person who had made it.

Selling by an inch of a candle seems to have been a common enough practice in earlier centuries (the practice is mentioned by Samuel Pepys in his diary of 1660). During the bidding, a small piece — about an inch — of candle was burned and the last bidder before the candle went out was declared the buyer. Two objects were to be attended by this practice, our scribe notes: in the first place, the flickering and expiring light proved a stimulant to bidders and, in the second, the candle marked the extent of the auctioneer's authority. Dutch auctions were also frequent. "A 'Dutch Auction' was like a crab — it went backways," the scribe elaborates. "The course of bidding was reversed, the seller naming at the outset a price beyond the value of his goods, and gradually lowered it until some one closed with the offer. Thus, of necessity, there was only one bidding."

Auctioneering dates back to the earliest times. According to IAA president L. V. Bennett, writing in 1931, a reference can be found in Herodotus to the custom of the Babylonians holding a marriage market at which women were sold by auction — "No information is given as to the disposal of the unattractive and consequently unsold lots, nor are we told if the auctioneer received his commission in kind!" By Roman times, the process of selling by auction had come to be recognised as the most convenient and equitable method of disposing of property in the best interests of buyer and seller. A name was duly provided for the custom which has remained to this day: "auction", from the Latin *augere*, meaning to increase — the essence of the transaction being that the sale was conducted by bids of increasing magnitude. The catalogues were called "auctionaries", the seller termed *auctor* and the bidders *sectores* who bid by lifting their fingers. At this period, the auctioneer was a soldier who, as a signal of commencing the auction, stuck a spear in the ground — hence the sale described as being held *sub hasta* (under the spear).

"Every conceivable variety of property, every known commodity, wild animals and even human beings were disposed of by this means," the IAA president elaborated.

> The Roman Empire was sold by a Praetorian guard when the Emperor Julian became the highest bidder and even the Holy See itself, according to history, was sold by auction to Virgilius for 200 pounds weight of gold! We are not told how, at these ancient Sales, a time limit was determined for the biddings; at a later period of Roman History the Sale was proclaimed by trumpet, when we also find that a Roman Government levied a duty of 2 per cent on the proceeds of the Sales. More recent History tells us that a Charter of Henry VII confined the business of an Auctioneer to an officer called a Crier whose duty it was to cry aloud the goods he had to dispose of and attract further attention by ringing a bell; the latter intimation may still be heard in this country.

By the eighteenth century, the scope for professional property work had been considerably amplified and "those adjuncts which have gradually become an essential part of the auctioneer's business" gradually became a commonplace of normal commercial practice. The legal profession had hitherto dominated this sphere, but the scope for property specialists began to win acceptance — particularly in urban areas. Raymond Judd of Battersby & Co. related in the IAA yearbook:

About 1750, the Auctioneer came to be looked upon as the best person to undertake the sale of Lands and Estates, and as far as records show, it had become the usual practice for the Agent or Auctioneer to prepare the particulars of sale after he had inspected the Property, and subsequently offer it for auction, the Lawyer, as happens today, dealing solely with the Legal aspect. From then on and for a number of years, such Auctions were mostly held in a convenient and popular Coffee House, but towards the close of the Eighteenth Century sales in Marts or in Auction Rooms were initiated.

The following notice dates from 1758:

To Be Sold by AUCTION, (for Payment of RENT) On Thursday the 15th June, 1758 at Dick's Coffee-House in Skinner Row, the Collection of Books, a Case of Pistols, a Sword, a Tea Chest, and Wearing Apparel, of the late Andrew Murray Esq., Councillor at Law, deceased. The Sale to begin at Six O'clock on the Evening and continue till all are Sold.

The earliest auction poster Mr Judd could find in his offices dealt with the sale of "Profit Rents arising out of Premises in the City and County of Dublin To Be Sold Together or Separate". The sale was advertised to take place on Monday August 25 at 3.00 o'clock in the afternoon at the Royal Exchange Coffee Room, Dublin. Although the poster does not disclose the year, the auctioneer believed that it must have been prior to 1820. The poster goes on to say that "Statements of Title are posted at the Bar of the Royal Exchange Coffee Room, which is in comparison with the present-day practice of their being available at the Offices of the Solicitors having Carriage". The property on offer comprised some twelve lots, in locations as far apart as Raheny, Ballymore-Eustace, Abbey Street, Beresford Place and Kilcullen, County Kildare — the latter item being "A Moiety of the Patent of the Fairs and Markets of Kilcullen", while another item included a distillery, then owned by Costigan & Company, "which would have been very welcome today by our purchasers from America". Another old poster mentioned by the auctioneer dealt with eleven lots of property in O'Connell Street, Smithfield, Marlboro Street, Mecklenburgh Lane, Bride Street, Thomas Street, Watling

Street, High Street, "part of it let by the Month until sold" and some eight houses "three on the North side of Black Rock and five on the South side of Black Rock".

The tide of acute economic depression and general uncertainty at the inauguration of the new Free State ultimately began to turn as the decade progressed. The Dublin Chamber of Commerce was expressing optimism on the economic outlook by 1927, although the burden of rates was a source of continuing concern. By the end of the 1920s, the auction room habit had caught on in earnest in Ireland. J. B. Hall wrote in the *Irish Independent* on August 24, 1927:

> Commend me to the auction room when in search of studies in temperament, pathos or humour, but above all, of a "genuine bargain".The auction room, apart from its importance as a great centre of commercial activity, and a mart essential to the requirements of modern life, is a wonderful place for the study of character. The primary object of most people who attend is unquestionably to secure a valuable painting, a rare book, or curious antique, which he has had the good fortune to secure for a "mere song", and fired with ambition to go and do likewise, one hurries off to the sale. Sound judgement, a cool head and quick eye are essential. And yet it not infrequently happens that such is the anxiety of rival bidders, such the seductive eloquence of the auctioneer, and so great the fear of losing a coveted prize, that people have been known to gladly pay a higher price for a second-hand and perhaps damaged article than would have been required for a new one.

The writer divided bargainers and bidders into two classes — "those who respond to 'any advance' for the sake of the article, the possession of which they covet, and those who do so simply from a spirit of emulation, or love of out-bidding". He concluded that one could generally discriminate between the two by studying their countenances as they try to catch the speaker's eye. There are auctions and auctions, Hall continued, but the most unique is that at which "lost or unclaimed" goods and chattels are disposed of at the railway terminus. At one such, lots included a double perambulator, an iron pump, a kettle-drum and trombone! "Umbrellas, walking sticks, or pipes and pouches one can readily account for, but not so easily for hunting coats and breeches, artificial teeth, a pair of corsets and, wonder of wonders, an iron bedstead," he concluded.

According to its booklet celebrating *100 Years & More A-Growing*, Battersby was "looked upon generally as the leading firm in the profession in Ireland". Its list of transactions over the previous century reads like a veritable Irish property Debrett, a "Who's Who" of the Irish propertied set. Taking up no less than eight pages, the detailed list of major property transactions runs alphabetically from "Airfield" in Donnybrook for Lord O'Brien of Kilfenora through to "Wilford" in Bray for the late Col. Rowan Hamilton, also including a lengthy catalogue of industrial/commercial deals — involving everything from breweries and distilleries through theatres/cinemas to aerodromes and munitions factories. Undoubtedly the most notable sale by the Dublin-based firm was Stormont Castle in Belfast on behalf of the Cleland family to the Government of Northern Ireland for its Houses of Parliament — a signal testament to the esteem in which auctioneers in the south were held at that time. The firm also disposed of No. 80 St. Stephen's Green and its contents for The Earl of Iveagh, handing over the keys to Eamon de Valera on behalf of its new owner, the Irish Government. The auctioneering firm also disposed of "The world-famous Mines and Valley of Glendalough", Kilkenny Castle for Right Hon. the Earl of Ossory (five kings and two queens stayed there); Dunloe Castle, Killarney for the Executors of the late Howard Harrington, USA; Addison Lodge, Dublin (16th Century residence of the poet); Gosford Castle, County Armagh (seat of the Earls of Gosford); "Gortleitragh," Dun Laoghaire, to His Excellency the last Governor-General of the Irish Free State and then to His Excellency, the German Minister to the Irish Free State; etc., etc.

The chronicle of commercial transactions is no less exhaustive. Included were The Royal Hibernian Academy, Abbey Street, sold to Raleigh Cycle Company; Carlisle Buildings, D'Olier Street to Independent Newspapers; premises in O'Connell Street after its rebuilding in 1916 to Messrs. Clery & Company, Messrs. Lawrence's, Sir James W. Mackey Ltd., J. and G. Campbell, George Mitchell Ltd., Elvery's etc; Dublin Stock Exchange; Dublin Municipal Art Gallery; Lord Clonmel's mansion to Messrs. Hoover Ltd. and Arks Ltd.; Gallaher's Buildings (tobacco manufacturers), D'Olier Street; Dennehy's Motor Works, Bray; Shamrock Cycle Factory; John Fulton & Company's building in Howard Street and Victoria Street, Belfast; Connemara Marble Quarries; Durrow Brick & Tile Works; and many other major properties. Hotels were likewise a feature of the Battersby business, with the Gresham, Hammam & Edinburgh, the Metropole, the Brazen Head (dating from Charles II), Buswell's, University Club, Leinster Club (described as one of the oldest clubs in the British Isles) and several others given pride of place in the listing. Breweries and distilleries cited were D'Arcy's Brewery, Dublin; Phoenix Park Distillery; Banagher Distillery; Dublin Distillery Company; Phoenix Brewery; Bewley & Draper's; and Schweppes Ltd., London.

Dublin theatres and cinemas were another feature, the latter heralding the dawn of a new entertainment era. Battersby was involved in the sale of the Metropole Cinema Theatre & Restaurant; the Capitol Theatre; the Queen's Theatre; the Tivoli; Savoy Cinema Theatre & Restaurant; Plaza Ballroom & Restaurant; Bohemian Picture House, Phibsboro; Sandford Cinema; Rinn Cinema, Ringsend; the Masterpiece Theatre; Dame Street Picture House; Adelphi Cinema & Café; and Pavilion Cinema Theatre, Sligo. At the other end of the spectrum, the auctioneering firm negotiated the sale of Tallaght and Gormanstown Aerodromes for the British Government; the National Shell Factory at Galway; plus Marrowbone Lane and Island Bridge Munitions Works for HM Disposal Board. The Battersby booklet commented:

> We have made a speciality of dealing with factories and we are in a position to furnish particulars of premises and sites in Dublin and district and throughout Eire. During recent years, we have secured premises and sites for numerous cross-Channel and local firms . . . and we are constantly in touch with manufacturers and others requiring such. Since the advent of the tariffs, the demand has greatly increased, and we shall be pleased to place our expert services at the disposal of parties interested.

Among the companies for whom Battersby acted were John Player & Sons, Nottingham; W. D. & H. O. Wills, Bristol; Wm. Clarke & Son, Liverpool, tobacco manufacturers; Evered & Co., bedstead manufacturers, Birmingham; May, Roberts & Co., wholesale druggists, London; Crosse & Blackwell, Liverpool; R. W. Scott & Company, jam manufacturers; Dictaphone Company; and Messrs Rathborne's Candle Factory at Castleknock, "the oldest firm in Ireland, having been established in the year 1488 AD".

Shipping and insurance companies added a further dimension. Under the former classification, Battersby negotiated the sale of Sailing Ship Louthside to Norwegian Fishing Fleet and SS Meathside, property of the Drogheda Meat Factory; SS Hamburg; Howth Lifeboat ON 429; and the Steamship Fawn. Insurance transactions included Friends' Provident Buildings, College Green and Trinity Street; Law Union and Rock Insurance Company's Buildings, Dame Street to Hibernian Insurance Company; North British and Mercantile Company; Irish National Assurance Company; and Munster & Leinster Assurance Company. Last, but by no means least, the Battersby sales roster features hospitals and institutions such as Grangegorman and Portrane Mental Hospitals; Royal City of Dublin; The Orthopaedic; Peamount Sanatorium; Glasnevin Cemetery and Botanical Gardens, Dublin; and the County Gaol, Naas.

The auctioneering profession at the turn of the century was accordingly much more diverse than might initially have been believed and demanded a high degree of professionalism. First president of the newly formed IAA George H. Lennon was a jovial, burly individual with a resplendent beard who operated from No. 29 Prussia Street, Dublin. A man of strong personality whose experience as a valuer of land and other property was always accepted as reliable, he was a keen judge of livestock and built up an extensive business as a salesmaster in the Dublin Cattle Market. His son, G. H. Lennon, continued to carry on all branches of his business following the death of his father in 1927. Lennon was succeeded as president at the 1923 general meeting by L. C. Cuffe, with George Greene and James McMahon as vice-presidents.

"The daily routine of a city auctioneer is very varied," his successor James McMahon of Thomas Dockrell Ltd., Dublin, wrote in 1926 — by which time he could already claim that most of the top auctioneering firms in the country belonged to the fledgling association.

> When the daily correspondence is read it means dictation to a typist at once, if letters are to be got away, as callers start early to come in, and interviews go on practically all day. Time must be seized to inspect properties, write up

reports, etc, and every day seems all too short for the amount of work to be got through. No Auctioneer can ever claim an eight-hour day.

The hard-working president has provided us with a revealing and detailed discourse on auctioneering as a profession during the 1920s: "Auctioneering is a very comprehensive term, and allied, as it very often is with the letting of houses and the management of properties, embraces a wide field of activity full of diversified work and scope," he elaborated.

> The activities comprise not only the letting and sale of houses and properties by private treaty, but the sale by auction of business premises, factories, residences of every description, farms, estates, cattle, sheep, horses, pigs, and all kinds of live and dead stock; machinery, timber, furniture, drapery and other stock; ships, jewellery, tailors' stock; hay, farming implements, etc; so it will be perceived an auctioneers' work is widely varied.

> In addition to selling property, he often has to value same, whether for probate, family division, loans, mortgages, etc., and also be capable of giving evidence as to the rateable value of leasehold and other property, and its letting or saleable interest. He has also to be able to let land for building; to advise as to the laying out and development of building estates, so that his knowledge must be comprehensive and extensive. It must not, however, be considered that he will have to undertake all these duties; but he must be in a position, if called upon, to give competent advice and assistance. In many cases, the profession is divided up as in the legal profession — some auctioneers dealing mostly with the sale of live stock and letting of grazing lands, sale of hay, etc; others deal solely with the sale of licensed premises.

> There is another, and large class, which, especially in the larger cities and towns, confines its activities to the sale and letting of houses and business premises, ground rents and disposal of furniture and effects; others specialise in the letting and sale of shops and business premises. It can thus be seen that the work of an auctioneer calls for a wide and varied experience of men and things, and a broad

knowledge of property, and how to dispose of it to the best advantage. As he also has to make inventories of furniture and chattels, especially in the letting of furnished houses, he must be capable of describing correctly and appraising its value. Another branch of work is to report upon the state of property, its condition of repair, and to be capable of giving a general idea of the cost of necessary alterations and repairs.

Despite this daunting schedule, the IAA president was nevertheless concerned not to inflate or exaggerate the importance of his chosen avocation:

Although this list of requirements and knowledge sounds very formidable, it is not so great in reality; and day by day actual experience soon helps a fairly intelligent individual to acquire necessary knowledge. Like many other professions, it takes, however, long experience and much exercise of the intellect to bring one into the foremost ranks of what is a most interesting career.

President McMahon summed up the attributes of a successful auctioneer in terms with which modern day practitioners would scarcely disagree:

An Auctioneer, to be successful, must have infinite patience, rare tact, and great energy. He must be a man of wide knowledge and a keen judge of the value of property and things. Practical experience is most essential, and in no profession does it count for more.

There are shades too of the kind of criticism still levelled at auctioneers by disgruntled vendors today in the following apologia from the IAA president:

People often imagine that the work of an auctioneer merely consists of occupying the rostrum for some minutes or longer, reading aloud conditions of sale, and then inviting bids, and if successful, knocking down the property to the highest bid. But before this successful consummation is reached there are weeks of preparation beforehand; the property must be inspected carefully, notes made for

descriptions, and its advantages and disadvantages wisely
ascertained; then follows an advertisement, which must be
judiciously drawn so as to present in proper perspective its
relative advantages. All these matters require careful
handling and much experience is necessary to do this effectively. Prospective buyers must be sought out, written
to, or interviewed personally; and here again long experience is necessary to know who is likely to buy or not.

It will thus be seen an auction is a series of progressive
workings, entailing time, much thought and knowledge;
and the actual auction itself is only the final ending. When
it is borne in mind that many auctions prove abortive, to
the keen disappointment of the vendor as well as the auctioneer, it will be seen that the remuneration of a successful
sale is not by any means too generous.

Entry to the major auctioneering firms was much sought after. Young
entrants regularly paid an apprenticeship fee — generally around
£100, but later rising to as much as £300 — to secure a position with a
leading practice. The apprenticeship period typically lasted for three
years, at the end of which membership of the Association was
sought. This practice persisted right though into the mid-1950s at
Battersby's. Properties varied greatly then, as ever — some held in
fee-simple (free of rent for ever); others fee-farm (lease for ever, subject to a ground rent); and others held for varying terms of years, at
different rents. The role of the valuer was thus indeed a complex one,
with evidence required in connection with probate valuations, as to
the value of ground and other rents, leasehold/reversionary interest
and the like. Ground rents were regularly bought and sold, often at
auction. In 1933, for example, the ground rent at No. 35 Lower Abbey Street of £65-0s-9d a year was sold by James H. North for £1,150.

Auctions of farms, hay and livestock were mostly conducted by
provincial auctioneers, although in Dublin and the larger cities there
were firms dealing mostly with this particular specialisation. The
auctioneer was very often a practical farmer himself, especially in
country districts — often owning and managing his own farm in
addition to his auctioneering business. Agriculture was, as we have
seen, paramount in early twentieth-century Ireland — as testified by
detailed articles in early IAA yearbooks on everything from market-

ing Irish dairy produce to live/dead weight of fat cattle, how to ascertain the weight of hay and sheep-dipping. An outstanding example of this trend was the firm of Gavin Low Ltd. of No. 50 Prussia Street, auctioneers to the Royal Dublin Society and secretaries to the Irish Shorthorn, Aberdeen Angus & Hereford Breeders Association as well as the Irish Pedigree Sheep Breeders' Association. The firm sold fat cattle, dairy cows and sheep at the Dublin Market every Thursday and held store cattle sales at its own premises. Sales of breeding ewes, store sheep and lambs were held at the Dublin Cattle Market fortnightly during September and October.

From the outset, the IAA drew up a scale of fees applicable to private sales, auction sales, valuations, inventories and other services — recognised by Government departments, courts of law and the public. The fee scale was suggested as a minimum and could vary according to usage in various localities — but any attempt to cut fees was frowned upon as contrary to all the principles of the Association. "These fees are both moderate and reasonable, and are justified by the character of the work done, which is of a responsible and highly skilled nature," James McMahon asserted. "It is, perhaps, not generally known how often an auctioneer, after infinite trouble and devotion of time, does not sell, and all his valuable work ends in no remuneration." Auctioneers were urged to obtain instruction in writing in all cases and to state clearly in the conditions of sale that purchasers pay 5 per cent auction fees. In response to a query from a member over fees in 1925, the Council expressed its opinion that auctioneers were entitled to a fee for inspection, valuation or advice as to the purchase of property — the fees usually charged for negotiating a purchase being 1.25 per cent, or two/three guineas for attending an auction on behalf of a purchaser.

One of the earliest pronouncements by the IAA was that properties for sale by auction should not be handled by a member while it was on the books of another member. The practice of solicitors holding deposits for sales of property was deemed "undesirable" in the 1924 IAA annual report "as the Auctioneer should in all cases be the stake holder" and representation to this effect was made by the Incorporated Law Society. The letting and sale of lands by solicitors was also criticised as "most unfair" to members of the auctioneering profession, while the attention of the Incorporated Law Society was drawn to the practice of solicitors' clerks acting as auctioneers. Several advertisements from solicitors offering properties for sale and also for letting lands by private treaty were brought to the attention of the IAA council which responded that all such activities should be entrusted to a reputable auctioneer. The Council of the Law Society expressed its disapproval of this latter practice.

Representations were likewise made to the Valuation Office and the Incorporated Law Society with a view to ensuring that only qualified valuers were employed and, so far as possible, members of the Association. The level of remuneration for court work was considered inadequate and the matter was referred to the Ministry for Home Affairs. The Department of Agriculture was requested by the IAA to have all sales and lettings of land carried out where possible through its members. Several cases of intimidation in the carrying out of auction sales and letting of lands were reported by the Association to the Minister for Home Affairs who gave an undertaking that every possible step would be taken to prevent any such interference and to afford protection to auctioneers in the discharge of their business. By 1926, a "Cash in Transit" policy insuring money collected at auctions against robbery was available at 6/- per hundred pounds.

A new form of agreement was drawn up by the IAA in 1924 for the letting of lands. "It has been mentioned that in some districts when conacres and meadows are let, the takers are never asked for a deposit, and no Bills are taken; serious losses have occurred in consequence," the annual report noted. "This practice should be discontinued and the approved Form of Agreement adopted in future." At the request of several members, a uniform instruction to be signed by vendors of property was also prepared the following year.

The new association was quick off the mark to object to "the appointment of auctioneers other than Irish Auctioneers" by the Royal Dublin Society. Their objection proved successful and a firm whose members were enrolled on the IAA list was appointed. "The condition, however, making it imperative for the Auctioneer for refund to the Society four-fifths of the Auction Fees" was, however, considered most unfair. An application was received from the Jewellers' & Allied Trades' Association in 1925 to co-operate in stopping "mock auctions". The IAA replied that the matter of unqualified and undesirable persons acting as auctioneers was in hand with the Minister for Justice and suggested that a bond be required of all persons applying for new licences similar to that which applies for other professions. In 1928, an IAA member complained that the fees offered for Government valuations were inadequate and instituted proceedings against the Minister for Defence and Attorney General. The case was heard in July in the High Courts, when James McMahon and the secretary attended to given evidence on behalf of the member who succeeded in obtaining a decree.

The following resolution was passed at a meeting of the Cork Branch on August 30, 1928:

> It having come to the knowledge of members of the Association that certain members are hampering its work by approaching Vendors or their solicitors subsequent to abortive sales; we consider such conduct is most unprofessional and that it should be made a rule of the Association that no member should on any account interfere with another unless directly approached by vendor or his Solicitor.

The council meeting of September 12 unanimously approved the resolution.

In November 1928, an IAA sub-committee was formed to enquire into and report on the advisability of the Association promoting a Bill in the Oireachtas for the protection of the auctioneering profession.

> It was pointed out that unlicensed persons are constantly offering properties for sale and that solicitors were also advertising properties without employing an auctioneer or estate agent; which is very unfair to members of our profession who have to pay licences annually.

A public meeting was held in Jury's Hotel on June 10, 1929 in connection with a proposed Bill for the Protection of Auctioneers, Valuers, House & Estate Agents. The chief aim of this bill was to protect the interests of its members and of the public. Its strategy was to have all qualified auctioneers in the country become members of the IAA. The Association was to be empowered to maintain a register of persons entitled to carry on the business of auctioneers and estate agents in Saorstát Eireann. This was, however, destined to prove an elusive dream despite long years of intensive lobbying ahead. The 1929 annual report stated:

> One of the measures of the proposed Bill stipulates that persons applying for registration, may be examined as to their qualifications. The importance of such a procedure is evident when it is borne in mind how wide is the scope of an Auctioneer, Valuer and Estate Agent. He should have a knowledge of the disposal by sale for Valuation of Houses, Landed Estates, Live and Dead Stock, Crops, Furniture, Pictures, Jewellery, Books, Plant and Machinery, and Chattels of all kinds. As an Estate Agent, he may be called upon to advise on the Management of Properties; indeed he must have a knowledge of everything pertaining to Land. Further, he must be acquainted with all legislation relating to the Sales or Lettings of Houses, Lands and Chattels, and all items accompanying such Sales.

The Association hoped that ultimately a board of examiners would be appointed as in the case of its cross-Channel counterpart. The cost of making application for the bill was estimated at £500 minimum and donations were sought from members towards a fund for this purpose. The response was, however, lukewarm, with only £302 subscribed by members and the Association was forced to halt its campaign at the end of 1929 until the shortfall of £200 was forthcoming. The task of preparing the bill proved more complex than anticipated too and the final draft of the bill was not agreed until end 1930, with the intention of submitting it to the Dail early the following year.

Efforts to increase membership and improve awareness of the Association continued with the appointment of McConnell's Advertising Services from the beginning of 1929 to "undertake a campaign to bring the Association under public notice". The publicity gambit paid off, with 119 new members enrolling over the following twelve months. By end 1929, it was considered that about three-quarters of the practising auctioneers, valuers, house and estates agents in the Saorstát were now members of the IAA. Yet the finances of the Association were nevertheless severely stretched and the council publicly expressed the fear that the 1930 yearbook might not appear due to lack of advertising support.

The potential of the emerging property industry was not lost on the newspapers of the day who were ultimately to draw a significant proportion of their overall revenue from auctioneering and new house sales. The national dailies were quick off the mark with advertisements in the IAA yearbook. Special pages dealing with "Business and Re-Construction" were published on alternate Thursdays in the *Irish Times*. The "Westmoreland Street Oracle" underlined its extensive farming readership by quoting John Sadlier, auctioneer to the Tipperary branch, Irish Dairy Shorthorn Breeders' Society who attested that "the Society considers that *The Irish Times*, through the medium of its important Press and agricultural page has done more, perhaps than any other medium in the Irish Free State to improve dairying and agricultural conditions in this country". Middle Abbey Street hit back by claiming that the net daily sale of the *Irish Independent* was at least three times greater than of any other Irish morning newspaper "which explains the packed auction page of this paper every Saturday". Two years later, the newspaper was laying claims to at least five times greater daily sales than its rivals.

The cost of advertising in newspapers was a sore point from the outset. A special IAA committee approached the principal newspapers as early as 1923 about their "excessive" charges. "As a result of our interview, a better position has been obtained and *The Irish Times* have agreed to publish a Calendar of Auctions weekly in their paper," the 1923 annual report states. A year later, however, the desired reductions in the cost of advertising had not been achieved. The Association responded by suggesting that members confine their advertisements to one day weekly and curtail all newspaper advertisements as far as possible.

The influence of the IAA grew in proportion to its membership in these formative years and the Association was well represented in new establishment circles from the outset. The members of the Dublin Chamber of Commerce were now either Catholic or Protestant businessmen who were not prominently identified with the old regime, notably families like the Dockrells and the Goods. In a significant appointment, IAA vice-president (and former president) Mr L. Cuffe was nominated by the Minister of Finance to the 1927 Currency Commission "to manage and control the issue and redemption of legal tender notes and the issue of consolidated bank notes". Luke

Elcock, Mayor of Drogheda, was a council member in 1926–27, while Mrs Albert MacArthur, MIAA, wife of a prominent Dublin auctioneer became the first lady to hold an auctioneer's licence in the Irish Free State. Reputed to have a strong and pleasant personality, she remained principally on the administrative side of her husband's practice. Albert McArthur promoted himself aggressively as "The House Finder" (the first agent in this country, indeed, to personalise his practice). He was one of the founder members of the Publicity Club of Ireland and, recognising the chauvinism evident in those days, took responsibility for most of the selling aspect involved in the business. However, he declared that the granting of a licence to his wife was the greatest advertisement for their practice as it attracted a large amount of publicity.

The IAA provincial presence was likewise considerable at this time. A Cork branch of the IAA was formed in 1927, together with a Westmeath branch. But the IAA horizons were never narrowed to purely national boundaries. The previous year, a letter was sent to the Auctioneers' Institute of the United Kingdom stating that the IAA would be glad to send representatives to any special meetings where matters of mutual advantage might be discussed. The declared aim of the founders of the IAA was to elevate the status of their profession, to protect its members, and to maintain professional conduct generally at a high level. An immediate objective was to start professional examinations as in Great Britain and to confer the title of fellow or associate upon those passing these examinations. At the 1927 AGM, it was resolved that a certificate of membership be issued to each member — the certificate to be the property of the Association and to be returned in the event of ceasing membership. The foreword to the inaugural yearbook and diary of the Association stated in 1926–27:

> The fact that any person applying for a licence to practice as an Auctioneer, Valuer etc, can obtain it on paying the necessary licence duty and without any question as to his qualifications, previous experience or financial position leaves the public open to certain grave risks in employing persons who may not be either competent or satisfactory. We are hopeful that it may be possible to obtain legislation whereby only persons who have served a proper

apprenticeship, and can give proof of their good standing may procure licences, and it may be pointed out that no persons are admitted to membership of this organisation until the Council have satisfied themselves on these points.

The ground rules and parameters for future generations of auctioneers and their clients were forged in these early years of the new Free State. A succession of cases involving auctioneering commissions and fees were settled by the courts, while law and practice continued to evolve on a continuing basis. The advent of the new Free State triggered a flurry of legislation relating to lands, rents and property. These included the State Lands Act 1924; the State Land Bill 1925; Land (Finance) Rules 1925; the Land Registry Rules 1926; and the Land Act 1926. Section 29 of the Land Act 1927 was of particular importance to auctioneers as it made them personally liable for all arrears due to the Land Commission on any lands let by them.

Rules, forms and schedules of fees were issued under the new Saorstát code. But the main corpus of legislation relating to the auctioneering profession traces back well into the previous century. Auctioneering licences were governed by a variety of Victorian statutes dating from 1845, while the law relating to appraisers' licences dates back to King George III in 1806. Thus, when it came to providing a legal definition of an auctioneer, the IAA fell back on the following quotation from Victorian times:

> Every person who exercises or carries on the trade or business of an auctioneer, or who sells in such capacity at any sale or roup, and every person who sells or offers for sale any goods or chattels, lands tenements, or hereditaments or any interest therein, at any sale or roup where any person or persons become the purchaser of the same by competition and being the highest bidder, either by being the single bidder or increasing upon the biddings made by others, or decreasing upon sums named by the auctioneer or persons acting as auctioneer or other person at such sale, or by any other mode of sale by competition, shall be deemed to carry on the trade or business of an auctioneer (8&9 Vict. c15s 4).

The first book on the tenure of land in Ireland since 1910 was provided for the legal profession in 1928 by Hector Hughes KC on the

Land Acts 1923–27. Auctioneers were also required to know the law relating to Town Tenants and the Land Acts. The position became very complicated after the Great War, however, when the passing of the Increase of Rent Acts made legal relations between landlords and tenants highly technical. The 1906 Town Tenants Act was passed to improve the position of tenants of houses, shops and other buildings in Ireland. It gave the tenant the right to compensation for improvements and also for unreasonable disturbance in certain cases. After the outbreak of war, a whole series of Rent Restrictions Acts were passed. The legislation was designed originally to deal with problems accentuated, but not created, by the conflict. The outbreak of war on August 4, 1914 abruptly stopped housebuilding, while the persistent flow of people from rural districts into the towns diminished supply and increased demand for living accommodation in large population centres. In England, where the problem assumed larger proportions than in Ireland, the need for better and cheaper houses, particularly for the poorer working classes, had already resulted in a considerable body of remedial legislation.

Every person exercising or carrying on the trade or business of an auctioneer was required to take out a licence and pay the annual sum or duty of excise of £10. This licence commenced and expired on July 5 each year. The statute required every licence to be renewed annually at least ten days before expiration. There were, however, several exceptions to this ruling: no auctioneer's licence was, for example, required by any person selling any goods or chattels by auction under a distress for non-payment of rent or tithes less than £20. Sales could also be conducted by any person acting under orders of the Chancery Division of the High Court of Justice, while no licence was required for sales of goods taken in execution by County Court bailiffs or sales under process of civil bill courts in Ireland. Other activities exempted from the licensing requirement included sales of fish where first landed under the seashore, the letting of lands or any interest therein, the letting of tolls to farm by trustees of the tolls, sales "by ticket" of mineral ore, sales by customs officials, inland revenue and sales of the effects of deceased officers, soldiers and deserters by direction of the War Office. Any person selling excise commodities was required to take out a separate excise licence.

Persons acting as house agents were required to take out an annual licence and pay a duty of £2. The following were deemed to be house agents:

> Every person who, as agent for any other person, shall for or in expectation of fee, gain or reward of any kind, advertise for sale or for letting any furnished house, or part of any furnished house, or who shall by any public notice or advertisement or by any inscription in or upon any house, shop or place, used or occupied by him, or by any other ways or means, hold himself out to the public as an agent for selling or letting furnished houses, and who shall let or sell, or agree to let or sell, or make or offer or receive any proposal, or in any way negotiate for the selling or letting of any furnished house, or any part of any furnished house.

These provisions did not apply to houses which did not exceed an annual rent or value of £5. Persons acting as appraisers were also required to take out an annual licence and pay a duty of £2. However, those holding an auctioneer's or appraiser's licence were not obliged to hold a house agent's licence. By the same token, holders of an auctioneer's licence required neither a house agent's licence nor an appraiser's licence. Appraisers were defined as:

> Every person who shall value or appraise any estate or property, real or personal, or any interest in possession or reversion, remainder or contingency, in any estate or property, real or personal, or any goods, merchandise, or effects, of whatsoever kind or description the same may be, for or in expectation of any hire, gain, fee or reward, or valuable consideration to be therefore paid him.

At sales by auction, an auctioneer was required by law to exhibit their full Christian name, surname and residence in large letters on a ticket or board "affixed or suspended in a conspicuous part of the room or place" where a sale took place. If challenged by an officer at the time of a sale by auction, they had to produce a proper licence or deposit £10 with the official. Upon producing a proper licence within a week of the sale, the deposit would be returned. The following penalties were imposed for breach of the auctioneering rules:

- For carrying on the trade or business of an auctioneer without a proper licence, £100
- For not exhibiting names and addresses at a sale by auction, £20
- For refusing to produce licence or pay the necessary deposit of £10 at a sale by auction, imprisonment not exceeding one calendar month
- Acting as an appraiser without a licence, £50
- Acting as a house agent without a licence, £20.

Where two or more auctioneers acted in partnership, each was required to have a separate licence. An auctioneer was not confined to one place of business — they could pursue their calling upon as many sets of premises as they chose. Any person not holding an auctioneer's licence who put up any words or letters importing that they were carrying on the trade or business of an auctioneer or were licensed to do so, was liable to a £20 penalty. Any person obstructing or molesting a revenue officer or any person employed in the service in the execution of their duty was liable to a £100 fine.

CHAPTER TWO

GOING, GOING, GONE — THE THIRTIES

"For this I used to pray: a little land, not large,
whereon my modest home would stand;
A garden, and a grove of sycamore,
a living river rippling at the door;
By Heaven with these, and more, I have been blest;
I have come home at last and am at rest." — Horace, *Satire VI.*

Going, going, gone,' or the Gaelic equivalent 'Ag imtheacht, ag imtheacht, imthighthe' are the words to which the auctioneer is most indebted," IAA vice-president Raymond Judd of Battersby & Company wrote in the 1935 Yearbook.

> It is from these accrue his 5 per cent commission and he grows not weary of their repetition. A successful auctioneer ought to be a good talker, but a better listener if he is to be favoured with instructions. He need not be rich, but he may always hope to be without suffering any disqualification. He ought to know Irish, or at least be learning it. He must be a farmer to the extent of knowing what grows on the surface and what is under the surface. Where is the auctioneer who has not been asked the nature of the grasses on the land he is selling, whether it is timothy, cockstail, meadow fescue or otherwise and whether the soil under contains sufficient silica, phosphates or hydrogen?

In the typically grandiloquent style of those loquacious times, Mr Judd gave his personal précis of the attributes of a good estate agent as follows:

> An auctioneer must have the patience of Job, the strength of a David, the wisdom of a Solomon, the learning of a philosopher and the virtue of a saint. . . . A slight

acquaintance with Bacchus might be forgiven on occasions such as the annual meetings and my Lady Nicotine, though so much in the clouds, need not be entirely neglected. Neither of these need, however, to be regarded as a necessity. . . . [The Ideal Auctioneer] ought to be a Connoisseur of the arts. He should be familiar with the works of Michelangelo, Van Dyck, Rubens, Reynolds, Gainsborough, Rembrandt, Franz Hals, Murillo, Velázquez, Poussin, Paul, Veronese, Teniers, Simon de Vos, Quintin Matsys, Wouvermans, Castigliona, Salvator Rosa and others, and he should be able readily to distinguish a copy from an original. Needless to say he should know the value of each. Furniture, china and glass are valued for their antiquity and craftsmanship; and Hepplewhite, Sheraton, Adams and Chippendale are familiar names in the former and demand the craftsman's knowledge to discriminate and appreciate, and, here too, the "Ideal Auctioneer" must not fall short; while in the china and glass section, he has to distinguish between Wedgwood, Dresden, Sevres, Lowestoft, Donovan, Beleek, Coalsport, Waterford, Cork, Bristol and Old English.

By 1930, total membership of the IAA stood at around 330 auctioneers. But the geographic spread of the new association was patchy. A letter was, for example, received from the secretary of the Cork branch pointing out that it had been found impossible to get a quorum at their meetings and suggesting that it would be best not to summon any further meetings in Cork. The council accordingly decided to discontinue the Cork branch. There was little hint in Ireland of the disastrous economic depression about to beset the international financial community. At a sale of antiques at the galleries of Messrs Bennett & Son, No. 6 Upper Ormond Quay, Dublin, a dinner service (part only), made in London in 1772, of dishes, tureens and plate, weighing about 400 ounces, fetched a record 780 guineas. An Irish Chippendale table sold at 21 guineas by Patrick Smith & Son, Navan, while the same firm sold an Adams-style sideboard formerly in the possession of Dean Swift at 200 guineas and a mahogany sarcophagus at six-and-a-half guineas.

At the other end of the scale, one-in-eight children suffered from malnutrition in 1932, over half from dental caries and one in five from eye trouble.

The old order was nevertheless inexorably on the wane, with the first stirrings of a new and modern Ireland beginning to emerge. In 1932, the first ever Fianna Fáil Government came to power, ending the ascendancy of Cumann na nGaedheal and castigated by critics as "a moment full of menace". Reconstruction costs at the end of the Civil War have been estimated at around £20 million. Although almost 5,000 dwellings had been erected in Dublin alone between 1923 and 1930, the Government reckoned that a further 18,000 new dwellings were required to deal with the capital's housing problem. Other even more progressive movements were in full flow. The spread of electricity throughout Ireland was one of the most far-reaching developments in the country this century. A hundred years ago, Ireland was dependent upon coal, turf and wood as its sole sources of energy supply for domestic and industrial needs. Industry had to import coal and this was one of the factors hindering the progress of industrialisation here.

All changed utterly, however, when supplies of energy in the form of electric current became readily available nationwide. Electricity was first supplied on a small scale in Ireland at the end of the nineteenth century. Although Dublin Corporation's Pigeon House Power Station near the mouth of the Liffey came into operation as early as 1903, many Dublin suburbs were still without electricity in 1925. In the 1920s, however, the concept of establishing an electricity network for the entire country began to be explored. By this time, some 300 small electricity companies were supplying various parts of the country. Yet most towns and villages were still without any form of supply. Over the years 1925–29, the Government accordingly constructed the giant £5 million hydro-electrical power station at Ardnacrusha on the River Shannon. Irish engineer Dr Thomas McLoughlin, employed by the German electrical firm of Siemens-Schuckert, designed the new power station, with Germanic style concrete buildings and structures like the huge dam and in-take buildings on a scale never before seen in this rural setting. The Shannon scheme was the greatest civil engineering and construction project ever undertaken in Ireland — yet its introduction was greeted by a vocal lobby decrying its infringement of property rights, enshrined from the outset in the legislature of the new state.

Auctioneers were quick to adapt to the altering demands of society, although proven methods of transacting business died hard. A revealing insight into the world of pre-war auctioneering practice is provided by the Battersby & Co. booklet *100 Years And More A-Growing* published around 1940. The booklet states:

> An Estate Agent's claim to public confidence must be based on service and his adoption to modern requirements. Our firm recognised this at its establishment in 1815. This recognition has been maintained since, and our experience of over a century can guarantee the service required. We accordingly direct special attention to the varied services we can give in the different departments of our business.

Based at No. 39 Westmoreland Street, Dublin, Battersby boasted over a century's experience in valuations and sales of house property, farms, furniture, factories, plants and machinery. Its services included valuations for insurance, probate rating, estate management, rent collection and general agency. For private treaty sales, Battersby had a "direct representative" to look after each district, with the latter grouped into areas — each of which was under the control of a more experienced "area supervisor". When a member of the public contemplated a disposal of their property, the direct representative was dispatched to advise as to value and the best method to adopt. The area supervisor inspected the property subsequently to make additional suggestions. Particulars were then sent to everyone likely to be interested in the property — "as carefully selected from our registers, built up during many years past". One of the firm's representatives subsequently interviewed interested parties and advised generally "regarding the purchase, and when financial accommodation is required, introduced them to a Building Society or other concern affording such facilities". A special free service provided by Battersby was that "the property is advertised for a week free of charge to the owner and, if desired, the address of the property is not mentioned".

Prospective purchasers were driven in one of the firm's cars to inspect the property, accompanied by one of the firm's area supervisors with a view to facilitating the inspections and negotiations. By arrangement, the Battersby photographer took photographs of the property, which were then displayed in the window of the firm's city centre offices. "This attracts great attention, as the window is illuminated nightly till close on midnight," the auctioneers proclaimed. "It is also convenient to have photographs to show to enquirers at our offices, particularly to enquirers from the country and abroad." For sales by auction:

> . . . on receipt of instructions, our representative inspects the property, notes particulars as to accommodation, tenure, etc. and, if desired, advises generally as to value. This will help owners in fixing a reserve price. Later, our District Representative, who is in possession of a carefully prepared list of seekers after property inspects and recommends to all likely parties on his list, whilst our Area Supervisor acts similarly.

The importance of correct sales publicity of property was given a high priority by the auctioneering firm. Advertisements appeared during the weeks preceding the auction in the Dublin daily and evening newspapers, and also the chief provincial and cross-Channel journals as selected, "after they have been carefully prepared and submitted for approval by us to the owner or his solicitor". If so desired, a photograph was inserted with the advert — which "adds greatly to the publicity to be gained from advertising". Battersby regularly printed close on 3,000 copies of the particulars of individual properties and posted them to solicitors, various professional/public interests and others.

> Special letters are written to those parties whose names are on our registers of property seekers and who are most likely to be interested in the particular type of property and one of our representatives calls on them and advises them generally concerning the purchase

the auctioneers elaborate.

> Over one hundred posters are printed and posted on our reserved advertising stations at Dublin Chamber of Commerce Buildings in Dame Street, Westland Row and Amiens Street Railway Station and other prominent sites

throughout the city. The remainder are prominently displayed by special contract on our reserved spaces on various hoardings throughout the city and suburbs and particularly in the neighbourhood where the property is situated, also special boards on the property itself.

From the founding of the State until 1982, the total number of building societies operating in Ireland varied between 16 and 23. Building societies with whom Battersby's were concerned included the Irish Industrial Benefit, National Union of Railwaymen, Economic & Public Utility, Dublin Workingmen's Benefit, London Provident Association, the Second Equitable Benefit, the Second Victoria Mutual, Royal Liver Friendly Society, the Dublin Model, Second Dublin Mutual Benefit, the Second Co-Operative Benefit, Dublin Building Operatives' Public Utility, Irish Civil Service and the Iveagh Trust.

The firm's high profile in the sale of Irish country houses also opened the door for a significant furniture auction business:

> Treasure of furniture from many of the famous houses in every Irish county . . . since 1815 have come "under our hammer," thus enabling us to ensure in auctions of furniture the very best results only obtainable with the highly-trained staff, expert services and confident Irish, English, American and Continental clientele, born of our wealth of experience during the Nineteenth and Twentieth Centuries.

The Battersby network was widened still further by "Agencies in the chief English, Scottish, Colonial and American Cities".

Housing had often been overshadowed by more immediate political and economic issues for much of the previous decade. Dublin Chamber of Commerce, however, invited the Minister for Local Government to address its general meeting on this topic in May 1930. The preliminary meeting urged that rent restrictions should be removed, subsidies stopped and steps taken to re-establish confidence in housebuilding as an investment. While there was general agreement that slums were undoubtedly the biggest problem and that more attention should be given to slum families compelled to live in one room, members were clearly fearful of extending local government authority and anxious to protect the role of private enterprise in housebuilding. The Minister indeed anticipated the mood of the members when he declared in his address that "the question that had to be kept prominent was: who should build the houses for the worker earning £3 to £7 a week?" The council report of the chamber stated in 1931 that the "big question" to be settled was "are local authorities to be the landlords of the working classes?"

Paradoxically, the Irish Free State was one of the areas least affected by the prevailing global depression at the beginning of the decade. But the pressure was on by 1932 (one symptom being the failure to publish the IAA yearbook due to lack of advertising support). The movement towards protectionism, occasioned internationally by the world depression, was abruptly accelerated in Ireland by the coming to power of the Fianna Fail government in that year. The party adopted a policy of strong economic nationalism, with the objective of maximum self-sufficiency and greater commercial detachment from Britain. A broad range of tariffs, quotas and other measures were introduced to protect and promote home production, both in manufacturing/agriculture. The so-called "Economic War" with Britain broke out in 1932, when the Irish Government withheld payment of land annuities arising from tenant purchase under land reform schemes prior to independence. Normal trading relations were not restored until 1938 when the Anglo-Irish Trade Agreement was implemented, restoring free entry to the British market in return for preferential treatment of most imports from across the Channel. Irish manufacturing industry expanded slowly during this period, but Irish farmers suffered considerable hardship, with the volume of gross national product declining by an annual average of 0.4 per cent for the duration of the economic confrontation.

Meanwhile, it was a buyer's market in residential property — provided you were one of the privileged few with the prerequisite cash (trivial as the sums involved may seem to us with the hindsight of history). A "pretty" bungalow in Dublin's exclusive Mount Merrion would have set you back a mere £700 in January 1931. Other properties advertised at this time included a "bright house, basementless, four bedrooms, detached, garage, tennis space" in Glenageary at £1,150; a semi-detached house in Dalkey at £750; a "conveniently situated house just off tram line: seven rooms, bath, garden" in Rathmines, £800; and an "attractive house at Kimmage, seven apartments, bath and lavatory, hot and cold, electric light, gas; remission of rates" £1,000; a "handsome semi-detached villa-type residence on tram line, every modern convenience, electric light, eight rooms, bath, good garden and garage" in Terenure, £1,800; and a "four-storey residence, ten apartments, suitable for flats or private guest house" in Fairview, £750. Wages were, of course, correspondingly lower — a qualified national school teacher, for example, earned £140 a year in 1932 (£2 13s a week), rising to £300.

In December 1933, Harry Selfridge Junior surprised the business community by disposing of his Irish Brown Thomas store to "Irish interests" — namely, former Clerys manager John McGuire and his two sons Edward and James. The first Royal Institute of the Architects of Ireland (RIAI) triennial medal award went to F. E. Hicks in 1932 for the Church of St Thomas, Dublin, an elegant Lombardo-Romanesque building. The award in 1943 went to Desmond FitzGerald for his starkly modernist Dublin Airport terminal building completed three years earlier. The stark design differences in both projects highlights the profound forces that were transforming both Irish architecture and society in general. The RIAI was indeed instrumental in promoting a number of landmark architectural competitions around this time, foremost amongst them being the Corporation's Municipal Offices and the new University Building at Earlsfort Terrace. In 1935, J. R. Boyd Barrett won the competition for new Department of Industry and Commerce offices in Kildare Street.

Housing activity continued at a high level during the early 1930s, but, despite widespread compulsory acquisition, it was estimated that some 18,000 families lived in single-room tenements in 1934, more than endured such conditions a decade previously. Dublin Corporation accordingly set itself a target of providing 2,300 dwellings a year and launched an intensive housing programme that was destined to continue over the next fifteen years. The population of Ireland declined by almost 10,000 between 1926 and 1936, but that of Dublin grew by 20,000 as a result of migration from the country. The numbers employed in the construction industry doubled in the period 1930–34, while imports of cement likewise surged. In May 1935, the Saorstát Eireann Federation of Building Trades Employers — forerunner of the Construction Industry Federation — was founded under director Thomas Kelleher. One of its first actions was to initiate a standard building contract agreement with the Royal Institute of Architects of Ireland. In 1937, the workforce made their voice heard by staging a historic 28-week strike over wages and conditions of employment — the final offer was an increase of one penny in June 1937 and a halfpenny on November 5. During the six years to August 1938, *The Irish Builders' & Decorators' Review* reported that private enterprise, aided by small state grants and by remissions of local rates, provided 8,000 new houses in the city and suburbs of Dublin. In addition, many hundreds of new dwellings, other than those eligible for state subsidies, were provided, representing a capital outlay of almost £8 million.

Ireland's first comprehensive town planning bill was introduced in May 1929, spurred by the desire to regulate the rebuilding of devastated city areas and to ensure proper control of urban/suburban housing schemes. It was supported among others by Senator Gogarty who saw the urgent need for a town planning act, especially in Dublin — a city with "the most varied architectural experiments and the most unvaried failures." The Town and Regional Planning Act 1934 was a milestone, but was of its time — making a contribution to development control and the protection of amenities, but in a pre-ecology, pre-environmental era.

By the mid-1930s, a feeling of economic confidence had begun to prevail, but long-standing social abuses proved hard to eradicate. The financing of Corporation schemes was coming to be accepted, but Dublin Chamber of Commerce president Hubbard Clark declared at the Dublin Housing Inquiry 1939 that "there is little use in preaching against Socialism and Communism so long as there is a great multitude of our fellow citizens compelled to live in hovels". In Dublin, land which ten or twelve years previously could have been bought for £10 per acre was now offered for sale at £300 or £500 per acre in 1935. "Why is this?" IAA president T. Morgan Good asked rhetorically in 1936.

> First, because the motor car and ubiquitous omnibus have suddenly turned agricultural lands into suburban building sites. Secondly, because the State is courageously spending millions of pounds yearly on housing schemes. Thirdly, because the populations of Dublin and other large towns are now showing signs of rapid increase. And fourthly, be-

cause manufacturers, as well as private citizens, are beginning to discover the drawbacks of operating in crowded
central areas.

One consequence of these combined forces of change alluded to by
Mr Good was an abiding evil even then commonly referred to as
"ribbon development" — a term destined to become all too familiar
throughout the country for many years to come. The IAA president
likewise went on to hit out at what he referred to as "Jerry-built"
dwellings — "roofed with concrete tiles, little else than petrified
sponges".

In the more opulent districts, technology was improving lifestyles
for the more fortunate in Irish society. Brown Thomas (BT) opened a
new electrical home equipment department, selling electric cookers,
refrigerators and every modern convenience for washing, cleaning
and ironing. A fleet of new BT delivery vans daily served houses as
far away as Bray, Foxrock and Howth. Porters at the fashionable
store were told to make use of the new mode of conveyance and not
to despatch parcels by post "as our customers prefer to receive their
purchases by means of our vans". The sight of a Brown Thomas delivery van drawing up at one's gate was even then an immediate
source of prestige and pride throughout the far-flung suburbs of the
capital. But the majority of the populace were much less pampered.
By far the most serious aspect of Dublin life remained the appalling
extent of the squalor still endemic in its crowded tenements which,
as late as 1938, averaged 18 persons per dwelling in the central area.

Decay and obsolescence in the older parts of the city, disused ca-
nals, new cramped housing areas at Ringsend and Fairview, sat uneasily with the lofty aspirations of a new nationhood and slowly
pricked the collective conscience into action. Slum clearance programmes were gradually initiated and suburban developments embarked upon. Whole new districts gradually emerged — Cabra,
Inchicore, Drimnagh, Marino, Clontarf, Donnycarney and Ballyfermot. The circle of development widened with every year that passed,
but the drive to provide low-cost housing quickly and cheaply was
in its turn fated to replace the old slums by what were effectively
one-class districts — too often dreary and monotonous serried rows
of anonymous estates, lacking in character and identity.

Ireland still lagged behind the pace of international development in many key respects and such domestic shortcomings were not lost on visitors from abroad. The country was being ignored in the itineraries of American tourist agencies because its hotel accommodation was poor and inadequate, J.J. Laughlin, manager of Capital Tours, Washington, told *The Irish Times* during a tour of the country in July 1929 with a party of 130 visitors. While acknowledging that the Irish Tourist Association was doing "magnificent" work in many respects, the American castigated the lack of adequate hotel accommodation outside Dublin. Our telephone system came in for particular fire — in Killarney, for example, communications had not been possible with other sections of the visiting party scattered throughout four or five hotels in the town because the local telephone exchange was shut down on Sundays. McLaughlin wondered what was going to happen when the expected hundreds of thousands of visitors came to Dublin for the Eucharistic Congress in 1932. There simply was not, as far as the US commentator could see, any accommodation for them.

Socially, the Land Acts had brought about dramatic social changes throughout the country in previous decades, shifting economic power from the elite landlord class to a wider and more prosperous property-owning democracy. The ownership of agricultural land had eventually been given back to Irish tenants through the Land Purchase Acts. These legislative measures did not, however, apply to urban property, where the ancient landlord retained ownership. The cities were thus largely developed by the granting of building leases, whereby the landlord granted a lease to a builder who then constructed houses or other buildings approved by the landlord and sold or sublet them to tenants. By this means, landlords were able to control the types of buildings constructed and therefore ultimately determined the shape of the cities. They were effectively the town planners of their day and, while the appalling squalor of the tenements can be laid at their door, the credit for the development of Dublin's great Georgian squares and streetscapes must likewise be conceded largely to the landlords of Dublin.

Celebrated architect Walter Gropius travelled to Ireland around this time to deliver a lecture to the RIAI entitled "The International Trend of Modern Architecture". The renowned head of the Bauhaus was wined and dined, taking time out to view places of interest including Glendalough in County Wicklow. He declared that Ireland was a lovely country, especially its splendid eighteenth-century quality. But the great designer was horrified at the most recent buildings in the capital, particularly the flat complexes that Dublin Corporation was then building. "He couldn't believe his eyes; he thought they were the world's worst," according to young Irish contemporary Michael Scott.

For his part, the local architect gives a graphic account of his first job on behalf of the Board of Works in a highly diverting collection of his published conversations. The task was to make an inspection of a tenement house in Aungier Street — a property that transpired to be in a terrible state of dilapidation, with a terrible smell at the top of the landing where a cat had lain dead for ten days. Scott asked one of the tenants why no one had taken it away. "Take it away, Sir!" said the old lady in question. "Jayzus, if you took it away you'd be blamed for puttin' it there." So the architect asked how did she stand this appalling situation. "Well, Sir," she said. "I run out meself, for daycentcy's sake, and I throw a sup of Jayzus Fluid over it to keep it down. Ah God, this is a terrible house."

There were, however, redeeming contemporary design features. Michael Scott's splendid house "Geragh" at Sandycove in County Dublin was designed in 1937/38. The sketch plans were completed overnight, but the finished house with its curved bays — flanked by the James Joyce Tower — was one of the most enduring examples of residential architecture ever conceived in this country (apart from some problems with weathering due to the exposed location), owing much to the new international style. Elements of Arts & Crafts continued to be used in Ireland well into the decade, the large housing estate in Mount Merrion being a good example — the planning of which was influenced by Garden City principles with wide roads, tree planting and Lutyens-style tiled roofs. Manning Robertson's housing scheme at Temple Hill in Blackrock, County Dublin was another commendable effort.

The auctioneering business prospered in stride with urban development. Several cases in which solicitors having the carriage of sales tried to induce auctioneers to cut their fees were reported to the IAA — which insisted upon full fees and expenses in all cases.

Complaints were received by the Association "of a practice by certain Auctioneers canvassing for business which they were fully aware other members would receive and in some cases offering to do the business at reduced fees". The council "strongly deprecated" such practices, as not only a breach of professional etiquette but also at variance with the principles of the Association. It also came to light around this time that certain banks were employing auctioneers who were not members of the Association to undertake property transactions. The Association lost little time in pointing out to the institutions concerned that all IAA members put substantial business their way in the various localities and that its members should therefore be employed to conduct sales. This unsubtle hint had the desired effect, with many members receiving instructions within a matter of months to sell lands and other property on behalf of the banks concerned.

The case law on auctioneering was being written literally by trial and error throughout the early decades of the new century. Justices were regularly called upon to settle differences over commissions and fees. In one important case, it was held that it is the duty of an agent to take the customary deposit unless authorised to take less and to hold the key of the premises unless authorised to hand it over to the proposed purchaser. The agent in this particular case had taken a smaller deposit from the purchaser and given him the key of the premises. He never completed the contract and eventually left the premises in a bad state. The vendor claimed the balance of the customary deposit from the agent and succeeded in two courts. Another judgement determined to what extent an auctioneer was responsible for injuries caused to persons during an auction in the event of the collapse of a floor in his own auction room or in a private house. In the case of *Brannigan v Brannigan* (1921), it was adjudged that the auctioneer should use reasonable care to ascertain that the floor was capable of bearing safely the weight of those whom he had invited to the sale in his room. In the case of a private house, the occupant would be liable.

Misdescription was another regular source of grievance. In one typical case, a violin described in a catalogue as being by a famous maker, whose name was not reported, was sold at a high price. Subsequently, the purchaser discovered that it was worth only a few

pounds. Counsel in this case expressed the opinion that an auctioneer's conditions of sale do not necessarily hold good in point of law
and advised that action should be taken against the vendor. House
agents' advertisements were likewise contentious items. In one early
case, the plaintiff purchased a house which the defendants had described in a newspaper advertisement as being "a desirable residence in perfect order". After entering into occupation, the purchaser
had to spend £260 in repairs and sought to recover that sum from the
defendants. The judge, in giving judgement for the defendant, said
that there was a distinction between a mere innocent misrepresentation and a warranty. An innocent misrepresentation might justify the
other party to decline to go with the contract, but if he went on he
had no remedy. To get a remedy, he must have a warranty.

In *Pilgrim v Wraby* (1921), it was held that a representation made
by the auctioneer and based on a statement of the vendor could not
be construed by the purchaser as a warranty. The plaintiff bought a
sow belonging to the defendant. The auctioneer represented it as
being due to farrow in three weeks, whereas it did not farrow until
twelve weeks had elapsed. The defendant said that his representation was made as a result of information given by the vendor. Likewise, in 1934, an auctioneer had to sue to get his fee because the defendant said an advert describing the horse as quiet was not correct.

There were frequent altercations too over sole agency and related
issues. James Etchingham, estate agent, 7 Lower Pembroke Street,
failed to recover £78 14d commission at the rate of 2.5 per cent on
£3,150 for negotiating the sale of No. 56 Henry Street, Dublin at the
request of defendants James H. Webb & Co, Cornmarket. Although it
was deemed that the plaintiff had originally introduced the purchaser to the seller, he did not bring about the ultimate sale which
was negotiated through rival estate agency North's. Raymond V.
Judd, trading as Messrs Battersby & Co, estate agents, Westmoreland
Street, made a similar claim against Messrs Webb concerning the sale
of the same premises. This claim was likewise dismissed.

With affluence increasing, builders too were now beginning to
take advertisements on a regular basis to sell their houses. J.
O'Connell invited inspection of his six-roomed houses for sale at
£900 in Kimmage Cross. W. Goulding advised housebuyers to purchase directly from the builder "who buys his materials in large

quantities from the merchants and the sanitary fittings, grates, ranges and mantels direct from the manufacturers. By doing so, you have your individual requirements executed at no extra cost." But buyers had to tread warily, whether the method of sale was private treaty or public auction. The *Connacht Tribune* reported a case involving an auction "puffer" who pushed the price of three acres of land half-way between Barna and Salthill to a "ridiculous" £320.

By the mid-1930s, the main landlord and tenant acts which auctioneers and valuers had to make themselves conversant with were the Increase of Rent and Mortgage Interest (Restrictions) Acts 1923/1926 and the Landlord & Tenant Act 1931. The former legislation set out the method of determining "standard rent", while the latter repealed The Town Tenants (Ireland) Act 1906 and set out rights to new tenancy, measures for compensation of disturbance, compensation for improvements, proprietary leases, special provisions in relation to building leases, terms of reversionary leases and lease covenants. The increasingly complex legal climate duly prompted the association to take action to help protect its members. Roger Greene & Sons, Solicitors, 11 Wellington Quay, Dublin were appointed law agents to the IAA in 1935, providing free legal advice through the secretary to members on all matters connected with their business. The service covered technicalities of freeholds, leaseholds of various types, ground rents, reversionary interests, fee farms, quit rents and other topics.

Irish rating and valuation law was also evolving apace. The Local Government (Rates on Small Dwellings) Act 1928 was passed to simplify the collection of rates on small dwellings. By mid-decade, auctioneers were already in search of a scientific formula for the assessment of the valuation of properties. The system in use was even then deemed haphazard and far from exact. Some valuers based their calculations almost exclusively on wildly fluctuating letting values, whereas the IAA believed that a valuation based on capital value would have a more solid foundation.

The Landlord & Tenant Act 1931 was one of the most important legal reforms made by the legislature since the setting up of the Irish Free State. Unfortunately, it bore marks of hasty draftsmanship and gave rise to great difficulties in interpretation, which were only slowly resolved by the decisions of the courts. In Ireland, the law of landlord and tenant was codified by Deasy's Act 1860. A landlord could give a lease to a tenant for 21 years; at the end of that time, the tenant was bound to give it up. A tenant covenanted to repair a house and not to assign or sublet it was bound to do the repairs and any attempt to assign or sublet was void. By the old law, a tenant who had made great improvements to his house had to give them up to his landlord when his term ran out, for he had not bargained to stay any longer. If he had built up a business in a particular place, it might involve him in a very severe loss to leave it, but he had no right to compensation when his lease expired. He was bound by covenants which he could not break, however unreasonable they had become with changed times and circumstances.

A certain amount of protection had been given by the Town Tenants Act 1906 and the Increase of Rent & Mortgage (Restrictions) Acts. But these were deemed not to go far enough and the new act, which repealed the Town Tenants Act, was an attempt to meet the difficulties in a reasonable way. The main objects of the new act were: compensation for improvements; right to a new tenancy or reversionary lease; modification of the stringency of covenants; and increased facilities for the grant of building leases.

The two wars in the first half of this century both caused a scarcity of building materials and a shortage of labour. Many of the houses existing at the beginning of each war were ceasing to be habitable or were situated in districts from which population was drifting. The net result was that tenantable houses obtained a monopoly value due to no effort of the landlord. If the old freedom of contract had been permitted and landlords had been able to terminate periodic tenancies by the simple process of serving a notice to quit, followed by proceedings in ejectment, rents would have soared and dwellings would have become impossible for any but the rich to obtain. The problem raised by both wars was thus the same. The rent restriction legislation designed to solve it in each case followed the same general lines. Landlords were prohibited from ejecting their tenants except in very special circumstances and rents could only be raised to a limited degree.

Richard Griffith, first Commissioner of Valuation, completed the primary (and only) national valuation of all properties in Ireland between 1853 and 1865. The 1852 Act provided for general revaluation of all properties every 14 years at the request of the Grand Jury (later county council). No such request was ever made and hence there has been no general revaluation from 1865 to the present day in the Republic. Legislation governing valuations consists mainly of core legislation passed between 1838 and 1864, various adoptions under local government law to reflect the establishment of county councils and other institutional changes and two modern statutes in 1986 and 1988.

Quite the most significant legal milestone for the IAA, however, was the promotion of a new bill for the protection of auctioneers, valuers, house and estate agents: "The main object of this Association is to protect the interests of its Members and of the public, and its chief desire is to have all qualified Auctioneers in the Country as Members," the 1929 annual report stated.

> The Association believes that if this Act is passed, all Auctioneers whose names will appear on the Auctioneers' and Estate Agents' Register will find themselves Members of this Organisation. One of the measures of the proposed Bill stipulates that persons applying for Registration may be examined as to their qualifications. The importance of such a procedure is evident when it is borne in mind how wide is the scope of an Auctioneer, Valuer and Estate Agent. He should have a knowledge of the disposal by Sale for Valuation of Houses, Landed Estates, Live and Dead Stock, Crops, Furniture, Pictures, Jewellery, Books, Plant and Machinery, and Chattels of all kinds. As an Estate Agent, he may be called upon to advise on the Management of Properties; indeed, he must have a knowledge of everything pertaining to land. Further, he must be acquainted with all Legislation relating to the Sales or Lettings of Houses, Lands, and Chattels, and all items accompanying such Sales. This Association considers that such important duties as are outlined in the foregoing should be carried out by qualified persons only, and hopes that ultimately a Board of Examiners will be appointed as in the case of the Institute in England.

The new bill was a private measure sponsored by the Association. The IAA envisaged the measure as effectively completing the organisation of the profession and the regulation of its practice: "To ensure its becoming Law, all non-members of this Association practising as Auctioneers, etc., should be induced to send forward their names for membership." The Auctioneers, Valuers, House and Estate Agents Bill 1931 was quite a radical measure — it even envisaged the dissolution of the Irish Auctioneers' & Estate Agents' Association, in whose place a new body to be styled The General Council of Registered Auctioneers, House & Estate Agents was to be established. The Council would consist of 35 members, two of whom would be nominated by the Minister for Justice. The assets of the IAA would be vested in the newly established Council. The new body was to establish a "Register of Auctioneers, Valuers and House and Estate Agents" in such form as they prescribed by regulations to be made by them — the date on which the register was established being published in *Iris Oifigiúil*, the official Government publication for such matters.

The following persons were to be subject to the provisions of the proposed Act:

- Every person who is a member of the Irish Auctioneers' & Estate Agents' Association at the time of the passing of the Act and who shall give notice to the council of his intention to practice as a registered person in Saorstát Eireann.

- Any person who at the time of the passing of this Act was a practising auctioneer, valuer or house and estate agent, and who agreed to pay such fees and conform to such conditions as the council would prescribe.

- Any person who applied to the council to be registered as an auctioneer, valuer or house and estate agent who complied with the regulations concerning registration under this Act.

The council would be empowered to refuse to register under this Act any person who had been convicted by any court or competent jurisdiction of any offence which in its opinion rendered them unfit for registration or who had been found guilty of any fraud. Likewise, any person guilty of any act, default or practice which the council considered dishonourable or discreditable in his business or profession could be debarred, as also would bankrupts and those refused a licence in Britain.

By the end of 1931, the new Auctioneers' Bill had passed its second reading and reached the committee stage in the Dáil. Legal costs of the Bill were around £1,000, with a further £200 required for organising expenses. Members subscribed only £480 towards the cost of the Bill, leaving a substantial deficit and fears arose about financing the measure through its final stages. "It is regretted that many of our members have so far not contributed anything although they all realise that the Bill when passed will be of material benefit to all members of the auctioneering profession," the Association chided in its annual report. Members of the parliamentary committee Raymond Judd, IAA president, L.C. Cuffe and Albert MacArthur spent long hours at Leinster House discussing the Bill with various parties, while a representative of the Association briefed deputies both in country constituencies and in Dublin. Two rapid elections in quick succession, however, necessitated some modifications in the Bill. The following motion was passed unanimously at a public meeting on March 8, 1932: "That we, the Auctioneers, Valuers, House & Estate Agents of Saorstát Eireann, assembled in public meeting, approve of the Auctioneers, Valuers, House & Estate Agents Bill about to be introduced in the Dáil and pledge support of the measure."

The Auctioneers, Valuers, House & Estate Agents Bill 1933 reached its second stage in the Dáil on November 28, 1934. Minister for Finance Mr MacEntee said that, while the Government was not prepared to accept the provisions of the measure, it recognised that certain steps should be taken against dishonest practitioners and, accordingly, a bill was in preparation which he believed would afford the public the necessary protection. It was therefore the Government's view, he declared, that the bill under discussion should not be proceeded with at this stage. A new government bill would be available next session. and the second reading of the IAA bill before the house was accordingly adjourned.

Contacts between the Association and the Government were sustained throughout the following year, with various memoranda circulated and meetings arranged. Progress proved painfully slow again in 1936. This was attributed mainly to the heavy volume of government bills passed through the house. At last, however, the

efforts of the IAA parliamentary committee appeared to have finally
paid dividends. The 1937 annual report trumpeted jubilantly:

> As a result of many deputations to Leinster House and fre-
> quent interviews and discussions with the Minister for
> Justice and Parliamentary Secretary to the President, Mr
> P.J. Little TD, your Committee were definitely informed on
> the 10th November 1937 that the Minister for Justice had
> given instructions to the draughtsmen to proceed at once
> with drafting a new Bill.

The council acknowledged the "great work" done by ex-TD Alexander Haslett when a member of the Dáil, John J. Cole TD and Daniel
Morrissey TD.

The elation proved premature. Another general election in June
1938 derailed the Auctioneers' Bill yet again, with a fresh flow of
government bills taking precedence over the long-awaited legislative
measure. The IAA annual report at the end of the year commented
petulantly:

> Members should realise that they have a duty to them-
> selves and the Association by seeing their Deputy or
> Deputies during the Parliamentary Recess and to express
> in no uncertain way their and the Association's keen regret
> at the undue delay and policy of *laissez faire* adopted to-
> wards legislation by the present Government.

Early in March 1939, IAA president D.P. Hoey, Senator Martin Conlon, Raymond V. Judd and secretary Michael Grey met the Minister
for Justice at Government Buildings to impress upon him the urgent
need for a speedy passage of the Bill. The Minister assured the delegation that the matter would be promptly dealt with by means of
legislation on the lines of the existing Bill. A further meeting with the
Minister took place on June 15, again to little evident avail as international events and the threat of war were now clouding over all
other considerations. The IAA council agreed following this statement: "That in view of the present emergency, further activities with
regard to the Bill be postponed for six months until the Annual General Meeting to be held in March 1940."

The Association had better fortune in other less momentous pursuits. It approached the Department of Agriculture in 1932 with a

view to securing the sale of breeding heifers for the Department. Several members were duly employed, but a member reported the same year that an unnamed agricultural society had suggested that he should refund a large percentage of his fees on livestock sold by auction. The IAA council rallied to his cause, agreeing that the cut was "most unreasonable" and would not be sanctioned.

A newspaper advertisement advertising a house for rent with the remark "will not be let through House Agents" was reported to council who promptly wrote to the newspaper in question, complaining that the phraseology of this advertisement was most objectionable and cast a slur on recognised house agents. The newspaper apologised, regretting the publication and promising not to accept advertisements worded in this manner in future. Also, on the litigation front, a case was reported where a man sustained injury when falling in an auction mart and made a claim. The Association availed of the occasion to impress upon auctioneers the advisability of insuring against third-party accidents of this kind. It also reminded members that insurance companies would not pay for fire losses to third parties and urged them to point this out to owners so that they could arrange to have their goods properly covered by insurance.

At a council meeting in December 1934, an IAA advisory committee put forward resolutions aimed at reorganising the Association in order to improve its services to members. Among the matters discussed were: legal advice; library; arbitration; subscription; election/ballots; debates; and the pursuance of a vigorous policy for the protection of its members. One of the first reforms implemented was the setting up of an arbitration court to deal with disputes between members, while a house agency committee was also appointed. It was decided in March 1936 that general meetings of the Association should be held every four months to promote the general interests of the profession and to extend the usefulness of the Association. The first such meetings were held at the Gresham Hotel in Dublin and proved highly successful, with members attending from all around the country. Meetings were soon also organised in Galway, Cork and Limerick Junction. To further the educational needs of members, a series of lectures was organised; topics in 1937 ranged from "The Contractual Relations of an Auctioneer with His Public" through "A Chat on Furniture" to "Irish Rating & Valuation Law".

It was also decided to establish an IAA library. Members were requested to present "any spare books of a technical character" which they possessed or to make a small donation to help buy books. In 1938, the Association announced its intention to establish a benevolent fund for members. The social activities of the Association (until now limited to an annual dinner) were also given more priority and a golf match was organised with the Chartered Surveyors' Institution at Headfort Golf Club, Kells, County Meath on July 12, 1939. This innovation was considered a signal success and it was agreed that the event should be the first of many such contests.

Under the new system of Seanad elections, the Association was appointed a nominating body for the industrial and commercial panel in 1938. Messrs Henry Connolly and Martin Conlon were nominated, the latter being successfully elected. Two other members of the Association were likewise successful in this election — James T. McGee (Kieran & McGee), Ardee, County Louth, and John Butler, Dungarvan, County Waterford.

A row erupted between members of the Irish Leaseholders' Association and the IAA in 1936 over the sale of ground rents in the city. In 1938, cases where firms were using the letters MIAA without authorisation became so frequent that council requested members to forward copies of papers printed in their district so that the necessary steps could be taken to stamp out this abuse. The IAA law agent was instructed by council to draw the attention of the Department of Justice to the Affidavit of Market Value being used by the Probate Office for the purpose of valuing real estate. This affidavit stated "that it may be made by any practical farmer with a knowledge of the lands in the vicinity where the holding is situated, and it need not be made by an Auctioneer or Professional Valuer". The IAA denounced any such suggestion, deputing its agent to make a case and to instruct counsel to appear before the Chief Justice in Chambers pointing out the merits of its claim.

Two important commissions — on agriculture and vocational organisation — were set up during 1939. IAA president Alexander Haslett of Alex Haslett & Son, Monaghan and John N. Greene, Greene Brothers, Mageney, County Kildare, were appointed to sit as members on the agriculture commission. An IAA deputation gave evidence before the Vocational Education Commission on December

14, 1939. The text of the Re-Valuation Bill introduced by the Minister for Finance in the early part of the same year was studied in detail by council, with many amendments and suggestions forwarded to members of the Dáil. "*En passant* it may be added, as was natural to expect, the Bill received a cold reception," the annual report stated. "Seldom has the Legislature had before it a Measure which aroused more misgivings. Public bodies all over the country protested strongly against its introduction. For the moment it is safely pigeon-holed."

A new Town Planning Act was put on the statute book in 1939, but neither it nor its predecessor delivered the results of which they were capable. According to planning experts, the fact that so little damage was done to the country and its amenities was a consequence of the low level of development pressure prevailing. Population was falling and emigration was rising fast. Both industry and agriculture were "suffering from the inward-looking and very nationalistic policies of government and from 1939 to 1946 the war concentrated the nation's activities on survival".

House values, meanwhile, continued at pre-inflationary levels. Properties advertised in December 1939 included: Rathfarnham (Terenure end) — "Delightful, brick-built modern house, three good reception rooms, five bedrooms, tiled kitchen and scullery, reception rooms, five bedrooms, tiled kitchen and scullery, cloakroom, bathroom (terrazzo), separate wc, open situation back and front, good garden, garage, rates remission for five years" £1,550; Drumcondra — "semi-detached pre-War built; seven apartments, bathroom etc., garage, greenhouse, well-stocked fruit garden" £950; Ballsbridge — "Leopardstown Park, Ideal homes, conveniently situated 1 1/2d fare to city" £650–£675; Palmerston Road — three receptions, five bedrooms, garage £1,700; Mount Merrion, modern house, four bedrooms, garage £1,100; Rathmines — semi-detached, non-basement house, two reception, four bedrooms, bathroom, garden and side entrance £700. Wages were in a different league also: cook £740 per annum; food analyst £1,990 per annum. For purposes of comparison, "Ellesmere", Crosthwaite Park in Dun Laoghaire, was auctioned in June 1940 by Lisney's for £1,000 (with electric light, Beeston Boiler, gas cooker, garage and garden). The same property was sold by Lisney's for £92,000 in 1991.

By the end of the decade, the IAA was on the move — in all senses of the word. It was unanimously agreed that "more commodious and more centrally placed offices should be procured, where there would be an Auction Mart, rooms where provincial members could call and transact business when in the city". The Association, however, did not rush into relocation and several years were to pass before a suitable premises was eventually found.

On December 31, 1929 T.P. McKenna, who carried on an extensive auctioneering business in Cavan and Meath for over 40 years, passed on. He took an active part in the public life of the country and was for years a distinguished member of many important public bodies, including the Governing body of the National University, the General Council of County Councils, the Council of Agriculture and the Ard Comhairle of Cumann na nGaedheal. In its 1930 yearbook, the IAA reported the death of two of its most prominent members: T. Elliott Potterton, a highly respected auctioneer and valuer in County Meath, and George Armstrong, who operated a successful estate agency in Kells and was also a salesmaster in the Dublin Cattle Market. Laurence C. Cuffe, L. Cuffe & Sons, president 1934 and a member of the Council since its inception, died in 1938. Denis P. Hoey, Thomas Dockrell & Son, Dublin, president 1938, likewise passed away, while the death of Frank North, James J. North & Co, Dublin, is marked in the 1939 yearbook.

But, if the old guard was passing on, a new era had already dawned. An *Irish Press* headline on November 21, 1939 proclaimed "History Made in the Insurance World" over its report that the Minister for Industry & Commerce had appointed Battersby & Company under the Insurance Amalgamation Agreement of 1938 to value the various properties of the four Irish participating companies included in the merger. The approximate value of the properties taken over by the Irish Assurance Company under the agreement was £4.5 million.

Meanwhile, the New York World's Fair, opened on April 30, 1939 on a 1,200-acre site, gave the newly-fledged sovereign state of Éire an ideal forum to make a statement of identity. Rising architectural star Michael Scott was chosen to design the Irish pavilion — soon popularly acclaimed as "the shamrock building". Stylistically, the building showed the influence of Le Corbusier, with glass walls and steel-framed windows. The only piece of sculpture was a figure of Éire designed by Friedrich Herkner, professor of sculpture at the National College of Art & Design. The interior of the building was decorated with two large murals by artists Maurice MacGonigal and Sean Keating. "I tried a whole range of forms which were recognisably Irish, starting with beehive huts!" the architect recalled. "Then suddenly I thought of the fair's theme, 'a new world of tomorrow', and of how the airplane had given architecture a new top elevation. So I started on the shamrock plan. . . . "

CHAPTER THREE

WAR AND PEACE — THE FORTIES

"God hates violence. He has ordained that all men
Fairly possess their property, not seize it." — Euripides, *Helen.*

The gathering storm clouds over Europe heralded a period of prolonged anxiety and deepening austerity for Ireland. Building slowed down discernibly after the tanks rolled into Poland and auctioneering activity suffered a corresponding decline. But the Irish Auctioneers' & Estate Agents' Association made a conscious effort to sustain normality, holding council meetings every second month for the duration of the conflict. The worsening global scenario nevertheless preyed on everyone's mind and security measures were an increasing priority — as witness items in the IAA yearbook on the protection offered by linoleum against fire from incendiary bombs and the most effective methods of glass protection in air raids.

Ireland had managed to side-step the rampant inflation that had torn apart pre-war Germany. Now it was likewise destined to escape the worst consequences of military conflict. In property terms, there were bargains to be had even before hostilities commenced, particularly in Ireland's rural outposts. In 1938, a Georgian mansion in Munster "in need of modernisation" but "with 27 acres of prime pasture land" sold for £1,000. The average holding in Connacht was less than 15 acres, to which might usually be added turf-cutting rights in an adjoining bog and sheep-grazing rights on a nearby mountainside. The accounts for a country house include "Groom's wages, £1 10s per week"; "To purchases, Cart and 2 ladders, £5; 2 manure Forks, 1 shovel, 1 spade £1 5s; A donkey, £1 5s; collar and harness £1 15s". The sale of ten head of cattle brought in £132 10s, of which the ten shillings was returned to the buyer as "luck money".

The remoteness of the Emerald Isle proved its salvation. "Sound Business Despite Adverse Conditions" was the headline on *The Irish Times* property market review published on December 22, 1939. In an interview with the newspaper's correspondent, Mr Judd of Battersby & Co. summed up as follows:

> It would be too much to expect that the property market should remain unaffected by the unsettled international conditions during the year now closing. Our neutrality in Eire could not have saved us entirely from the ill-effects of the catastrophe, but we may at least congratulate ourselves that we are less seriously affected than most other European countries. The first immediate effect upon the property market was the curtailment of the necessary credit facilities for the purchase of new houses, with the consequent result of a cessation of building and an unfortunate increase in unemployment, but it's an ill wind that blows nobody good, for increased favour was shown for all forms of property as an investment, apparently due to the uncertainty of stock securities, and more property has been sold for investment purposes during the past six months than for any corresponding period for a number of years past. Ground rents particularly have been sought after and prices have been hardened substantially, and the demand at present is greater than the supply. This situation will probably now be eased by the Government issue of 7,000,000 Exchequer Bonds at 4 per cent, and I shall be interested to see how much money will be available for investment in property after this issue is taken up. I can hazard the opinion, however, that there are always enough people so partial to property as an investment security that they will not change for any other.

> From what I have said, it will, of course, be obvious that the demand for building land, which was such a strong feature of the property market up till recently, has declined, but it may be assumed that this is only temporary, and in view of this very extensive building development in and around Dublin in recent years, the supply of available building land within the metropolitan area is limited, and a fall in prices is not anticipated. Generally speaking, property has maintained a steady level in prices, during the

year, and although the building costs had increased, prices did not react correspondingly, except in the case of new property, where sales could not be effected at a loss. There was a steady demand for first-class suburban property, consisting of detached residences, with grounds within reach of the city, and it was difficult to supply the demand in some of the more favourite districts, such as Pembroke and Castleknock. Turning to business property, it is gratifying to note the small number of vacant shops in Dublin at present, and in really good business centres they are taken over as quickly as they become available. As was anticipated in the early stages of our industrial development, many premises then taken over are now found to be inadequate for the expansion of business which has taken place, and more extensive premises are being sought, but unfortunately, there is a dearth of good modern factory premises and the only alternative will be the erection of new buildings.

Another Dublin-based auctioneering firm, Jackson-Stops & McCabe — claiming "a remarkably successful year in spite of adverse conditions" — opined that the property market generally remained in "a sound condition". Ever since estate and forestry consultant Herbert Jackson-Stops teamed up with Mr Joyce in 1934, the new Dublin-based auctioneering concern lost no time in making an impact. In his review, Mr Laurence J. McCabe, principal of the Kildare Street firm, stated that he did not see why property for investment purposes should not maintain its popularity — "more particularly nowadays, investors looking for security cannot do better than invest in a small landed estate," he commented. In a similar review three years before, the firm pointed out in *The Irish Times* the advisability of investing in land. Many people availed of this advice and Mr McCabe reported that his firm had sold over 5,000 acres of land throughout the country in 1939. "The introduction of the new Tillage Act may have an effect in the future on the value of lands per acre," the auctioneer stated. A notable sale during the year indicating the value of grazing fields in the County Dublin area was that of Glencairn Estate at Sandyford — comprising 400 acres, this land sold at approximately £50 per acre fee simple.

"There always seems to be a good demand for first class, well-secured ground rents, and, although it is difficult to obtain more than sixteen to seventeen years purchase for these, rents which are available at this figure find a ready market," Mr McCabe continued. He added that blocks of houses, let and producing an income, were a very favoured investment in Dublin, and always sold readily. Difficulty was experienced in obtaining really good detached houses on about two acres. Ordinary suburban houses between £800 and £1,300 found a ready sale and, in some instances, made more than the actual market value. Business premises remained steady, no big changes being noted during the year — a sign of confidence in the stability of the market by the larger investor.

Henry Dockrell, TD of Messrs Thomas Dockrell & Sons, said that the international situation and its uncertainties had a depressing effect on the property market as far as the buying of ordinary residences was concerned. Borrowing powers became restricted and large insurance companies, who operated to a very large extent previously, curtailed their operations, he commented. Moreover, would-be purchasers hesitated owing to the prevailing uneasiness. Albert MacArthur, "The Housefinder," was decidedly more sanguine, reporting that there had not been any appreciable decline in values; on the contrary, some properties realised higher prices than in former years. The outstanding feature of the year, he asserted, was the marked success of the auctions market. Over 80 per cent of the property offered for sale through his firm was sold, "thus bearing out his contention that auction is still the favourite and most successful method of disposing of all classes of property".

The Irish Free State escaped serious damage during the Second World War because of its policy of neutrality. By contrast, an estimated 3,200 houses in Northern Ireland were destroyed and a further 50,000 badly damaged there during World War II. But living standards and economic conditions steadily deteriorated throughout the island as the global industrial effort was redirected towards feeding the military machine. Agricultural output increased, but shortages of supplies severely impeded manufacturing production — resulting in static national output. During the War, some 550 special orders were made under various forms of legislation and unquestionably accepted by stoic, public-spirited consumers. The year

1943 was the darkest hour, with virtually every commodity in short supply and hardship widespread. Building materials were increasingly hard to come by and builders were obliged to negotiate their individual needs with the Department of Supplies. As commercial activity slowed, efforts were made to encourage tillage and domestic cultivation. The IAA discussed the Emergency Powers (No. 12) Order 1939 relating to the cultivation of land at a general meeting in 1940. "Hardships under the Order were put forward, but it was the desired wish of the Organisation that hearty co-operation should be given to the Government in their efforts to procure increased tillage during the present emergency," the Association commented in its annual report. Notes on this order were procured from the Department of Agriculture and forwarded to each member.

Emergency measures by their nature breed equally quixotic responses. "Quidnunc" of *The Irish Times* reported a story from Wexford on February 13, 1943 of an auctioneer who invited bids for a bicycle and who was immediately offered the maximum "controlled" price of £9 by three separate bidders present at the sale. Every one of the trio claimed to have made the successful bid. The man on the dais solved the problem by handing them pennies and asking them to toss; the odd man out got the machine for his nine pounds. It is not recorded whether he was allowed to keep the auctioneer's coin as "luck money"!

As the gloom of wartime austerity enveloped everything in its path, the "glimmer man" became a familiar figure on city streets during blackout hours and motor cars began to give way again to horse and pedal power, with petrol shortages becoming ever more acute. There were an estimated 3,000 horses in Dublin alone and bicycles or horse-drawn carriages were the chief method of conveyance. Petrol rationing was introduced from September 16, 1939 by the Minister for Supplies to conserve energy stocks and ensure adequate provision for essential public services. On and after that date, motor spirit could be purchased only on production of a licence from the Minister. Within weeks of the introduction of rationing, the IAA was deluged with letters from members who found their mobility severely constrained by the meagre allowances granted under the national scheme. A deputation from the Association met with the Minister for Supplies on November 16 and sought supplementary supplies for auctioneers — a concession that was granted, to the relief of all concerned.

But the respite was temporary. The petrol rationing system continued to put severe strains upon both provincial and city members despite this concession. An IAA deputation met Mr P.G. Dardis, Department of Supplies, at Earlsfort Terrace in Dublin and impressed upon him the "dire straits" in which members found themselves owing to the shortage of petrol. The important work being undertaken by auctioneers in supporting the Increased Tillage Campaign was pressed home by the Association. The official regretted that auctioneering could not be considered an essential service and no extra allowance could therefore be granted at that point in time. The only exceptions to this ruling were doctors, clergymen, veterinary surgeons and those engaged in essential services. In view of the difficulty in travelling and more particularly in response to Government forebodings about the serious economic outlook ahead, the annual dinner of the Association was cancelled. The IAA, in the meantime, gave its full support to a fine arts auction aimed at raising funds for the Irish Red Cross Society. This took place at the Gresham Hotel, Dublin in July 1942 and raised the very satisfactory sum of £2,500.

Prior to the 1947 Auctioneers and House Agents Act, it was possible to hold a licence before the age of 21. So it was that future IAVI president Liam Maher of Roscrea became a licensed auctioneer at 18. Due to the wartime regulations, the normal transport for his and other auctioneering firms at that time was pony-and-trap or bicycle, he related later. Like most provincial auctioneers, Liam recalled cycling several miles to meadow auctions, conacre lettings and clearance sales of pedigree cattle, antique furniture and farm machinery. When cars eventually were allowed in late 1945, he was forced to continue cycling and to use the car sparingly as the petrol ration was only 8 gallons per month.

Paradoxically, the war years were an active period for the building/architectural profession, although the ever-increasing difficulty in locating materials meant that builders had in the main to make do with wet Irish timber. The severe shortage of coal meant that there were no means to burn brick and the brick industry dried up almost completely. Construction activity did not cease entirely during the war, but continued on a fairly large scale considering the difficulties.

A long-drawn-out review of the standard form of building contract was commenced in 1940 and the resultant document published in 1947 formed the basis of the contract document used today in both the public and private sector. Dublin Airport was completed in 1940 (apart from the four covered walkways to the aircraft which were not built for another twenty years), but due to wartime restrictions, the building — designed by Desmond Fitzgerald — did not get the public recognition it deserved. Details of the most important building in the international style seen in Ireland until that time could not be published until after the end of the war. The project was indeed a major breakthrough in terms of "total design", with the architects choosing fabrics, cutlery and even designing the menu cards. The building not surprisingly played an important role as the embodiment of the new national airline.

Irish Estates (Management), eventually to become Ireland's largest property management company, was formed in 1946. Busáras, another landmark building in Dublin, was completed during the period 1946–53. Architect Michael Scott assembled a talented multidisciplinary team including top Danish engineers Ove Arup and Jorgen Varming who only completed this widely acclaimed building after many vicissitudes and in the face of vehement opposition from *The Irish Times* among others. The design was highly innovative and materials used included mosaics and bronze windows — the latter purchased from Denmark at the same price as steel windows because that country was desperately in need of sterling at the time and thus prepared to offer bronze at a bargain basement price. A series of elections meant that the design concept changed several times during its construction phase. Originally planned as the headquarters of CIE, various other uses were contemplated, including at one stage an unemployment exchange for women (inspiring the wry quip from humorist Myles na gCopaleen that the name should be changed to the "bust terminus"!)

Despite Ireland's neutrality, the ever-present threat of war and its consequences remained a constant concern throughout these turbulent years. Daniel Morrissey, TD, requested that IAA members dealing with claims under the Neutrality (War Damage to Property) Bill 1941 should supply him with amendments to be inserted in the new measure — for example, the basis upon which valuations were to be

made of real and personal property when they were wholly destroyed; reinstatement and reconstruction of premises; consequential
loss; provision of alternative accommodation/removal; and loss of
personal jewellery.

New administrative inconveniences had to be dealt with too as
fresh sources of red tape emerged and bureaucrats began to win their
own private war. In June 1943, the Minister for Supplies made an
order entitled "Emergency Powers (Retail Sale of Second-hand
Clothes and Bed-clothes) Order, 1943". Under this order, it was illegal for any person to sell rationed second-hand clothes and bed-
clothes by retail on and after July 1, 1943, unless registered by the
Minister. Registered retailers of such articles were required to furnish
a statement of sales to the Minister each month and to surrender
coupons collected. As the order applied to members of the Association who might have sales where blankets and sheets were sold at £1
or more, the IAA immediately made representations to the Department of Supplies and pointed out the inconvenience caused to members in having to apply for registration under this order. The Department duly relented and the obligation of registration by members conducting such sales was cancelled. However, the concession
did not relieve members selling second-hand blankets and sheets or
clothes which were rationed from the obligation of collecting the required number of coupons from the purchaser and sending them to
the Department in Kildare Street.

The interminable negotiations to secure reform of the profession
continued doggedly on throughout this decade also. On March 27,
1939, the Association was back at Government Buildings with the
Minister for Justice to discuss the proposed Auctioneers' Bill. The
Minister informed the IAA delegation that the Government had decided that legislation was indeed necessary and that a bill had now
been drafted. He outlined its various headings and said that the
Cabinet was not prepared to go as far as outlined in the Association's
1933 Bill. While regretting the protracted delay in introducing the
desired legislation, council agreed that no undue pressure relating to
the Bill should be resorted to during the present crisis. The IAA nevertheless repeated its criticism of the Government's *laissez-faire* attitude in its annual report.

A lengthy memorandum on the main points at issue — competency and registration — was forwarded to the Department of Justice in April 1941. A reply followed in due course, stating that "the Minister regretted that during the present emergency no legislation other than that of an urgent or essential nature could be proceeded with". With a general election looming at the end of the following year, members of the Association were asked to impress upon sitting deputies and prospective candidates "their regret at the undue delay in the introduction of legislation which was admitted on all sides to be a necessity".

Lobbying persisted throughout the next twelve months, when a brochure explaining the necessity of the bill was circulated — but again to no avail. At the next two annual dinners of the Association, the Minister for Justice as guest of honour repeated his intention to introduce a bill dealing with the auctioneering profession. But nothing was done towards this end. "Rumour has it that the proposed measure would not be on the lines suggested by your Council and for this reason it was decided not to press the matter," the 1945 annual report stated petulantly.

> No Bill, it was agreed, would be better than a measure introduced on the lines envisaged by the Government. Members can rest assured that the Parliamentary Committee is fully alive to the situation and will avail of every opportunity of impressing upon the Department concerned the urgent and absolute necessity for protective legislation.

The persistence of the Association did, indeed, finally pay off — but not fully. The text of the Government-drafted Auctioneers & House Agents Bill was eventually issued in October 1946 and became law on March 27, 1947, introducing new licensing requirements. The IAA commented:

> Whilst the measure does not give all the Association has advocated and striven for for years, your Council welcomes the measure as a step in the right direction, but considers that the qualifications under the Bill do not go far enough to protect and safeguard the interests of the public.

In the event, the Auctioneers and House Agents Act, 1947 required that auctioneers' licences be renewed annually at least 28 days before expiry each year. There was no register or educational qualifications. The Act instead required that a £2,000 deposit be lodged with the High Court or a guarantee bond to that amount issued by a licensed company. The provision of a collective bond on behalf of members of the Association at a reduced rate was immediately considered by the Association and insurance brokers Hamilton & Hamilton of Dawson Street in Dublin were approached towards that end. Auctioneers' indemnity insurance cover had already been arranged for IAA members through the same firm of brokers at advantageous rates in 1943 and the following year, council also obtained public liability "third part" risks insurance for members at very attractive rates from the same source.

A circular from the Banks' Standing Committee raised the wrath of the business community in 1941, auctioneers included. At a meeting on September 10, the following resolution was unanimously adopted:

> That the Council of the Irish Auctioneers' and Estate Agents' Association strongly protest against the new bank charges to be introduced on 1st October, 1941. We consider them to be excessive, unjustifiable and the time for their imposition inopportune.

Due to widespread protests from all sections of the community, the proposed increase in charges was postponed to allow the Minister for Finance and, later, the Minister for Supplies to investigate the position. The general furore notwithstanding, the higher charges became operative from January 1, 1942 — a pattern that was destined to become all too familiar in future years.

Educational development was not neglected by the Association during the war — despite the following item in the IAA yearbook dating from that time:

> Limited knowledge often leads obscure auctioneers into ridiculous errors in cataloguing the lots at a sale of antiques, but we are glad to think that the standard is nowadays seldom as low as that of an auctioneer referred to by the author of a recent article urging the public to take up

the collecting of old furniture, silver and *objets d'art*. "I once saw the catalogue of a country sale. There was an early (but worthless) Italian panel of St Francis of Assisi. The auctioneer did not know what to make of the saint's halo, so he catalogued it as 'Portrait of a Gentleman Wearing a Straw Hat'!"

An important educational milestone was, on the contrary, reached in 1942 when the IAA education committee contacted the College of Estate Management in London with a view to opening a branch college in Dublin similar to the courses on offer at the time in Bristol, Cardiff, Liverpool and Manchester. Owing to the War, it was decided that there was no possibility of providing such facilities in Dublin at that juncture. "It is hoped that facilities may soon be provided in Eire to assist aspirants to qualify as Auctioneers, Valuers, House and Estate Agents," the Association stated in its annual report.

Your Council is desirous that entrants to the profession of Auctioneering and its kindred branches here should have the same or at least some of the facilities afforded to aspirants on the other side of the Channel. Today Auctioneering, Valuing and Estate Agency needs especial training and education for the protection of the public who rely so much on advice tendered.

A two-and-a-half year course was, however, arranged for aspirants to the auctioneering and estate agency profession with the City of Dublin Vocational Education Committee in 1943. The courses were based on the syllabus of the Auctioneers' & Estate Agents' Institute of the United Kingdom and were drafted in consultation with the IAA. "Your Council is happy to state that the Courses in the Technical Schools, Bolton Street, Dublin, are well attended and proving highly successful," the Association stated at the end of the inaugural year. "It is hoped at a later date to extend such facilities to the provincial cities and towns of Ireland." As an incentive to the students attending these courses, the IAA offered a prize of £5 5s 0d, to be allocated on the basis of attendance and examination results. It was hoped at a later date to extend such facilities to provincial cities and towns.

Neither of the IAA nominees was successful in being elected to the Industrial and Commercial Panel at the Senate Election held in August 1943. However, three members of the Association were re-elected — Senator James T. McGee (Kieran & McGee), Ardee, County Louth; Senator John Butler, Dungarvan, County Waterford; and Senator William Quirke (Stokes & Quirke), Clonmel, County Tipperary and Dublin.

The trio were again re-elected in the Senate Election twelve months later, together with Senator David J. Madden (D.J. Madden and Son), Rathkeale, County Limerick. Senator James McGee was also elected chairman of the general council of county councils.

At a special council meeting held on May 31, 1944, the question of extending the activities of the Association in Northern Ireland was raised by a council member resident there. The proposal was "very favourably received" and it was formally agreed in 1948 to establish a committee of the Association in the Six Counties. The Association had established a cross-border presence from the outset, but this move was a further significant step in copper-fastening the 32-county aspect of the auctioneering body. This is yet another example of how the IAA continued to make headway despite the turbulence of the times. Its 1944 annual report noted that agreement was reached that the IAA offices in Dublin were now "totally inadequate" for the present needs of the Association. A committee headed by president William Corry of Dublin was accordingly given full powers to purchase suitable centrally located premises, subject to the sanction of council. A fund was launched to help defray the cost of the move and the sum of £8,000 was allocated towards securing new headquarters.

The nightmare of global conflict at last receded and the Irish shared in the jubilation when the spectre of war was finally laid to rest. With the ending of the Emergency in 1945, Grafton Street was thronged with euphoric crowds. Students at Trinity College hung out the Union Jack and were rumoured to have burned the tricolour in a show of contempt at Ireland's neutrality. The ribbon counter in Switzer's, wrote Éamonn Mac Thomáis, did a roaring trade: "One end of it was selling red, white and blue ribbon and the other end was selling green, white and orange ribbon!"

But the euphoria quickly evaporated. A report by the Planning Advisory Board in 1944 underlined the extent of the challenge confronting Northern Ireland in particular:

> We have now for the first time a comprehensive picture of housing conditions in the Province. The survey shows that to provide decent housing conditions approximately 100,000 houses will be required. This is a tremendous task. About 50,000 houses of all types were built in the 20 years from 1919 to 1939, and it will be appreciated that the most energetic steps will have to be taken if the task is to be completed within a reasonable period of years after the end of the war.

The war apart, auctioneers had a continual battle of their own on their hands to maintain their professional status throughout the decade. Complaints regarding solicitors requesting a share of auctioneers' fees were a recurring theme. Following a particular complaint at the annual general meeting on March 14, 1945, an IAA deputation met the President of the Incorporated Law Society, P.F. O'Reilly, on April 16 and gave formal notice of their dissatisfaction in this regard. Summing up, the President of the Incorporated Law Society stated that solicitors had no right to demand a share of auctioneers' fees. He further requested that the matter under review would be placed before his council and the illegality of such a demand brought to the notice of members through the medium of the *Law Society Gazette*.

The following communication was subsequently received by the Association from the Incorporated Law Society:

> Dear Sir,
> In connection with the recent Deputation from your Association which was met by representatives of the Council, I am directed to inform you that the following resolution has been passed by the Council: "The Council is of the opinion that it is both illegal and unprofessional for a solicitor to seek or accept for his own benefit a share of the commission or fees payable to an auctioneer on a sale by public auction or by private contract. The Council has no evidence before it of any case of a solicitor seeking or taking for his own benefit from an auctioneer a part of the auctioneer's commission, but if any case of the kind be brought to the

notice of the Council it will be investigated and appropriate action will be taken."

The resolution will be brought to the attention of the members of the Society.
Yours faithfully,

(Signed) Eric Plunkett, Secretary,
Incorporated Law Society of Ireland.

The IAA annual report also observed:

Instances in which Solicitors having the Carriage of Sale
endeavoured to induce the Auctioneers to cut their fees
were reported, but it was pointed out that the full fees and
expenses should be insisted upon. Such practices cannot be
too strongly deprecated; not only are they a breach of professional etiquette, but also at variance with the principles
of the Association which was formed and established for
the protection of its members.

Another attempt at inter-professional fraternity proved abortive,
however. The holding of an annual dance under the auspices of the
IAA and the Chartered Surveyors' Institution was considered at a
meeting in January 1945. As the Institution was unwilling to share
liability in the event of a loss, the project was not proceeded with.

Early in 1945, applications were received by many city and provincial members from the Department of Defence to tender for sales
for the disposal of second-hand army lorries and vans. At a meeting
on May 9, 1945, the IAA council "took exception to the method
adopted by the Department concerned with regard to these sales"
and sought an interview with the Minister of Defence to discuss the
matter. A reply on August 21 stated: "I am directed by the Minister
for Defence to state that it is not proposed to depart from the present
practice of inviting tenders from auctioneers for this service." The
council pledged to continue to press that a deputation be received by
the Department and to recommend that these auctions should be
allotted on a wider basis.

Members were invited to submit suggestions for a "Code of Conduct" following a decision reached at the annual general meeting of
March 14, 1945. Recommendations received from members from all

over the country were unanimously agreed and ratified at a general meeting on November 14. The matter was subsequently put into the hands of the law agent with a view to having the new code incorporated into the articles of association. It was deferred pending the passage of the new legislation, but the 1947 annual report contained the following five-point statement on conduct of members:

1. No member shall engage in any occupation which in the opinion of the Council is inconsistent with the practice of the profession.

2. No member shall conduct himself either in his personal or professional capacity, in such a manner as would be likely to prejudicially affect his own professional status, or injure the reputation of the Association.

3. No member shall directly or indirectly, in writing or verbally, canvass for or seek instructions to transact business which he knows, or with ordinary care could have ascertained, is in the hands of another member as Sole Agent.

4. No member shall offer any financial inducement to secure instructions for business, nor shall a member charge for effecting a sale, purchase, letting, taking, or valuing, an amount of commission which would be unfair to other members.

5. Where a vendor proposes to transfer business from one Auctioneer to another, the Auctioneer to whom the business is offered shall decline to act until he satisfies himself that all charges due to the Auctioneer originally employed *have been or shall be settled.*

The decision in 1945 to allow private motoring to be resumed after three-and-a-half years' suspension was applauded throughout the country — and by none more so than the members of the IAA. News that the issue of a basic ration of petrol would be made about the middle of November was released by the Department of Industry and Commerce at the end of October, but it was not until a week later that the actual date (November 12) was announced, together with details of the ration. Many applications were immediately received from city and provincial auctioneers on the question of a supplementary allowance. Representations were duly made by the IAA to the Department of Supplies, but without effect. A supplementary petrol allowance was, however, granted to members in 1946.

As occurred during the previous war, the subject of rent controls became a priority issue. A review was now undertaken by the Minister for Justice to decide whether rent control should be extended to furnished lettings of houses, flats or rooms. Before making any recommendation to Government, the Minister expressed an anxiety to seek the views of the principal house agents in Dublin. Accordingly, he sought the co-operation of the IAA who appointed a committee under president Arthur W. Bennett to consider the matter. A special meeting of the committee was held and an agreed memorandum on a questionnaire submitted by the Minister was forwarded to the Department of Justice. The Rent Restrictions Bill 1944 proposed to repeal entirely the existing Rents Acts, the principal of which were the Acts of 1923 and 1926. The provisions of these Acts were re-enacted with certain amendments, some of a substantive nature and others designed to improve the drafting or to remove anomalies. In addition, entirely new provisions were included to enable poorer classes of tenants to secure their legal rights in a cheap, simple and expeditious way. The Bill incorporated the provisions of various emergency orders. It was conceived as a temporary measure, to expire on December 31 unless previously renewed.

The main features of the Bill were:

- the extension of the Poor Law Valuation limits from £30 in Dublin and £25 elsewhere to £60 and £40 respectively, so as to bring within the scope of the Bill premises then controlled under the Emergency Powers orders

- provisions governing the determination of the "lawful rent"

- provisions for the relief of tenants of "small premises"

- the abolition of the tenant's right in certain cases to recover overpayments of rent made prior to the institution of proceedings for the determination of the basic rent

- the limitation on the recovery of overpayments of rent

- the absence of any provisions on the lines of the sections in the 1923 Act restricting the calling in of mortgages or rates of mortgage interest

- the absence of any provision such as was contained in the 1926 Act, for the decontrol of premises on the landlord obtaining vacant possession.

The bill was greeted by the IAA as "a matter of great concern" and a deputation headed by president Bennett was received at Government Buildings on October 30, 1945 when several amendments suggested by the Association were discussed.

The immediate post-war years were busy ones for the auctioneering body. In a bid to reduce the cost of newspaper advertising, an attempt was made by the IAA in 1946 to reduce the size of photographic blocks in advertisements to single column only, including fine art sales. The council regretted that its decision was not universally carried out. A special section of the Association for auctioneers operating in the wholesale fruit market was formed in October 1947. An IAA golfing society was established the same year, meeting annually in the spring and autumn. An IAA benevolent fund was inaugurated in November 1948, its purpose to assist members and their dependants in times of need.

The passage of the Finance (No. 2) Act 1947, whereby the stamp duties on the conveyance or transfer of properties were increased to 5 per cent in the case of an Irish citizen and in the case of a non-national to 25 per cent was the cause of much concern to the IAA council. A deputation from the Association visited Government buildings on April 23, 1948 "to put forward a very strong case for the reduction of the rates in the case of an Irish citizen to its original rate, 1 per cent and a substantial reduction in the case of a non-national". The Minister, whilst expressing himself sympathetic to the view put forward, informed the deputation "that there was no hope at present of a reduction in the new rates". The matter was raised at subsequent council meetings during the year and the abolition of the prevailing level of rates was a constant refrain.

The IAA ethos very much reflected the socio-political correctness of the era. A revealing case was, for example, brought to the notice of the IAA council in 1949 where a property for sale was opened for viewing on a Sunday. "It is a matter for concern that such a happening should take place and your Council strongly deprecates such an occurrence and recommends that the inclusion of Sunday as a 'View day' be discontinued," the annual report stated.

The IAA council decided in 1949 that it would be to the advantage of the Association to seek membership of the Dublin Chamber of Commerce. It was duly agreed on December 8 that IAA president Louis de Courcy, Limerick, should be chosen as its representative. New stars in the IAA firmament who came to the fore around this time included Harry Lisney, an eminent chartered surveyor and valuer operating from No. 23 St Stephen's Green. A former member of the IAA council and past chairman of the Chartered Surveyors Institute, he was the prime mover behind the establishment of one of our leading auctioneering firms, Lisney. He founded his company when he retired from the Valuation Office and practised as a valuer and consultant until he died in office in 1946. McMahon and Probert, then Probert and Franks and later Franks and Franks all practised as estate agents on the hall floor of No. 23 St Stephen's Green prior to the arrival of Lisney.

Harry Lisney had a specialised knowledge of rating and compulsory acquisition and was joined for a short time by his son who concentrated on estate agency, but later lost his life in Burma during the Second World War. In 1946, John Broadhead took over the firm. He was born in England, graduated from Cambridge University and had a six-year involvement in the war. It was in 1943 that he met his wife and married into Ireland. The firm slowly expanded out of the single front room and took over other leases until, at one stage, it was working from three different buildings. It then consolidated and occupied No. 23 St Stephen's Green and No. 15 Kildare Street. The firm gradually built up to 12 employees by 1958; by 1964, there were a total of 30 people on the payroll and the firm had soon outgrown temporary premises in both Nos. 18 and 20 St Stephen's Green. With a staff of 60 by the end of the decade, Lisney acquired vacant possession of the adjoining building, No. 24 St Stephen's Green, in 1972.

Other new names staked their claim around this time also. Hamilton & Hamilton at No. 17 Dawson Street booked a prime advertising position at the back of the IAA yearbook in 1942 and followed through by reserving the bookmark the next year — a token of further innovations to come from what was to prove one of our most dynamic auctioneering concerns. In 1947, James Osborne King took over his father's firm James King and formed Osborne King & Megran with Jervis Megran. Hamilton & Hamilton had been formed in 1935 as an insurance and estate agency by Willoughby Hamilton and his brother Blayney Hamilton. After a short time, the two brothers parted company, with Blayney concentrating on the insurance business and Willoughby on the estate agency. In 1954, Willoughby's son Hugh Hamilton joined and later became senior partner of the firm.

Further rising young auctioneering concerns also making their mark included Jackson-Stops & McCabe, No. 35 Kildare Street, who sold Ashford Castle Estate, County Mayo with 3,700 acres for Iveagh Trustees in 1939. The firm also sold Glencairn Estate, Sandyford, County Dublin with 400 acres the same year. In 1940, Jackson-Stops & McCabe kept up the sales momentum by disposing of the Mount Coote Estate, County Limerick with 550 acres for the executors of the late Lord Daresbury on two separate occasions — the ultimate buyer being Mr Luke Lillingstone. The auctioneering firm was officially appointed as valuers for Dublin Corporation to assess compensation in connection with the Liffey water supply scheme.

The older generation was, in the meantime, passing on. John D. Palmer, Waterford vice-president IAA died on August 20, 1939. The son of a cabinet-maker/undertaker, he was a very familiar figure in the lower and higher courts as a valuer. William Smith, Navan died on 18 April 1943. For half a century, he was principal of the firm of auctioneers, with headquarters at Navan, founded by his father in the previous century, and which on his death was carried on by his sons. He had been a member of the Association since its inception and became president in 1942. A successful breeder of bloodstock and cattle, his most notable success on the turf was as the breeder of Salisbury, winner of the 2,000 Guineas.

Mrs Albert MacArthur died on September 15, 1945 at her residence, No. 40 Sandycove Road, Sandycove, County Dublin. Wife of Albert MacArthur, PC, she was the first woman in Ireland to hold an auctioneer's licence. Mrs MacArthur travelled extensively and was involved in many Dublin charities. Albert MacArthur himself died in 1950. He came from a family established in the auctioneering and house agency profession for close on a century and was managing director of the well-known firm of Albert MacArthur Ltd., "The House Finder", D'Olier Street, Dublin. The auctioneer was a Freeman of the City of Dublin (an honour that had been accorded to the MacArthur family since 1768) and was appointed one of the first Peace Commissioners in 1922. He was a past-president of the Association, an honorary member of the Auctioneers' Association America, Fellow of the Valuers' Institution, London and Fellow of the Incorporated Society of Auctioneers and Landed Property Agents, London.

A detailed scale of professional charges was published in the 1941 yearbook. This provided a comprehensive and complicated breakdown of fees for valuations, sales, letting and collection of rents. All kinds of property transactions were covered, from houses and flats to activities like marketing and selling timber and underwood. Charges for dilapidations were included, as was the laying out or development. The fee for sales by private treaty of house property, ground rents etc. in the Dublin district was 5 per cent on the first £300 on property under £800; 1 per cent on the next £500; and 2.5 per cent throughout on property at £800 and over — the vendor to be responsible for payment of fees in all cases. On the sale of house property or business premises by auction, there was a 5 per cent fee paid by the purchaser on the amount realised plus fixtures, fittings, stocks, furniture or timber. The cost of advertisements was to be paid by the vendor. Sales by order of the Circuit Court were fixed at 2.5 per cent up to £500 and 1.25 per cent exceeding £500. The minimum fee for valuation of freehold or leasehold properties was 3 guineas up to £500; half a guinea per cent on the next £2,500; quarter guinea per cent on the residue, or in accordance with local custom. In case of several lots and greater difficulties, a special fee above this amount to be charged.

By 1945, *Bateman's Law of Actions* ran to 698 pages. Roger Greene, law agent to the Association, was advising auctioneers that they would be well advised to insure themselves in the running of their business just as solicitors, doctors and many other professional practitioners did. In order to have an enforceable contract for the sale of goods valued £10 or upwards, the legal expert advised members that buyers must either accept part of the goods, make a part payment or else record the matter in writing. With regard to the sale of land, in order to have a binding contract for the sale of land, there must be a note or memorandum in writing. Mr Greene wrote:

> From this you will see that the provisions of the two Acts are very clear and simple and you would all be well advised when transacting your business to reduce all matters to writing as far as possible. By this I do not mean that you should become enveloped in a positive mass of paper, but all sales or agreements for sale should be reduced to writing forthwith and signed by the various parties. Similarly, when you are taking instructions from your client to sell land or goods on their behalf, you should whenever possible reduce the instructions to writing on the spot, including the terms of commission and have them signed by your client so that there can be no question raised afterwards as to the validity of the instructions or the amount of your charges.

By the mid-1940s, it was acknowledged that an auctioneer's very existence depends on the words contract and agency, with the latter dependent on the former for its existence. The following extract from the 1945 IAA yearbook illustrates the point:

> Very often either the auctioneer or his client became what Judge Davitt described a defendant in the Circuit Court recently as "a victim of the slipshod habit of mixing friendship with business" which of necessity is very common in business transactions in this country. Very often persons with property for sale are approached by auctioneers with a request that they may put it on their books, sometimes giving as a reason that they have a particular client who is very interested in this class of property. As we all know, this is a common ruse for obtaining particulars. . . . The acid test boils down to a question of contract, that is to say, whether the principal contracted with the agent to pay his fees in the event of a sale or letting. The contract, of course, should be either direct or implied. It is situations such as these which arise every day of the week and which are a never-ending source of friction between the auctioneer and the public. Neither party knows exactly where he stands and this leads to constant worry and trouble.

Do not think that the only binding contracts are those that are in writing. This is not so. An oral (agency) contract is just as binding and as capable of being enforced as a written one. The main difficulty about an oral contract, however, is the difficulty of proving what actually were the terms of the contract and what agreement had been come to between the parties. It usually happens you have both parties, very often quite truthfully, swearing that they were under diametrically opposite impressions, one party swearing that he was under one impression, the other the direct opposite. . . . Thus, where a verbal contract has been arranged between parties, a letter confirming the arrangements by that evening's post will be of great assistance in the case of an eventual dispute.

The IAA articles of the Association were widened at the end of the decade to allow junior members of staffs be elected as Associate Members on the payment of £1 1s per annum. Architect Alan Hope won the Gold Medal of the Royal Institute of the Architects of Ireland in 1949 for the Aspro (Ireland) factory and offices built by G&T Crampton of Dublin. The building echoed German design influences and a circular entrance hall with self-supporting staircase formed its principal architectural feature. Grants for the improvement of houses by the installation of piped water and/or sewerage facilities were available from the late 1940s.

The first significant increase in the assets of building societies occurred in the 1940s, when assets grew from £1.4 million to £9.5 million — the start of a process of almost exponential growth thereafter, helped along the way by inflation. A modern detached house with three reception, four bedrooms, garage, large garden and conservatory in Raheny was for sale at £3,000 in 1949; a four-bedroom house in Ranelagh at £2,000; a semi-detached cottage-style property in Blackrock with two reception, four bedrooms, maid's bathroom, and garden £2,750; a pre-war property on Castlepark Road in Sandycove was £3,000; a four-bedroom red-brick house in Dundrum £1,500; a four-bedroom semi in Dun Laoghaire £2,600; a villa-style detached residence on an acre with three reception, four bedrooms, spacious fruit and vegetable gardens, greenhouses, out-offices and garage in Clontarf at £3,450; and a spacious cottage-style residence on two acres in Sandymount with six bedrooms, stabling and orchard was up for sale at £6,000. Outside the city, prices were lower still: a five-bedroom family residence on 150 acres in Leixlip, County Kildare was on the market at £2,500. The price of a family Morris Minor had escalated to £397, while an engineering assistant was earning £400 to £600 a year.

To its credit, the IAA achieved significant growth during these most demanding of times when notable strides were taken in the development of modern auctioneering. The Association may have failed in its overall goal of achieving formal registration under its auspices, but its efforts to raise standards made a major impact and membership numbers increased dramatically. There were some 340 IAA members in 1940. By the end of the decade, this figure had risen to 580.

CHAPTER FOUR

BACK TO THE FUTURE — THE FIFTIES

"'I'm sure it's your room that's partly responsible for your depression.' 'My room?' he replied absent-mindedly. 'Yes, I suppose my room has quite a lot to do with it. . . .'" — Dostoevsky, *Crime and Punishment.*

The combined impact of the Economic War in the 1930s followed by World War II served to intensify Ireland's innate insularity. "It would be a fine thing for us in this country if we could shut ourselves off from the rest of the world and get back to the simple world I knew as a boy in Bruree," Eamon de Valera mused. But the advent of the 1950s paved the way for a more outward-looking attitude. An advertisement in the 1952 IAA yearbook urging prospective cross-Channel property buyers to turn to the Irish page of *Dalton's London Weekly* was an early sign of the dawning of a more expansive approach by a hitherto largely insular property industry. The variety of options available showed that the country was moving away from its earlier reliance on agriculture. "Auction sales, houses for sale, houses wanted, houses furnished, shops & businesses, offices, factories, land, farms, storage, nurseries, small holdings, valuation, rent collection, management, flats furnished and unfurnished" were listed — all on offer at an insertion rate of £1 5s per single column inch display or 1s 6d per line.

Some things had not altered, however, and the agricultural roots were still only too evident — as witness the entry in the mensuration tables appended to the 1950 IAA yearbook on how "to estimate the contents of dung heaps":

> To whom it may concern, this was achieved by multiplying the mean area by the mean depth, the quotient being the solid contents in cubic yards (Note — the mean area of a heap is found by adding to half the area of the base half the

area of the top. The mean depth is the average of the various depths; this being found by dividing the sum of the
several depths by the number. A cubic yard weighs from 15
to 20 cwt. Fifteen to twenty tons may be lifted by a labourer
into a cart per day).

But the pendulum was most assuredly on the move. The pace of life
quickened discernibly in a post-war building drive, with cities commencing their relentless sprawl into the rural countryside. Dublin
led the way, its peripheral expansion continuing in an arc from
Howth to Killiney. Public and private housing areas developed separately, driving an invisible but divisive social wedge between both.
In less fashionable locations, serried rows of two-storey semi-
detached or terraced housing multiplied with monotonous regular-
ity. To ensure that scarce labour/materials were directed towards
socially desirable ends such as housing or hospitals and not dissi-
pated on more frivolous pursuits like leisure centres or shopping. a
Control of Building Order was introduced by the Government.
Builder's Federation president W.K. Cleere hit out against what he
described as an influx of "irresponsible persons" entering the building industry in a bid to exploit the public. "Since 1945, the industry
has rolled its unruffled way along the smooth broad highway of pos-
terity," Mr Cleere fulminated. "Yet it now seems to have turned onto
a second-class road and at present it has descended with alarming
rapidity to the category of a mere boreen."

The *Irish Press* review of property auctions in September 1950
provides a flavour of values at the start of the decade. In the residential sphere, No. 24 Park Drive, Rathmines, Dublin, a detached
four-bedroom red brick residence changed hands before auction for
£3,525; No. 4 Belgrave Square, Monkstown, a three-storey semi-
detached house with two reception and three bedrooms sold privately for £2,050; "The Pelican", No. 12 Windsor Terrace, Dun
Laoghaire, a three-storey house on the seafront with five bedrooms,
fetched £3,325; and No. 19 Myrtle Park, Dun Laoghaire, a three-
bedroom semi sold for £2,250. Torca Cottage, Dalkey, County Dublin,
a one-storey property with six rooms where George Bernard Shaw
lived for some years as a boy, went for £2,750 (vendor was retired
judge Sir Oscar Daly). To wind up the estate, the executors of a
"gentleman's residence" on 33 acres in Rathfarnham, County Dublin

withdrew the property at £5,000 from auction and sold it later in trust for an undisclosed sum. There was plenty of demand for pubs, then as now. Bourke's, No. 4 George's Quay, Dublin was purchased privately by Kevin O'Flaherty, the former owner of the Blandford Arms in Cloughran, County Dublin for £10,600. The interest and goodwill in the lock-up fish-and-chip, minerals and ice-cream shop at No. 7 George's Avenue, Blackrock, County Dublin was purchased in trust for £2,450. The shop, which was sold with fittings and held on a yearly tenancy at £71 10s, had average weekly takings of between £21 and £26.

In the provinces, Peter Murphy sold his residential farm at Knowth, Slane, County Meath containing 24 acres 3 roods and 15 perches statute measure to Kate McCarthy, Keenogue, Duleek for £1,925. "Glencove", Newtown, Waterford, property of R.L. Dempster, was acquired for £3,800 in trust. The property was built by the late Sir William Goff 50 years earlier. Matthew Langan's holding of about 30 statute acres with bungalow at Bryanstown, Drogheda was acquired by Michael Convery, Newry for £3,000. Rockfield House, on over 24 acres near Ballybofey, was disposed of for £1,625 and fees. The residential one-acre farm "Brookside", Redcross, County Wicklow changed hands for £650 and fees. James Sharkey, Mohill, County Leitrim sold his 39-acre farm to Michael J. Winters for £500. Turner's Bar, Templeshannon, Enniscorthy, with restaurant was bought for £800, while another seven-day licensed premises, Mooney's, No. 9 Main Street, Enniscorthy, made £1,000. The two-storey drapery business premises at Fermanagh Street, Clones, owned by Miss M. Cox, sold for £725. Miss M. Dowling's three-room cottage at Old Leighlin was purchased by Miss E. O'Meara, Monaduff for £325.

Residential flats were now beginning to make a mark as a lucrative property investment. Irish Life commenced construction of the Mespil Estate in Dublin in the mid-1950s. Completed in 1972, this was the largest privately-owned development of modern apartments undertaken in the country, featuring many modern amenities including a swimming pool. "Progress" came at a price, however, as development demands now came into conflict with conservation — with the demolition of houses in Leinster Place off Kildare Street starting the process and duly becoming a *cause célèbre* in architectural heritage circles. The early years of the decade saw mounting building costs and a substantial fall in productivity despite the introduction of new mechanical aids. Construction output lagged behind that achieved at the start of the war. Higher wages rapidly triggered a general recession in the building trade. In August 1953, the Taoiseach promised that building and civil engineering work would be made available to relieve unemployment. A Government programme of housing and public works was embarked upon. Steps were taken to remove restrictions imposed by the Control of Manufacturers Act in a bid to exploit the country's export potential and encourage foreign investors to locate in Ireland.

Nevertheless, by 1954, almost 95 per cent of Irish architectural graduates were leaving the country. Unlike other European countries, the Irish economy underwent a period of economic stagnation during this period. After marking time in the earlier part of the decade, output declined abruptly and the average rate of change of GNP was –0.3 per cent from 1950-58. A balance of payments crisis loomed, accompanied by rising unemployment, falling living standards, record emigration levels and a general air of gloom and despondency. In the 1950s, an estimated 400,000 Irish citizens out of a total population of just under three million decided that de Valera's rustic idyll was not for them — it has been claimed indeed that around 80 per cent of the generation born between 1931 and 1941 emigrated during these trying times. From September 1956 to March 1957, the total value of building contracts recorded by CIF members fell by an alarming 49 per cent. Irish emigration to Britain peaked, with Irish labourers leading the way. In some cases, householders simply turned the key in their door and walked away from their homes. During the period 1951–61, there was a net decline from the Dublin area of more than 70,000 people.

Dublin Corporation revealed that more than 1,500 of its houses were being abandoned by their tenants at the height of the depression. House values were badly hit, with building societies instructing their auctioneers to sell at rock-bottom prices. One story from this time illustrating just how severe a hammer blow was dealt to the industry relates to a property on the Merlin Estate in Ballsbridge where a builder developed two identical semi-detached houses, selling one for £4,000 and the other on the opposite side soon afterwards for £2,000.

There was some noteworthy construction activity despite the overall stagnation. The post-war years to 1958 nevertheless saw the development of new Dublin suburbs at Ballyfermot, Crumlin and Finglas. Other forces were at work in the provinces, notably Bord na Móna, which created new towns beside its turf and peat stations in the Midlands. Nevertheless, the 1961 Census revealed that at least half of all houses outside the urban areas had no fixed lavatory facilities whatsoever: in Longford, there were only 1,600 indoor lavatories in a county of 30,000 souls. Commentators at the end of the decade spoke of "threadbare cottages, half-ruins and half-tacky shops, almost as dreary as ghost towns . . . rank country towns spreading out and out like spilt drink".

For its part, the IAA had in the meantime gained significant ground north of the Border. The first meeting of the newly formed IAA Six Counties of Northern Ireland Committee was held in Belfast on June 29, 1950. Jack Heather of Banbridge was elected chairman, while Richard P. Napier of Belfast became honorary secretary. Among the main items on the agenda of the new offshoot were the collective guarantee bond and auctioneers' indemnity insurance. But old traditions died hard and social mores were slow to change — further cases were brought to the notice of IAA council in the same year regarding properties for sale which were open on Sunday as (a) A View Day; (b) A View Day for Furniture; and (c) A Delivery Day. The annual report stated:

> As regards (a) your Council wishes to point out that at a General Meeting of the Association held 10th November, 1949, it was decided "That this practice was to be strongly deprecated and it was the wish of the meeting that the inclusion of Sunday as a 'View Day' should be discontinued". With reference to (b) and (c) at a Special Council Meeting held on Monday, 2nd October, it was unanimously agreed "That Sunday Delivery of Furniture was a contravention of Article 78, Section 2 of the Articles of Association" and "That Sunday Viewing of Furniture is to be avoided".

An IAA delegation met with the Minister for Lands Mr J. Blowick on October 2 to complain about the acquisition of land by the Land Commission in the wake of the new Land Act introduced the previous year. The Minister in reply stated that the Land Commission would not at any time interfere with the free sale of lands, but was non-committal regarding the key issue of fees. The annual report observed:

> On the question of the payment of fees — a point very much stressed by the deputation — the Minister did not seem to think that the Land Commission were liable for the payment of auctioneers' fees. The attention of the Minister was also drawn to the fact that payment for land was made in 3 per cent Land Bonds at par value of £100, but these land bonds which in the great majority of cases had to be cashed by the vendor had been quoted on the stock exchange as low as 89 and from that up to 95, showing a substantial loss. In this matter, the Minister did not hold out much hope for any remedy from this unsatisfactory state of affairs.

On July 3, it was unanimously decided that the IAA Senate nominating committee give their number one preference to secretary Michael Grey. Much to the regret of council, however, the IAA nominee was not returned, although many of its members were on the electoral roll. A commission presided over by Judge John Conroy was appointed in October 1950 to enquire into the workings of the Rent Restrictions Act 1946 and 1949. The Association took an active role and provided expert advice throughout.

A special "emergency committee" of the Association was appointed on September 13, 1951. The committee was to meet when in the opinion of the president (or of the two vice-presidents) it was desirable with full authority to dispose of any matter or matters requiring immediate attention. The powers of the emergency committee were "not, however, to extend to affairs of the Association" for the regulation of which a special committee was in existence. The members of this new committee were all Dublin-based: Arthur W. Bennett, Hubert L. Corrigan, William S. Corry, Arthur Ganly, Frederick J. Holden, Raymond Judd and Reginald N. MacArthur.

Following an excess of expenditure over revenue during the previous few years, the financial position of the Association was put under the microscope in 1953. The upshot was a decision to invest accumulated monies from the capital fund in gilt-edged securities.

Charles Judd, No. 17 Eustace Street, was retained as stockbroker to the Association and duly purchased £4,700 4.5 per cent National Loan 1973/78 at 98.5 on its behalf. At the special council meeting on May 22, 1954, the secretary was selected as the nominee to the industrial and commercial panel for election to the senate. The IAA nominee was again not returned. Subsequently, a majority of the Seanad nominating bodies including the Association met at Jury's Hotel in Dublin on November 24 to discuss what they described as the "present unsatisfactory method" of election to Seanad Éireann.

A communication from the Lord Mayor for the IAA to contribute to the Dublin Tóstal fund in 1953 met with a cool response from provincial members who considered it unfair that the Association should be asked to contribute to a Dublin fund. After due discussion, it was decided "that the Secretary enquire if there be a 'Central Fund' and if such exists that a donation of £25 be forwarded to such a Fund". The necessary enquiries were made as directed, but it was established that there was no such fund.

The IAA committee dealing with the acquisition of new premises visited three premises during 1951: Nos. 4 Wilton Place, 94 Merrion Square and 21 Parnell Square. None of these properties was, however, pursued further due to location and/or financial reasons. Members were urged by council to suggest alternatives. The following excerpt from a letter by a provincial member provides an insight into the thinking of members on the need for new headquarters:

> I wish to thank you for letting me have the use of your Office for the purpose of interviewing a client in Dublin yesterday. It is a great convenience to country members to be able to make appointments to see their clients at the Offices of the Association. I was just wondering if your Council had got any further with the purchase of new premises, the existing premises are quite obviously too small and badly situated. In view of the size of the Membership, surely the time has arrived when more attractive and spacious premises, including a library and two or three private rooms, should be available, particularly to Country Members. A more imposing and better situated building would create a much better public opinion on the dignity of the profession. The existing premises are so shabby that one hesitates to invite a client to meet one there. I hope that the matter

will receive attention and I am sure that the vast majority
of the Members would lend every possible assistance necessary towards procuring a more suitable suite of Offices.

In 1952, Nos. 6 Merrion Square, 11 Fitzwilliam Square and 3 Eustace
Street were likewise considered, but found unsuitable. So too the
following year were Nos. 72 St Stephen's Green, 84 Harcourt Street
and 29 Merrion Square. In 1954, No. 29 Merrion Square was again
inspected and now deemed "ideally situated". However, no further
steps were taken as the ground floor and other parts of the property
were let on lease. It was agreed in October of the following year that
60 Merrion Square had possibilities, but this location was also re-
jected on the grounds that the position was not central, the ground
floor was not available and the price too high. In considering future
likely properties, council decided that the ground and first floors
must be vacant. No. 22 Merrion Square was viewed in 1956, but the
£8,000 price tag was deemed too expensive. The vendor's solicitors
intimated to the Association that an offer of £5,000 would be accepted, but nothing further was heard in this regard.

No. 38 Merrion Square was inspected on October 26. The acquisition committee unanimously decided to recommend that the council
purchase the premises which were considered ideal for the purposes
of the Association at £7,000 and 2.5 per cent fees payable to the auctioneers, subject to an architect's report and possession of the whole
premises with the exception of hall floor and mews. The fact that the
hall floor was occupied proved a stumbling-block with council, although the discussion was terminated in any case when the owner
changed her mind and declared that she was not prepared to sell after all. But No. 38 was back on the IAA agenda by 1957, when the
earlier decision to buy only with vacant possession of the ground
floor was rescinded. At a committee meeting on May 20, it was
unanimously decided that 38 Merrion Square East be purchased at a
price not exceeding £7,000 to include agent's fees and provided that
repairs in the architect's report and repairs to the roof were carried
out at a cost of no more than £1,200.

The IAA decided to approach the Pembroke Estate to ease the
terms of the lease with regard to the holding of property auctions on
the premises. An offer of £6,500 plus auctioneer's fees at 2.5 per cent
was duly made and the president reported at a council meeting on

Mr. Daniel Morrisey, T.D.
(Daniel Morrisey & Sons, Dublin)
President, 1952-53

Mr. Noel Judd, B.A., B.A.I., P.C.
President, 1955-56

Mr. Daniel F. Stephenson, P.C., F.V.I
(James H. North & Co., Ltd.) Dublin
President 1957-58

Mr. Geo. H. Lennon
First President of the Association

Mr. James Adam
(James Adam & Son)
President 1961-62

Mr. Seán Meehan,
Bundoran, Co. Donegal.
President 1969-70

Mr. Desmond G. Scales,
Dublin
President 1968-69 and 1984-85

SAORSTÁT ÉIREANN.

Auctioneers, Valuers, House and Estate Agents Bill, 1931.

AN ACT TO MAKE PROVISION FOR THE REGISTRATION AND CONTROL OF AUCTIONEERS, VALUERS, HOUSE AND ESTATE AGENTS, AND FOR OTHER PURPOSES CONNECTED THEREWITH.

BE IT ENACTED BY THE OIREACHTAS OF SAORSTAT EIREANN AS FOLLOWS:—

1.—This Act may for all purposes be cited as the Auctioneers, Valuers, House and Estate Agents Act, 1931.

2.—In this Act—

The expression "The Minister" means the Minister for Industry and Commerce.

The expression "The Association" means the Irish Auctioneers and Estate Agents Association.

The expression "The Register" means the Register of Auctioneers, Valuers, and House and Estate Agents to be established and maintained pursuant to the provisions of this Act.

The expression "The Official List" means the Official List of Registered Persons to be published by the Council in accordance with the provisions of section 12 of this Act.

The farseeing 1931 Bill (see page 46).

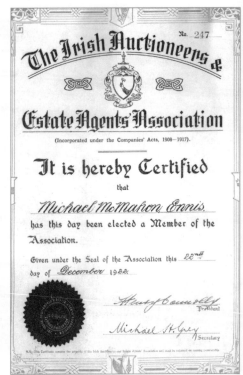

The Irish Auctioneers & Estate Agents' Association

(Incorporated under the Companies' Acts, 1908—1917).

It is hereby Certified

that

Michael McMahon Ennis

has this day been elected a Member of the Association.

Given under the Seal of the Association this 22ⁿᵈ day of *December 1922*.

Henry Connolly
President

Michael H. Grey
Secretary

No. 247

An original 1922 membership certificate.

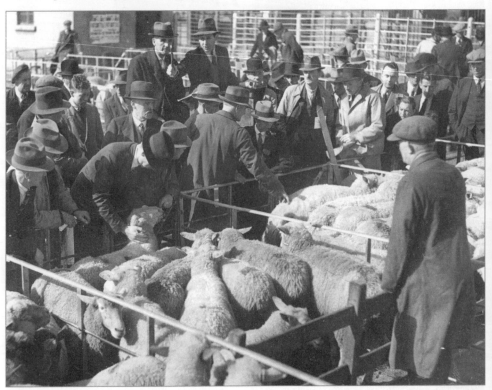

A 1913 Sheep Mart. Photograph by Ganly & Co.

Some Members of the Council 1927
Left to right: J.D. Palmer, Waterford; John S. Wilkinson, Dublin; M. Shields, Carrickmacross; Frank Warner, Secretary; J.F. Armstrong, Kells; Michael McMahon, Ennis; H.B. Hill, Dublin; S.F. Ebrill, Limerick; Geo. W. Greene, Dublin; N. Flood Davin, Mallow. Sitting: E. Rothwell, Ballinasloe; Raoul Joyce, Galway; Lee. C. Cuffe, Dublin; James S. McMahon, Dublin; Michael Quirke, Clonmel; Luke J. Elcock, Mayor of Drogheda; Wm. P. Smith , Navan.

Lakes of Killarney Auction, on Tuesday 21st of November 1899
James H. North at the rostrum.

"HOW can I buy Killarney?" wistfully queried the crooners some five or six years ago, and left their lyric question hanging in the air. They have been saved from a precise answer by the calendar. Time had made their question rhetorical. If they could have asked it 50 years before, they would have been given an opportunity to bid for them when the Lakes of Killarney came under the hammer in the Antient Concert Rooms!

For the Lakes of Killarney, 14,000 acres of land, water and beauty, Muckross Abbey, Torc Waterfall, the Devil's Punch Bowl, Dinish Island, Mangerton Mountain, O'Sullivan's Cascade, part of, and all the rest were put up for auction at 1 p.m. on Tuesday, November 21, 1899, at the Antient Concert Rooms, 52 Great Brunswick Street, (now Pearse St.) Dublin, by Mr. James H. North on behalf of his clients the Herberts of Muckross.

THE auction raised the greatest interest. Originally Mr. North had intended to hold the auction in his premises at 110 Grafton Street, where the business still continues, but it is safe to presume that the demand for space became so great that he had to move to the Concert Rooms.

"Ireland's greatest beauty spot" wrote the *Independent* on September 23, "under the hammer will constitute one of the most remarkable auctions ever held in the Irish capital. It is to be hoped that the result of the sale will be to preserve for the Irish people the rights which they have so long enjoyed and which they have extended to strangers in connection with the famous Kerry lakes."

That was the keynote of the months that preceded the auction. Several millionaires were rumoured to be taking an interest in the matter, including "a millionaire in Kingstown".

SIR THOMAS LIPTON was prepared to go up to £50,000, but as this was substantially under the reserve, it was plain that the Lakes of Killarney were not his cup of tea.

A pioneer of Irish tourism, Mr. F. W. Crossley, of the Irish Tourist Development, 118 Grafton Street, Dublin, worked might and main to ensure Killarney for the nation. His letters to the Dublin papers were many He stressed the reasons why it should be acquired for the country. He stressed too, its importance to tourism.

"I calculate," he wrote, "that the country has benefited to the extent of a million pounds from the tourist traffic during the past season."

HE seems to have conceived the raising of a million shillings to buy the Lakes. He was joint secretary of a committee formed under the National Trust to raise funds. Yet there seemed to be a certain pessimism about the future of the Lakes.

One Dublin paper commented that the Americans might carry away the pillars at Stonehenge, but at least they could not take the lakes or uproot the arbutus trees.

The day the Lakes fell beneath the hammer came. A photograph which has just been found among the archives of Messrs. North brings the scene to life. Taken by Chancellor, it is as fresh almost as the day it was mounted. It shows the front upstairs apartment of the Concert Rooms. There is not even standing room.

ON the rostrum is James North himself, suave, urbane and frock-coated in a pose that takes due regard of his professional dignity and the exposure time of the lens. In the immediate foreground is a slightly out of focus silk hat. It would belong to a solicitor. They had their silk hats and official place behind the auctioneer. Immediately beyond him is the Press table.

Those at it are recognisable as newspapermen anywhere, anytime.

The room is crowded. The men, with their bowler hats, beards and/or moustaches, stiff, starched, upright linen collars, starched cuffs, cravats, and velour-collared overcoats, are in the majority.

Most of the women, all voluminously draped, are wearing broad brimmed hats surmounted by herbaceous borders.

Some of them are left to stand against the end wall. Not all the men are seated. Those wearing cloth caps are lined up against the side wall at the end towards Mr. North's right.

IN the Bidding Book, entered in Mr. North's own hand, I found the 22 bids he received. They began at £35,000 and moved sluggishly by five hundreds and one thousands to £50,000. Fifty-one thousand was then offered by the vendor, and the Lakes of Killarney were withdrawn.

Then, under the final offer, comes the entry: "Sold, Messrs. Sutton and Sons. £60,000."

History had been made. The Lakes of Killarney had been sold. And if any ballad maker with prophetic vision had thought to sing, "Why didn't I buy Killarney?" who could blame him! If Killarney was not sold for a song, it has sold many a song since.

A cutting from the Irish Independent November 23, 1955.

THE MART, CORK.

In the Estate of AUGUSTINE ROCHE, Esq., M.P., Deceased.

CATALOGUE

OF

THE ENTIRE COLLECTION,

COMPRISING—

About 6000 ozs. of Old Irish and English Silver Plate embracing many beautiful examples in Tankards, Salvers, Two-handle and other Cups, Porringers, Salt-Cellars, Casters, Teapots, Coffee Pots, Sugar Basins, Cream Ewers, Milk Jugs, Centre Pieces, Cruets, Baskets, Old Chalices, and Patens.

Jewellery and Medals.   Bronzes and Clocks.
Old Irish Glass.   Oil Paintings.
China.   Water Colours.

Engravings and Prints.

A Collection of Antique Furniture, including Very Fine Old Carved Side Table and other examples in Early Chippendale and Sheraton.

TO BE SOLD BY AUCTION

AT THE MART, 70, SOUTH MALL, CORK,

3 rd July

.. ON ..

Monday, 1st May, 1916, and Four Following Days,

COMMENCING AT 11.30 A.M. EACH DAY.

2nd, 30th   1st July

On View 27th, 28th and 29th April.

J. J. McCABE, Esq., LL.B.,
Solicitor for Executors, No. 17, South Mall, Cork.

W. MARSH & SONS, Auctioneers, Cork.

A notice in respect of one of the auctions, no doubt postponed because of the 1916 Rising.

When " G.B.S." was a clerk

13º August 1873

Sunday leases handed Mr. Todd this day, see list endorsed in Mr. Manly's letter of 12th Aug. '73.

G.B. Shaw

The above is a reproduction of a document in the late George Bernard Shaw's handwriting, now in the possession of Mr. Arthur F. Bennett of Messrs. Townshend & Dickinson, M.I.A.A. George Bernard Shaw in his boyhood days was employed for a period by the old established Dublin firm as an estate agent's clerk.

The auctioneering profession's loss was the literary profession's gain.

Mrs. Albert McArthur, M.I.A.A.
First lady to hold an Auctioneer's Licence in the Irish
Free State

A View of Westmoreland Street in 1815.
From an Old Dublin Print.   McCleary.

MORE than One Hundred Years ago
THE HOUSE OF
BATTERSBY AND COMPANY

was established, and in the century that has elapsed,
the business has developed in such a manner, due
to its up-to-date methods, that to-day the concern
is looked upon generally as the leading firm in the
profession in Ireland.

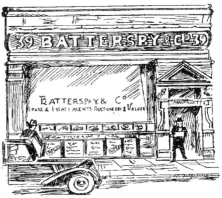

Our Head Offices in Westmoreland Street To-day.

"Who lasts a century can have no flaw."
—POPE.

AUCTION GALLERIES, SALEROOMS AND
OFFICES,
39 WESTMORELAND STREET, DUBLIN, C.3.
Our Auctions of Property, Estates and Furniture
are advertised regularly in the Daily Papers,
and are issued also in illustrated Brochure
form, which can be sent free on application.

Left to right; Mr. Michael Quirke, Vice President, 1925;
L.C. Cuffe, President, 1923-24, Vice President, 1925;
James S. McMahon, President, 1925-26

Extract from Battersby & Co. Centenary brochure
published 1915

THE
IRISH AUCTIONEERS AND ESTATE AGENTS' ASSOCIATION.

(Incorporated under the Companies Acts, 1908 to 1917.)

FRANK WARNER,
Secretary.

Telephone No.—Dublin 735.
Telegrams:—"Warner, Dublin."

23 LOWER ORMOND QUAY,

DUBLIN.

July, 20th, 1926.

YEAR BOOK, 1927.

Dear Sir(s),

I am directed to inform you that our Council have decided, at the suggestion of several members, that the next edition of our Year Book will date from 1st January to 31st December, 1927.

The first edition (although many Solicitors and Government officials expressed their appreciation of its usefulness), was in some respects disappointing, but the information in our next publication has been considerably added to, and will contain much additional information. In addition there will be a ruled and date printed Diary—three days to a page—for the year.

The printing and advertising departments have been entrusted to Messrs. George F. Healy & Coy., Ltd., 23 Lower Ormond Quay, Dublin, who may be relied upon to put the best workmanship into the publication, and it is hoped that those of our members who desire to secure spaces for advertisements, will lose no time in communicating with Messrs. Healy. Several members were disappointed last year owing to their advertisements failing to reach the printers in time, so that early application for space is essential.

I would remind you that the Year Book will be placed in the hands of all the leading Solicitors, Government Departments, &c., throughout Ireland, so that as an advertising medium the publication is a most valuable one. The Council hope, therefore, that all members will give it their support, as of course advertisements from Auctioneers other than members of this Association will not be accepted.

The rates for advertisements are as follows:—

Full Page (Members)	£10 10 0	Other Businesses		£12 12 0
Half Page	„	5 10 0	„	„	6 6 0
Third Page	„	4 0 0	„	„	4 4 0
Quarter Page	„	3 0 0	„	„	3 3 0

If special positions such as inside and back of cover, and top and bottom of Diary portion, are required, prices will be quoted by the printers on application.

Yours faithfully,
FRANK WARNER,
Secretary.

November 14 that a sale had been agreed. The housing committee reported that the cost of the house, £6,500, the house agent's commission £162 10s, repairs, alterations and decorations were to be met by sale of investments amounting to £4,703 11s and a £4,000 bank loan.

"The House occupies a commanding position in one of the most sought-after districts in the City and when repairs are completed will be worthy of the Association," the annual report stated. A "beautiful" room was immediately set aside for the use of members for property sales and this new "auction mart" was to be much availed of by both city and provincial members from the outset. Fee for the use of the new salesroom was £3 3s 0d per day or part thereof. In 1959, the suite of offices and return not occupied by the Association became vacant by the death of the late Dr D.J. Cummins and was let to a well-known Dublin solicitor, Mr Hugh J. Fitzpatrick, at a rental of £300 per annum, plus rates, RV £40.

The new IAA headquarters is an imposing Georgian edifice. Its history mirrors that of the other fine properties in this fashionable precinct — buildings that today are among the jewels in Dublin's architectural crown. When Samuel Sproule bought a vacant lot of ground where Merrion Square meets Mount Street near Holles Street in the late nineteenth century, he was not called a developer. The modern term — sometimes of distaste — had not yet been coined. Yet to all intents and purposes, that was what Sproule was. He was also, for a time at least, the employer of the great Francis Johnston. He was other things too, a man of all parts — developer, contractor, decorator and stuccadore, in the great tradition of Dublin stucco artists. Sproule is thought to have built five houses on the corner of Merrion Square East, probably selling them to their first owners before they were entirely finished so that the new occupant could have the house finished to his or her taste — a tradition once again currently in vogue with developers of luxury Dublin houses.

No. 38 is one of Sproule's original five buildings, alike in many respects to its fellows, but with many highly individual flourishes. Since it was built in the 1780s, the property has had the usual chequered career of all such Georgian houses — a private house of the "Upstairs Downstairs" variety, then a gradual shift into more professional use (James Joyce's dentist is reputed to have once held rooms there) and finally to the office function it fulfils today. The Association acquired the entire building, but occupied just the main two floors, with the upper and bottom floors held by tenants.

New brooms were soon sweeping clean at the new IAA HQ — but only after some little time had elapsed, and for the most mundane of reasons. At the general meeting on July 9, a member drew attention to the state of the hall door. This was referred to the house committee on July 17, where it was unanimously decided "that the Hall Door and Hall be painted". It was explained that this would have been attended to much earlier, but had been deferred at the request of solicitor Mr Fitzpatrick so that the paintwork would not be scratched during the removal of his furniture into the IAA building. Otherwise, it was business as usual. After the move.

No. 38 Merrion Square was destined to prove a more than appropriate headquarters building — a tall, Georgian red-brick terraced house flanked at one stage on either side by the British Embassy at No. 39 and the Deutches Kulturinstitut. A broad, tiled entrance hall, its walls decorated in abstract designs of mushroom and white, led to a sweeping eighteenth-century staircase. The brackets holding the original oil lamps were still below the white-painted fanlights, while the ceilings were decorated with intricate mouldings and elaborately carved woodwork. At the rear of the hallway stood a small cupboard with a wooden grille ventilating the top; in different times, this might well have served as a broom cupboard or a press where the housemaids kept their buckets and pails. In fact, this "cupboard" was none other than the living quarters of the footman in the days when the other half lived the way the other half would like to live today! A Wedgwood-blue and white interior decor scheme was chosen for the auctioneers' hall and council chamber, highlighted with thick seaweed-green fitted carpets throughout. A new 20-foot long oak conference table seated up to 24 members.

The Association, meanwhile, continued to progress in ways other than physical expansion. A group voluntary health insurance scheme was introduced through the Voluntary Health Insurance Board in 1958 for members, their families and staff. Due to serious claims against the collective guarantee bond for the year 1957/58, the Irish National Insurance Company sought a substantial increase in the bond premium. Council sought quotations elsewhere and obtained better terms from the Shield Insurance Co. A rate of £7 was accepted in the best interests of members.

Following representations from a provincial bar association, the council of the Incorporated Law Society approached the IAA in 1957 on the sensitive issue of relations between solicitors and auctioneers, with a view to joint action "to discourage certain objectionable practices". Standing arrangements between solicitors and auctioneers whereby each party habitually employed the other for clients' business were condemned in the annual report:

> Where there is a reciprocal understanding or arrangement with the Auctioneer, such conduct on the part of a Solicitor may very well fall within the prohibition against unfair attraction of business contained in the Solicitors' Act 1954 (Professional Practice Conduct and Discipline) Regulations 1955. The Irish Auctioneers' and Estate Agents' Association take the view that it forms no part of an Auctioneer's duty to advise vendors or purchasers of property as to the selection of a particular Solicitor and that any arrangement or understanding of the kind mentioned is greatly to be deplored.

Both the Society and the Association pointed out that "it is unprofessional and may be illegal for either a Solicitor or an Auctioneer to split costs or commission in consideration of the introduction of business".

At the suggestion of vice-president Anthony Sherry, a letter was forwarded to the Law Society regarding solicitors advertising properties for sale and letting by private treaty. Law Society secretary Eric Plunkett responded as follows at the end of the year:

> My Council direct me to say in reply that they would be unable to find themselves in agreement with your Association if it were suggested that Solicitors should not undertake Land Agency and Rent Collection work which has always been part of the normal practice of Solicitors, although they cannot claim an exclusive right in it any more than Auctioneers, Accountants or members of the public. With regard to the question of advertisements by Solicitors offering Property for Sale or Letting, my Council are in agreement with yours that in the interests of your

respective Bodies and their Members' Solicitors should not
hold themselves out as undertaking such work. It must,
however, be borne in mind that there is no legal prohibi-
tion which would prevent Solicitors or any other persons
from advertising Property for Sale or Letting on the instructions of clients and that cases do occur in which clients
may direct Solicitors to perform this work if so directed.
My Council feel that Members of this Society could not le-
gitimately refuse to accept instructions, having regard to
the particular relations which exist between Solicitors and
their clients. Subject to the foregoing considerations, my
Council are prepared to advise Members of this Society
that Solicitors should not undertake this business without
direct instructions from clients, and they hope that this will
meet the wishes of your Association.

Throughout this period, relations between both bodies remained
amicable, as witnessed again in 1958 when the Fitzwilliam Estates
invited solicitors to place properties on their books for sale by private treaty or public auction, and offered a percentage of fees earned
of 25 per cent to 33.3 per cent. The firm in question was not a member of the IAA, but the Law Society quickly wrote to each practising
solicitor in response to a letter from the Association pointing out
their professional obligations in the matter.

The matter of professional boundaries had, however, been causing friction for some time. The 1951 annual general meeting was
asked by a member "if it was professional and recognised by the Incorporated Law Society for Solicitors to act as Valuers". The law
agent in reply stated "that it is the practice where small properties
are concerned and there is a provision to that effect in the 'Statutory
Laws of Solicitors'". Provincial members pointed out that properties
amounting to £2,000-£3,000 and upwards had been valued by solicitors. The meeting determined that the Association should strongly
object to this practice and that the valuing of properties should be
left in the hands of qualified valuers. Representations were also
made by members in County Kildare to the undesirability of a law
clerk in possession of an auctioneer's licence carrying on business.
The matter was brought to the attention of the secretary of the Incorporated Law Society, which disapproved of the practice and condemned it in its gazette. Notwithstanding, the auctioneers in

question continued undaunted. In 1952, it was the turn of architects, engineers and builders to come under IAA fire for valuing properties offered as security for loans sought from building societies. The matter was reported to the Revenue Commissioners who responded that any person acting as an appraiser/valuer for a property chargeable with stamp duty is required to take out an appraiser's licence.

Inter-professional rivalries continued to surface throughout the decade. Eric Plunkett, secretary, Incorporated Law Society of Ireland, wrote the following letter to the IAA in September 1959:

> I have been directed by the Council to raise with your Association the question of the preparation of agreements for sale of property by auctioneers. It has come to the notice of the Council that in a number of cases auctioneers have drawn up open contracts for sale and had them signed by the purchaser or vendor or both parties before either had an opportunity of consulting a solicitor. It is obvious that this practice is contrary to the interests of clients and my Council would like to know whether your association is in a position to take action to prevent it. The Council have been surprised to learn that auctioneers of repute in the city of Dublin have engaged in this practice within recent years. It is also believed that the practice exists in country districts. In a number of cases in which these contracts or agreements were prepared by auctioneers, the interests of the parties were prejudicially affected because the contract was signed without legal advice as to its full meaning and implications and in some cases litigation between the parties has followed. I have also been asked by the Council to point out that they are advised that the preparation of such agreements by persons other than solicitors or barristers is contrary to the provisions of the Solicitors' Act, 1954. The Council will be greatly obliged if you submit this matter to your Council with a view to the prevention of the activities mentioned.

The IAA responded by drawing up a "preparation of agreements for sale" form. This was not intended to have any force as a binding contract, but to record an agreement in principle which must then be referred to the solicitors for the parties to be set out in proper form in a legal contract. At this juncture, the secretary reported that an action was being taken by the Law Society against a well-known provincial member in the west with regard to "drawing up agreements". In April of that year, a "widespread" practice of solicitors valuing properties for probate purposes was reported by council.

The vast majority of the queries submitted through the Association for legal advice in the early 1950s, however, were in connection with claims for commission. In a paper read at a general meeting of the IAA at the Clarence Hotel in Dublin in July 1952, a solicitor stressed that claims for commission can only succeed when it can be clearly established that there is a contractual obligation on the part of the auctioneer's client to pay the auctioneer. He urged auctioneers to have their retainers from their clients covered by a very clear agreement. If at all possible, that agreement should be in writing and should set out the fees payable for a particular transaction and the event upon which they were payable. The solicitor instanced a case where an auctioneer sued for commission in accordance with the scale of charges adopted by the IAA. "The Court did not recognise that sale as being binding on the client sued because he had not been put on notice that the Auctioneer would charge his fees according to it," the solicitor stated. "Furthermore, it was held that there was no evidence that that scale was so widely known to the public at large as to be established as a custom within the legal sense of the word." He added:

> The best way of all of avoiding misunderstandings as be-
> tween auctioneers and clients is to have the retainers of the
> former clearly set out in writing and signed by the latter.
> Many Auctioneers, while accepting fully the wisdom of
> this, feel that it is bad business to have such formality with
> clients. In reply, it can only be stated that it is even worse
> business having disputes which arise from a lack of formal-
> ity.

At the 1954 IAA annual dinner, the Minister for Justice, attending as guest speaker, said that Government would pay the Association the tribute of introducing legislation laying down rules and regulations for the auctioneers' profession. He added that he would like to see the Association sponsoring such legislation and taking full respon-sibility for it. "In cases where there was default on the part of Asso-ciation members, the persons placed at a loss should get compensation out of a fund provided by the Association," the Minister declared.

The following notice from IAA secretary Michael Grey appeared in the *Evening Mail*, *Irish Independent*, *Irish Press*, and *Irish Times* on March 19 and October 23, 1958:

> It has come to the notice of the Association that certain Dublin Auctioneers have within recent months imposed a charge for supplying lists of Properties available for sale and/or letting. NOTICE IS HEREBY GIVEN THAT SUCH A CHARGE IS NOT SANCTIONED BY THE ASSOCIATION. The furnishing of lists is a service which, for generations, has been available to the public FREE OF CHARGE. NO CHANGE IN THIS POSITION IS CONEMPLATED.

The directive arose from a complaint from a member of the public earlier in the year regarding a request for payment of a registration fee when seeking information on a house to rent.

An IAA delegation met the Dublin Newspaper Committee on April 5, 1955 at The Mail Chambers in Parliament Street to press for a reduction in the high cost of newspaper advertising. Their mission was unsuccessful, however, as the newspaper managers could not promise any reduction in the cost of display adverts or any corresponding increase on the prevailing rate of auctioneers' discount, owing to the high cost of newsprint and increases in wages, freight and storage.

Increases on market tolls and rentals caused alarm in 1956 when auctioneers operating in the wholesale food market were confronted by a demand for a 100 per cent increase in all tolls (including weighing tolls). Weekly rents of stands in the food market ranged from 1/3d to 3/9d per square yard. The Corporation proposed to fix a minimum rent of 2/6d per square yard, all stands becoming vacant to be offered for tender. The Association made representations to the parliamentary secretary to the Minister for Agriculture Mr Oliver J. Flanagan — to no avail, however, as the Minister was held to have no function as regards the fruit and vegetable market.

Two cases were received in 1956 from provincial members in which articles sold were found to be subject to hire purchase contracts. The cases were put before the law adviser who stated:

> In general, an Auctioneer who sells property without the
> authority of the true legal owner is liable to that Owner
> under a Hire Purchase agreement, the legal ownership of
> the goods remain vested in the Hire Purchase Company
> until the Hire Purchaser has fully discharged all the obli-
> gations of the Hire Purchase agreement so as to acquire
> ownership of the goods.

The Association pointed out that practically all hire purchase finance
companies operating in Ireland at the time were members of Hire
Purchase Information Ltd. and urged members to work in arrangement with this company.

The auctioneer's responsibility in connection with a deposit received on a sale of property was another frequent source of difficulty,
while auctioneers' liability in connection with seizure of cattle for
rates and annuities was a further flashpoint. In many cases, the stock
of the renter was seized because the rates or the Land Commission
Annuities on the land had not been paid. Under Section 29 of the
Land Act of 1927, the auctioneer was bound to pay the Land Commission first. This arose from the custom whereby auctioneers set
lands on the eleven months system. In such cases, in the absence of a
cash payment, the auctioneer took bills from the purchaser or renter
of the land, made payable to the auctioneer and not the vendor or
owner of the lands. It was deemed easier for the auctioneer to get the
bills discounted than for the owner of the lands.

In general, the late 1950s were bad times for the property business
— so bad, in fact, that Mrs Daisy MacArthur tells of young couples
emigrating who didn't even try to sell their houses, many simply
boarded up the houses and left. Whether it was the depressed state
of the market or perhaps a touch of male chauvinism, the bank she
approached for assistance in 1958 after the death of her husband
Reginald (and who had dealt with the family for three generations)
refused to help her to take over the running of the firm. Two years
later, however, Daniel Stephenson of James H. North & Co., asked
Daisy to join his firm and she agreed. Unusually for a woman in
those times, she preferred the commercial property market to the
residential and had an excellent rapport with the industrial-
ists/developers of the day. Daisy was indeed responsible for the letting of the first of a number of Ireland's purpose-built commercial

properties — O'Connell Bridge House in 1964 and the sale/letting of the first five units in the John F. Kennedy Industrial Estate on the Naas Road. Indeed, Daisy recalled later that she was rarely without her wellingtons and map of the latter location. She also worked in the retail sector and was involved in the development/letting of Dublin's first modern arcade — the Grafton Arcade, once the site of Knowles' fruit, flowers and vegetable shop.

By contrast, those years with James H. North in the 1960s were boom times for the property business and Daisy said in 1987 that she was lucky to have experienced them — times have never been quite so good since then, she declared. The grand old lady of Irish auctioneering also counted herself fortunate to have worked with Daniel Stephenson who, she related, was an excellent delegator and who gave her the confidence to follow through all deals alone. With a sense of propriety typical of a more refined era, Daisy asserted that in her years in the property business she never encountered any sexist discrimination within the profession and declared that she was always treated with respect and courtesy by both fellow professionals and clients alike.

Her story about the launch of *The Irish Press* will no doubt wryly amuse many agents who are today bombarded with requests from advertising salespeople. The newspaper launch was greeted with something akin to dismay by many agents and an informal agreement was reached that properties would only be advertised in *The Irish Times* and *Irish Independent*, because it was feared that, if one agency started to advertise with the new *Press*, they would all have to follow and advertising costs would increase. Advertising outlay was very carefully regulated in Daisy's time because in private treaty sales the advertisements were paid for by the agents themselves out of their 2.5 per cent fee, whereas the vendor paid for advertisements when the property was auctioned. Fees for auctions were normally 5 per cent and paid by the buyer. Perhaps this is one of the reasons auctions were such a popular form of sale in those days!

The MacArthurs had a long involvement with the Association. Daisy's husband Reginald was president from 1946–47 and his father Albert held that position in 1933. Daisy retired in 1969.

Things were scarcely any better on the Belfast property scene during the mid-1950s. Jonathan Baardon's history of the city explains why Belfast is sometimes referred to as the hub of the Black North:

> Despite its fine setting, Belfast is not built on a perfect site. Much of the land is low-lying, prone to flooding and composed of muddy sleech providing an uncertain base for buildings as the leaning Albert Clock indicates; in dockland after the Point Fields had been drained wooden piles 30 to 40 feet long had to be driven through the blue clay to the bedrock underneath to take the weight of the larger buildings. The semi-circle of hills encourage a pall of smoke to hang over the city; 425 tons of tar and soot per square mile were recorded as falling on the city centre in 1954. The choking atmosphere uniting with a penetrating dampness largely accounted for the high rates of death from tuberculosis and bronchitis until very recent times. . . . So uninviting was the Lagan mouth that it was not until the seventeenth Century that a town stood there at all. Belfast became a booming industrial city in the nineteenth Century, but the twentieth Century has been characterised in many ways by violence — firstly through two world wars and over the past two and a half decades by paramilitary activity and sectarian violence.

But the property market is nothing if not resilient and demand was perking up discernibly, at least in Dublin. Writing in *The Irish Times* in January 1959, William Browne, auctioneer and valuer, Rathgar, reported that there was a brighter tendency in the market during the autumn of the previous year, with a keen demand for the smaller type houses and bungalows, especially near Dublin. Old houses, needing repairs, were selling better and he attributed this to the Government grant for structural alterations. Business premises were selling well at greatly reduced prices, especially those properties suitable for factories. Among recent sales were a semi-detached house in Orwell Road at £3,200; a residence at Upper Rathmines £2,750; a house at Harold's Cross £1,800; and a residential property at Rathgar Road, £1,900.

At the end of the decade, their were 566 IAA members and 22 associates.

Chapter Five

Modern Times — The Sixties

"Men honour property above all else;
it has the greatest power in human life"
— Euripides, *The Phoenician Women.*

The first Programme for Economic Expansion 1958-63 represents a major watershed in Irish financial history. The property industry was a major beneficiary of the new drive to concentrate the national development effort on structural investment in terms of industry and production, inspired by Taoiseach Seán Lemass and celebrated secretary at the Department of Finance Mr T.K. Whitaker. The 1960s marked a period of economic expansion after years of at best static national output, sewing the seeds of Ireland's first ever "property boom". Over this period, the Irish economy registered a growth rate of 4 per cent were annum — four times the average rate since independence. By 1963, the economy was growing faster than any in Europe. The success of the new economic policy had a profound psychological effect, dispelling the prevailing pessimism and boosting confidence nationwide. In Shannon, *Irish Times* journalist Michael Viney scented "the sweet tang of optimism . . . like an aura of aftershave applied freshly every morning".

A new office-property era dawned in Dublin, demand for industrial space rose significantly and other forms of commercial property experienced corresponding growth. Up to the mid-1950s, the emphasis had been largely on local authority and speculative housebuilding, the rehousing of citizens from the slums of Dublin and of those who chose not to emigrate. Now productivity became the economic catchcry as prosperity gradually improved and private housing boomed. The Electricity Supply Board pumped out 50 per cent more electricity in 1963 than it supplied five years before. The Stock

Exchange Index lurched up from 94 at the beginning of 1958 to 252 in May 1963.

Progress, however, had its inevitable price. In 1961, the wages of building workers increased by 17 per cent and construction activity increased considerably also — only to be interrupted by a seven-week strike in 1964. During the five years from 1958, wage rates rose by 32 per cent in Dublin (and almost as much elsewhere). In 1962, there was a massive 10 to 12 per cent wage hike. However, even though the growth rate was in excess of 3 per cent per annum, a Second Programme for Economic Expansion was ultimately abandoned because its ambitious targets were not reached and the initial momentum was not maintained. This was replaced by a watered-down Third Programme, reflecting a gradual disillusionment with the efficacy of economic planning. More pertinently, between 1961 and 1971, employment in agriculture fell by 28 per cent — a drop, however, counterbalanced by jobs growth in other sectors. The increase in non-agricultural employment was concentrated in the towns, with the result that the urban population grew more rapidly at the expense of the rural. Major inflows of capital from outside the State played an important role in the process of expansion. Foreign investment in industrial development began to accelerate — to such an extent, indeed, that by the end of the decade, gross national product had grown by almost 50 per cent, an annualised average rate of around 4 per cent.

Ireland's employment structure was transformed as a result, with radical implications for commercial property, as the downturn in agricultural jobs was matched by a corresponding increase in the industrial and service sectors. The number of office jobs rose by nearly 40 per cent during the decade. This process had a marked effect on the centre of Dublin in particular, where the number of office workers increased from around 42,000 to 72,000. Government and semi-state sectors were to the fore in this new demand for modern office accommodation. The total lettable area of office space completed over the next twenty years was approximately 9 million square feet in just under 300 purpose-built office blocks. Urban design expert Professor Patrick Malone characterised the ensuing pattern as follows :

The production of completed office space over the period
1960-83 may be characterised in terms of the relatively low
average level of output in the period up to 1968; the build-
up in ouptut, giving rise to the first "boom" period of the
early Seventies; a relative decline in output in the middle
Seventies, and the build-up in output to the second
"boom" period of the early Eighties.

In a very real sense, the property industry can be said to have come
of age at this time: "Many strangers think we are nothing but lepre-
chauns and live in the past; indeed, in property terms, we were ex-
traordinarily unsophisticated until the early 1960s," J.H. Guinness,
joint managing director, Guinness & Mahon merchant bankers told a
real estate conference in Dublin some years later.

The idea of quoting rents in square footage was unheard of
and, if anyone bothered to work out their rents in these
terms, he would find that prime space in the city centre often was rented for less than 10/- per square foot! It was not
until 1965 that the first modern office block was constructed in Dublin. Ever since then, activity has increased
and all talk as if plot ratios, curtain walls, net lettable areas
and bridging finance has been taught at nursery schools.

Among the pioneering examples of the new Dublin office development phenomenon were Hawkins House and O'Connell Bridge
House in the mid-1960s. Outline planning permission was granted in
September 1968 to New Ireland Assurance Company and Hardwicke
Ltd. for a development totalling over 300,000 square feet in central
Dublin bounded by Nassau Street, South Frederick Street, Molesworth Street and Kildare Street. Formed in 1935, Hardwicke was one
of the first to foresee the potential of the Irish commercial property
scene. Its earliest developments included Lansdowne House, the
Irish Dunlop Company office/industrial complex at Adelaide Road
and offices for IBM, the Allied Irish Bank Group and Ryan's Tourist
(Holdings). Assurance giant Irish Life — destined to become our
largest property development combine — came to the fore in 1965–
67. Most of these prototype projects were undertaken predominantly
within the insurance sector, but significant development by owner-
occupiers in the commercial and public sectors also took place. Approximately 75 per cent of the total area of office space completed

between 1964 and 1973 was indeed developed by commercial development companies, many of them British.

The advent of purpose-built commercial properties was destined to have a palpable impact on the existing fabric of the capital, all the more so as the first tranche of developments were mainly located in the heartland of the city where the physical effect was most pronounced: "The sudden burgeoning of administrative work space came when people realised that eighteenth- and nineteenth-century conversions were no longer adequate," architect Brian Hogan of Tyndall, Hogan & Hurley observed. "The alarm that people feel at the construction of so many modern office blocks will be purely temporary." The architect stressed the need for mixing residential buildings with the new offices to avoid a situation developing in Dublin similar to the City of London, where everything went dead after six o'clock: "A city must have vitality — a viable organism providing facilities. A city has a spirit. It must have identity — a life of its own. A city must have heightened activity. If it is dead, it is dead."

The architectural correspondent of *The Irish Times* wrote on December 21, 1959: "It is well known that, as far as the central city is concerned, the days of Dublin's Georgian heritage are numbered and that when these decayed and obsolete monuments of a past age come to be demolished, many of their sites will be redeveloped with buildings much larger in bulk and greater in height than the present ones." The price of progress and development was the razing to the ground of much of the fabric of the historic city core. The outcry over these increasingly frequent demolitions led to the emergence of conservation group An Taisce and the formation of the Irish Georgian Society, pledged to awakening public interest in Ireland's heritage of outstanding eighteenth-century buildings and campaigning for their preservation.

Paradoxically, the desire to preserve our architectural heritage was by no means a matter of preaching to the converted. The public receptivity towards modern building of often dubious merit was predicated to some extent, initially at least, by an unspoken undercurrent of populist satisfaction that the ascendancy's Georgian building stock had finally come to the end of its useful life and was about to be replaced by a completely new order. The battle for

Fitzwilliam Street was the first of many bitter struggles fought out in the streets of Dublin "between the forces of barbarism and civilisation", to quote *Irish Times* environment correspondent Frank McDonald, in his impassioned book *The Destruction of Dublin*, which chronicled the ravages wrought by speculators on the capital's building fabric.

"At stake was the fate of 16 late eighteenth-century houses which formed part of the longest and arguably the finest Georgian streetscape in the world, extending three-fifths of a mile from Holles Street Hospital to Lower Leeson Street," McDonald wrote on the Fitzwilliam Street saga.

> For the sake of a mere convenience, the Electricity Supply Board was determined to demolish these houses to make way for a modern office block. But the Board's diabolical plan for Fitzwilliam Street was vigorously opposed by the Irish Georgian Society which, for once, organised a spirited campaign that won widespread public support. It was an immense cultural confrontation between two irreconcilable views of Ireland and the fact that, in the end, the ESB won the argument was an outright disaster for Dublin.

Industrial development was equally dramatic. Around 150 home-based industries were established nationwide during the 1960s, with a further 350 foreign investors also locating in this country — representing a total investment in excess of £100 million. Industrial production increased by about £500 million as a result and generated around 50,000 new jobs, while industrial exports rose from around £51 million at the start of the decade to £214 million in 1969. Hand-in-hand with this industrial expansion went an increasing demand for infrastructural development — roads, hospitals, water supply schemes, schools and public buildings. Dublin's main industrial estates by the end of the decade were situated at Ballyfermot, in the Kylemore Road/Killeen Road region; at Bluebell, Inchicore; at Clonshaugh/Coolock; and on the John F. Kennedy Estate on the Naas Road. Outside Dublin, the success of the Shannon Free Airport Estate was followed in 1967 by the Government-sponsored Waterford and Galway industrial estates.

Until the merits of this innovatory approach to property development began to become self-evident, none of the Irish banks became directly involved in property finance. In the past, when a business concern wished to build itself an office, the development would have been financed by a bank overdraft if cash was not available from its own resources. Banks were more than willing to lend money to good customers and not too many awkward questions were asked about the use of funds, or even the length of the borrowing provided the security was good. All this was destined to change utterly, however, and a terrible commercial beauty was gradually born. The late 1960s saw a proliferation of merchant banks, finance companies and branch offices of North American banks in this country — just as eager to lend, but applying new and ever more rigid criteria which had evolved elsewhere in more urbanised economies.

A more opulent society likewise provided fertile soil for new retail development as international influences began to percolate through to Irish consumers. The first planned suburban shopping development to open in the Republic — Stillorgan Shopping Centre — began trading in summer 1966 and was developed at a cost of £1.5 million by MEPC (Ireland). This non-enclosed centre was to be the first of many: during the period 1966–90, 51 planned shopping developments with a cumulative total of 3 million square feet net retail floorspace opened for trade in Dublin alone. Stillorgan Shopping Centre was duly purchased from MEPC in 1984 by Salix Trust, the staff pension fund of Bank of Ireland for £12.3 million and subsequently sold to Treasury Holdings/Jermyn Investments for around £40 million in 1996. Meantime, the first shopping arcade in this country outside Dublin was Market Parade, Patrick Street, Cork, at the former Grant's premises where developer Green Property secured the first letting in March 1968. Green Property's next development was the £1 million Northside Shopping Centre.

By the end of the decade, two property companies were quoted on the Irish Stock Exchange — Associated Properties and Dublin Artisans Dwellings. Shares in the other active Irish property development companies were still privately held, although public flotations were expected in the foreseeable future. The unit trust movement had not yet developed, but the low profile Irish Pension Fund Property Unit Trust was established and confined to self-administered pension funds. IPFPUT was to fund many of the largest commercial property developments in the capital over the next three decades, attaining a total value of £190 million by 1995.

The building societies were another major success story in the financial markets, emerging as a major force in the 1960s and 1970s. Although mostly founded in the late nineteenth century, building societies continued to be low-key mutual operations — much like the credit unions of today — during the first half of the twentieth century. In the late 1950s, the Irish Permanent started an aggressive advertising campaign for funds. The rest is history, as the IP moved from the number 12 society position to number one in the mortgage league. The total assets of the building society movement as a whole registered a remarkable 75-fold growth from £16 million in 1960 to £1.2 billion in 1980.

The 1963 Planning & Development Act was a major landmark, effectively laying the foundations for the newly emergent modern commercial property industry in Ireland. The measure followed closely the Town and County Planning Act 1961 of England and Wales. The principal provision of the Irish Act was the establishment of 87 planning authorities which were required to prepare development plans for their individual areas. The *Architects' Journal* commented that Ireland had made a late start to physical planning, but this could prove to be "a great advantage to a country; it is the pioneers who make the worst mistakes, and latecomers learn from them". Predictably, the development plan process was to spawn argument without end as zoning and other issues raised their heads over the years. But this again was the price of progress and "progress" is the most elusive of commodities — like "beauty", it is in the eye of the beholder.

"The resurgence of interest in all forms of planning is closely associated with the rise to power of Sean Lemass, who became Taoiseach in 1959 and who had demonstrated a consistent commitment to planning over the previous thirty years," comments Michael Bannon in his definitive study on planning history.

> Under his leadership, and with the support of a committed Minister for Local Government, there emerged a broadly based confidence in the role of development planning at local, regional and national level. Indeed, Ireland's achievements in the field of planning in the early 1960s

were to serve as a model to inspire action in other relatively underdeveloped societies and emerging nations.

Purpose-built office blocks, new shopping centres, commercial
investment properties and the wider availability of development finance presented unprecedented challenges together with corresponding opportunities. The largely unchanged face of Dublin city
centre was suddenly redrafted by the intrusion of taller buildings,
using modern materials which often stood ill-at-ease with older
neighbouring facades. Three new suburban towns were created to
the west — Tallaght, Blanchardstown and Clondalkin — as the capital sprawled ever outwards to ultimately comprise one million people, nearly a quarter of the entire population of the island. Section 4
of the Housing Act 1969 eventually imposed a control on the demolition of any habitable house or the use of it otherwise than for human habitation without the permission of the housing authority.

Fortunes were made by entrepreneurs willing to stake their all on
the new development phenomenon. These speculators topped the
Irish earnings lists, although its was impossible to quantify exactly
how much they made from the property boom. Ordinary lifestyles
were less lavish. Providing a flavour of Dublin domestic life in 1963,
Tony Farmar quotes the following in his revealing book on the Irish
middle class:

> Liam and Maureen lived in a six-roomed house near the
> Phoenix Park, for which they paid £73 a year. A slightly
> grander house, such as a three bedroom, two reception in
> Stillorgan was advertised for £4,100; one in Rathgar, five
> bedrooms, three reception, for £6,000 and a five-bedroom
> house on one-third of an acre in Foxrock for £8,500. This
> was two-and-a-half times the taxable income of the average
> surtax payer. In all, Dubliners spent only 10 per cent of
> their income on housing, which was less than they spent
> on drink and tobacco.

The dire urban poverty and exploitation that came about in the nineteenth century had by now been largely relieved by public provision
of houses and by legislation controlling the relationship of landlord
to tenant — although shortcomings in the latter sphere have persisted right down to the present day. The tenement problem too

proved remorselessly difficult to eradicate. In 1963, a house in Fenian Street collapsed with consequent loss of life. Efforts to improve the lot of inner-city dwellers in many cases merely transplanted social problems from decaying precincts into soulless and blighted new suburban ghettos. The decision to shift thousands of underprivileged people to gaunt high-rise tower blocks at Ballymun in 1967 spawned a whole new generation of socio-economic problems.

"The pattern of car ownership had now altered so radically that the design of roads for cars had become a dominant concern of planners," Fionnuala Hayes, architectural inspector, Department of the Environment, explained at the 1996 National Housing Conference.

> Concern also for pedestrian safety led to a near obsession with sight lines and visibility, so that the scale of roads and the spacing of houses was altered radically. The distance between the fronts of houses was increased significantly to accommodate front gardens long enough to park one or two cars in, a wide pavement, a wide grass verge for services to run in and a wide road.

> Even on a short cul-de-sac, the houses needed to be 28 metres apart, and this increased on more substantial housing roads. This pushing apart of small scale buildings (two storey semi-detached in the main) made it almost impossible to bring any sort of vibrancy to the street — no more "eyes on the street", no more carefully designed corners, no more intimacy, no more life and activity on the street — just lots of hard surfaces and a long ribbon of grass to be kept cut by the local authority, or to turn to mud in wet winter weather, an area to divide rather than unite. And these roads drive onwards, without punctuation or variation.

Such considerations, however, were as nothing compared to broader cosmic issues overhanging the new generation. "The answer, my friend, is blowin' in the wind," American folk idol Bob Dylan intoned — touching a global chord. In 1965, the Department of Civil Defence responded by issuing a 56-page booklet entitled "Survival in a Nuclear War — Advice on Protection in the Home and on the Farm". The text — re-issued in 1971 — pulled no punches:

Nuclear weapons have added a new and deadly peril to modern war — RADIOACTIVE FALL-OUT. It can come to us on the wind from other countries. It cannot be seen or felt, but we have instruments to tell us when it is about. In a nuclear war, thousands of our people could die from the effects of radioactive fall-out and thousands more could become seriously ill, if they did not know how to protect themselves. Protection is not too difficult for the householder to provide for himself and his family. . . .The risk of nuclear war, which has caused the Government to issue this booklet specially for householders, may remain for many years. So keep the booklet carefully. Hang it, or place it, where you can easily find it in an emergency — it could mean the difference between life and death for you and your family.

Such apocalyptic forebodings notwithstanding, the day-to-day concerns of the average householder were much more pedestrian. Property ownership was a burning issue. Urban development was generally achieved by way of building and/or proprietary leases. A building lease was made in respect of a property where the house was already built and the tenant paid the price of the house to the landlord from whom they were getting the property. Since the tenant either built the house or paid for it, the rent was usually referred to as a "ground rent" — that is, a rent that related to the ground that the house was built on rather than the house itself. Nevertheless, when the term of years in the lease ran out, the original position of the law was that the landlord could resume possession of the property — house and all. There was general questioning among those who had paid dearly for their houses as to why they and their children should have to pay a ground rent with nothing in return, or why the landlord should have the right to take their house off them when the lease ran out.

In the early 1960s, the Association of Combined Residents' Associations (ACRA) mounted an active campaign for the abolition of ground rents. Eventually, a number of acts were passed to enable and facilitate tenants in purchasing the fee simple from their landlords, thereby redeeming the ground rents. ACRA continued to seek total abolition of ground rents without compensating landlords — a demand considered impossible by the Government in view of the guarantee of property rights in the constitution. The principal acts passed in this field were the Landlord and Tenant (Ground Rents) Act 1967 and the Landlord and Tenant (Ground Rents) (No. 2) Act 1978. The latter Act had an original life of five years, but this was extended indefinitely by subsequent enabling acts. Proinnsias O Cillin, chief examiner of Titles in the Land Registry Centenary, 1892-1992, explains:

> It enabled the Land Registry to issue vesting certificates, vesting the fee simple in the tenant of a dwelling house whose lease comes within the Act, thus avoiding the necessity of paying the legal fees involved in getting deeds executed by the landlords. Where the consent of a landlord is not given, the Act enables the Land Registry to arbitrate the matter, to fix the purchase price and hold the purchase money until claimed by the landlord.

In 1978, it was thought that there were about 250,000 residential ground rents in existence. To date, around 59,000 vesting certificates have been issued by the Land Registry. This indicates that there are about 200,000 householders who have not yet bought out their ground rents.

New horizons were being exploited outside the country too. In 1963, the Irish Auctioneers' & Estate Agents' Association was admitted to membership of the International Real Estate Federation (FIABCI). The link-up with this influential world real estate body — founded in Paris in 1951 and today comprising some 7,000 members worldwide — ushered in a new cosmopolitan dimension to the affairs of the Association. IAA members have attended every subsequent council meeting in Paris and all world congresses in centres as far apart as Tokyo and Mexico City. Since 1954, FIABCI has had consultative status as a non-governmental organisation with the Committee of Housing, Building and Planning of the Economic Commission for Europe under the United Nations Economic & Social Council. It has a permanent representative with that body in Geneva and in New York, and is also represented at various meetings and seminars throughout the world. All things considered, Ireland has made a quite remarkable impact on this worldwide body considering its comparatively late arrival on the scene and its small population base.

Paris-based FIABCI secretary-general Jean Bailly travelled to Dublin on January 12, 1963 to pave the way for the initial Irish membership, while IAA president Liam Maher of Roscrea in turn travelled to Paris on the occasion of the actual application for membership and was cordially received there by FIABCI president Elie Cordier. R.E. Corish was elected president of the Irish chapter of FIABCI later that year and continued in this office until 1971 when Anthony Sherry assumed office. During the negotiations to establish the Irish link, proceedings were delayed because the international body was unable to decide what level of subscription it should demand from a country with such a small prospective membership base. A £5.00 subscription was ultimately decided. The Irish contingent was not long in making itself felt: the local chapter totalled some 160 members by the end of the decade and its efforts bore fruit in abundance when this country was chosen as the venue for the prestigious FIABCI annual congress in 1970. The final decision was taken by the FIABCI council in Mexico, with Ireland winning out against stiff international competition. The Dublin Congress was destined to prove an outstanding success and local chapter president Mr Corish was awarded a medal of honour in recognition of his outstanding services to the international body. At the Montreal Congress in 1971, Laurence J. McCabe, Dublin was awarded the same honour.

More humdrum domestic matters continued to exercise the majority of IAA members, however. The collapse of a floor at a furniture sale by a Dublin member was discussed at the annual general meeting on March 31, 1960. Similar earlier incidents at Ennistymon in 1950 and more recently in Ennis were recalled. After much discussion, it was agreed that members would be well advised to have ample third-party risk cover and that the secretary make enquiries with regard to a "block policy" for the benefit of members. A public liability insurance policy was duly arranged with a £100,000 limit.

Elsewhere, an auctioneer from Bray, County Wicklow brought to the notice of the meeting a case of a fellow-member undercutting his colleagues on fees. A lengthy debate ensued after which is was decided that the area of Dublin District be defined as Dublin City and County, to include Bray and Greystones. It was also agreed that a fee

2.5 per cent payable by the vendor be charged on private dwellings and business properties. The following rider was added:

> The Select Committee wishes to make it quite clear that the Member was within his rights in raising the question of 5 per cent fee as laid down in Scales of Charges. The Select Committee, however, would ask the Member to accept the recommendations now made in view of the fact that the 5 per cent fee is very strongly opposed by the Public and Solicitors.

Council was unable to negotiate a collective bond on favourable terms for 1961/62 and advised members to make their own individual bonding arrangements. A sliding scale was also agreed for Land Commission sales (5 per cent on the first £5,000; 3.75 per cent on the next £2,500; 2.5 per cent on the next £2,500; and 1.25 per cent on the balance). A Government Commission on Ground Rents was appointed in 1961 and former IAA president Daniel Stephenson of James H. North & Co. was appointed a member of the Commission on the nomination of the Minister for Finance. Council again "strongly deprecated" the inclusion of Sunday as a "View Day" in 1961, reminding members of their obligation not to act in a manner prejudicial to the reputation of the Association. The basement of the new IAA headquarters was let soon afterwards "at a very satisfactory rent". The housing committee was, in the meantime, also negotiating a letting of the rear of the headquarters building.

The problem of solicitors advertising private treaty sales resurfaced in 1962, when newspaper cuttings highlighting the practice were forwarded by the IAA to the Incorporated Law Society. A lengthy memorandum from a Dublin firm advocating that "this might be an opportune time to suggest a further innovation: that the Members should consider advertising in one daily paper only" was placed before the annual general meeting in March 1962. The proposal was referred to a subsequent general meeting in July, where opinion was divided. A committee to discuss "amongst other things, the question of cost, discount etc." with the Newspapers Managers' Committee was formed comprising representatives from leading Dublin auctioneering firms Jackson-Stops & McCabe; Hamilton & Hamilton (Estates); Daniel Morrissey & Sons; Murphy, Buckley & Keogh; and James H. North & Co.

The decision that members be advised to consult their own insurance company or brokers in connection with their bonds for 1963/64 was described by the secretary as "calamitous" for provincial members. Over 200 members had not received their bonds by the time the 1964 annual report was completed. "The position at the moment was chaotic," the 1964 annual report stated. "Members in Dublin and in the Provinces were clamouring for their Certificates of Deposit." With this end in mind, it was unanimously decided to revert to the collective bond procedure.

The law relating to the profession of auctioneers — the term now generally used to incorporate both auctioneers and estate agents — is governed by the licensing provisions of the Auctioneers and House Agents Acts 1947–73. "While the licensing law concerned is unique to Auctioneers and House Agents, the general legal principles that are relevant to the practice of estate agency are to be found for the most part in the Law of Contract and of Tort applicable to all aspects of commerce," Alan P. Mahon, SC, explains in his authoritative publication on auctioneering and estate agency law in Ireland. The term "auctioneer" is now generally used to incorporate auctioneers, estate agents and valuers of property. A simple definition of an auctioneer is an agent who is engaged or contracted to sell or dispose of property at auction or by private treaty. This will include actual sales or disposals of property and the letting of property. In more recent times, the business of many Auctioneers, particularly in larger towns and cities, has been expanded to include property management, property consultancy work and in some instances the management of building society sub-offices. Auctioneers frequently act as financial and mortgage brokers in an effort to offer the consumer the most comprehensive service possible, but their role in this regard is essentially separate from their role as auctioneer or estate agent. Mahon adds:

> While a professional qualification is not required for a person to practise as an Auctioneer, or House Agent, the entry into the practice of an Auctioneer or House Agent is nevertheless governed by statute, namely the Auctioneers and House Agents Acts of 1947, 1967 and 1973 and the regulations made thereunder, and in particular the Auctioneers and House Agents Act 1947 (Accountants Examination and

Certificate) Regulations 1968 (S.I. number 10 of 1968). The legislation effectively provides for the licensing of Auctioneers and for a fine of up to £500 for any person convicted of holding himself out or representing himself as carrying on the business of an Auctioneer or who conducts an auction without a licence.

The evolution of a new and more sophisticated property industry corresponded with — and was indeed determined by — a strong and resourceful IAA. It was no mere coincidence that 1964 marked a high point of the IAA's educational efforts with the establishment of a high-level structured course. In that year, a three-year part-time day and evening course of studies leading to a qualification for membership of the IAA was inaugurated at the School of Professional Studies, College of Commerce, Rathmines, Dublin. This was then to be the standard of academic qualification for entrance to membership of the Institute. No person could be admitted as a member unless he/she had successfully completed this course or an alternate academic course of instruction recognised by the Institute. Shortly afterwards, an additional facility was provided for students enabling them to qualify by correspondence through the College of Estate Management in London. Membership was restricted from 1970 to applicants who had either completed the programmes of study or held equivalent qualifications.

By this time, six regional committees had been formed within the Institute and the Association was functioning in a highly effective manner. Pressure was accordingly on again for a reform of overall auctioneering standards. A memorandum to the Minister for Justice from the IAA in early 1964 stated:

> The Association feels that the ease with which persons without suitable qualifications can set up in business as auctioneers, house agents and valuers is completely unsatisfactory and requires prompt remedial action in the public interest.

The memorandum declared that the 1947 Act was "very inadequate", pointing out that anyone wanting to set up in business solely as a valuer does not even have to get a certificate of qualification. The memo continued:

The Auctioneers & House Agents Act 1947 lays down a
procedure requiring a so-called Certificate of Qualification
to be obtained from a District Justice as a condition prece-
dent to getting an Auctioneer's or house agent's licence. It
is mandatory on a Justice to grant a certificate unless the
application therefor is opposed and an objection sustained
on one of the statutory grounds mentioned in the Act. It is
rare for an objection to be made and this type of negative
control serves little or no useful purpose in working practice. A person wanting to set up in business as a valuer
simply has to take out a £2 licence from the Revenue
Commissioners which can be obtained for the asking.

The IAA argued that persons holding themselves out as experts in
their business as auctioneers, house agents or valuers are not required by law to have any kind of training or practical working experience to qualify them to render a competent service to the public.
Neither were they required in any positive sense to satisfy the court
as to their financial strength and integrity notwithstanding the fact
that in the course of their business they might be handling very substantial sums of money entrusted to them. The Association stated:

The £2,000 bond required by the Act no longer provides
adequate protection to the public — assuming it was originally adequate. Firstly, the value of money has considerably depreciated since this sum was fixed in 1947. Secondly,
property values have gone up very considerably since 1947
with the result, for example, that one sale at current average prices for small properties can involve an amount
equal to or greater than the present bond value.

After lengthy consideration, it was decided that an auctioneers'
compensation fund was not a practical proposition at this stage. It
was felt that the only solution was therefore a substantial increase in
the existing £2,000 bond. Accordingly, insurance brokers Hamilton &
Hamilton issued quotations ranging from a £4,000 indemnity
(premium £18) to £10,000 (£420). Stressing that its reform efforts
stretched back over thirty years, the Association urged that the status
of auctioneers, house agents and valuers ought be raised to a proper
professional level based on minimum educational standards followed by proper courses of professional studies and examinations:

In the light of experience since 1932, the Association would suggest some modification of the 1932 Bill to enable the Association to function on a basis akin to, say, that of the Incorporated Law Society of Ireland, i.e. the Association would: (1) act as a registration and disciplinary authority and (2) act as a general representative body. Though its jurisdiction would be mandatory on all, membership in the Association in capacity (2) would be optional.

On the basis of its earlier experience, the IAA acknowledged that a system such as it was proposing could not commence to produce effective control for about five or six years. A minimum apprenticeship and study period of three years was, for example, envisaged by the Association, while it would take a good deal of time to get the requisite Bill on the statute book. Short-term amendments to the 1947 Act were thus urgently required to cover this five/six year period. The short-term action plan aimed at ensuring that a certificate of qualification could only be obtained by an applicant who satisfied the court that he or she had a minimum standard of technical competence and was financially sound so as to be worthy of public trust. The Association also urged that the amount of the bond be substantially increased. On the technical side, there should be a requirement for an applicant to show that he had served a proper period of apprenticeship of a minimum of three years or for a similar period had served as an assistant or clerk with an auctioneer in bona fide practice or had already been in practice as a licensed auctioneer for a minimum period of three years. On the financial side, the applicant should have at least to satisfy the court as to his solvency. An IAA deputation headed by president Arthur Bennett met Minister for Justice Mr Charles Haughey in Government Buildings on May 4, 1964 to discuss the IAA recommendations, but to no avail. "The result of the meeting was most disappointing," the 1964 annual report summed up tersely.

But the IAA lobbying eventually bore fruit two years later when The Auctioneers & House Agents Bill 1966 was introduced by Minister for Justice Mr Brian Lenihan, who agreed to consider various points raised by the Association and to introduce amendments to the Bill where necessary. The Minister told an IAA delegation that the current Bill should be accepted in conjunction with the IAA diploma course as stepping-stones to future legislation. The new Auctioneers & House Agents Act 1967 increased the auctioneers' bond to £5,000 — with 290 members availing of the IAA collective bond the following year. The new Act laid down strict rules as to the maintenance of a separate bank account for all monies received on behalf of clients. All auctioneers and house agents were thus required to keep all deposits or other money received on behalf of clients quite separate from their own funds. An accountant's certificate to the effect that this requirement had been complied with became a necessary condition for the renewal of a licence.

Meanwhile, the Land Act 1965 generated widespread controversy. A memorandum to the IAA from the Land Commission on Section 45 stated the following:

> General policy requires that the farmland of Ireland will not ordinarily pass into the control of non-citizens. Accordingly, it may be generally assumed that consent to sale of farm lands to non-citizens is unlikely to be granted except in very exceptional circumstances. Sales of land, which would in the opinion of the Land Commission be useful for present or future land settlement schemes, or sales which would interfere with State afforestation schemes or with existing land settlement schemes, would fall within the same category. . . . Any idea abroad that there is land to spare in Ireland and that people from outside the country are welcome to acquire it should be effectively discouraged. Everybody who is familiar with Irish conditions knows that the home demand for farmland far exceeds the supply.

> Decisions under this Section 45 (dealing with proposed sales of land to non-citizens) are ultimately in the hands of the Lay Commissioners and are so specifically stated in the Section to be a "reserved matter". The following general points may be made as a guidance for Auctioneers without in any way seeking to bind the Commissioners in any separate decision. Categories within which there may be reasonable prospects of consent being forthcoming are as follows:

> 1. Parcels of land not of any significant size having regard to the quality of land and local conditions generally

2. Large mansions which have become insupportably expensive for the ordinary purchaser i.e. "white elephant" properties

3. Remote estates of no agricultural value unsuitable for afforestation i.e. "snipe grass"

4. Existing bona fide stud farms being sold as going concerns, with reservations as to acreage.

Each case, however, will be judged individually and no assurance can be given that every property in these categories will be readily saleable to non-citizens.

Apart from the machinery of consent, there is a specific provision in the Act for the issue of a certificate covering a purchase "for private residential purposes where the land involved does not exceed five acres in extent." It is not necessary that there should be a residence on the land; a bona fide intent to build a residence suffices. In respect of all other non-urban properties, auctioneers are advised to discourage vendors from assuming that sales to non-citizens will be authorised. In this way, wasted effort, delays and disappointments can be brought to a minimum.

The Association at last formally addressed the ultra-sensitive issue of fees publicly on January 13, 1966. The pronouncement issued to the press and Telefís Éireann, however, proved almost an anti-climax:

The Irish Auctioneers' and Estate Agents' Association at its largest ever general meeting of members held today considered the desirability of revising the current scale of auctioneers' fees on sales, which has prevailed for many years. It was unanimously decided to retain it unchanged at its present level. The prevailing scale is 5 per cent, save in the case of Private Treaty Sales of property other than land in Dublin District to which a special scale of 2.5 per cent applies.

On April 20, 1967, a deputation from the IAA met Taoiseach Jack Lynch with a view to safeguarding the interests of auctioneers and estate agents in Ireland in the event of entry to the European Economic Community and getting the views of the Irish Government in relation to this matter. The deputation was most cordially received by the Taoiseach. IAA President Oliver J. Flanagan outlined the Association's links with FIABCI and through this organisation with other European states.

A new Pawnbroking Act of 1965 dispensed with the requirement to apply for letters patent from the Department of Justice. This was obligatory under a pre-union statute of 1788 to authorise agents to sell pawnbrokers unredeemed pledges "within the Barrack Division of the District of the Metropolis of the County of the City of Dublin." Kathleen Jordan, partner, O'Reilly's Auction Rooms, Merchant's Quay, Dublin, is believed to be the last practising auctioneer to hold such a patent: "I swore to enter into bond and provide sufficient sureties for the faithful discharge of the several trusts reposed in me," she recalled. There were about 25 pawnbrokers in the city when Kathleen originally joined the firm and she was kept busy with sales. A typical week, she related, would be as follows: Monday, Tuesday and Friday evenings — Soft Goods (clothes), Tuesday afternoon — Leather (footwear), Wednesday — Rummage Goods (hardware, cycles etc.) and Thursday — Jewellery. The new act also dispensed with the "Divisions" as they were known. At the end of the eighteenth century, the City of Dublin had been divided into four police divisions for the sale of unredeemed pawned goods and each auctioneer appointed could only sell in his designated division. These were in the gift of (1) The Lord Lieutenant who had the Workhouse and Barrack Divisions, (2) The City Swordbearer, the Rotunda and (3) The City Marshal, St Stephen's Green Division.

Ms Jordan recalled:

> The new Act removed many of the restrictions which we had been labouring under, and gave us more freedom to bring our methods and charges up to date. The Corporation wanted our premises (in a hurry!!!) to make way for the new Civic Offices, a number of pawnbroking clients went out of business. . . . We moved to Merchants Quay . . . and business began to expand. In addition to the unredeemed pledges, we were selling lost property from the public transport companies (still very popular), private and house property.

Skibbereen-born Joseph J. Healy succeeded Michael Grey as IAA secretary in 1968, having joined some time previously as assistant to the ageing secretary. During the year, a greatly increased public relations programme was activated by president Desmond Scales, ranging from a press conference to announce the FIABCI World Congress for Ireland in 1970 to many articles in the press outlining the Association's policies and activities. The public relations aspect was timely, as instances of staff members in auctioneering offices ringing up and obtaining particulars of properties by pretending that they were potential buyers came to light in 1966 and were deprecated in the annual report of that year. Sometimes advertisements under box numbers were published for the same purpose — "the information thus obtained was used to cut across the agencies of the auctioneers officially dealing with the properties". These practices were decried as "not only mean, but also most reprehensible" and a circular outlawing them was sent to the principals of firms/members throughout the country.

Auctioneering firms continued to undertake a wide variety of property activities, ranging from large Dublin firms dealing both in urban residential properties and in industrial/commercial premises to one-person businesses in the country dealing with small cottages and agricultural land. Not only did the nature of the business vary greatly, but so also did the scale of business: commercial transactions in Dublin could now involve hundreds of thousands of pounds, yet small country cottages in remote areas were still changing hands for several hundred pounds. "Not all auctioneers dealt in property: some were wholly or mainly dealers in livestock or were auctioneers of foodstuffs such as fruit, vegetables or fish," a National Prices Commission report published in April 1974 related. "Although in the past many country auctioneers have combined dealing in property and in livestock, with the growth in organised livestock marts the two businesses have tended to become separate."

In 1956, auctioneers Osborne King & Megran took over the Dublin firm of Smith Griffin & Company. OKM was located in Dawson Street at this stage in the present Norwich Union building. The firm was led by John McFarlane who came from Belfast in 1959 and had extensive contacts in Britain. In 1968, OKM moved to Molesworth Street, from where it acted as project manager and letting agent for Stillorgan Shopping Centre. It soon boasted many prominent office developments on its books, including Carrisbrook House in

Ballsbridge, Norwich Union on Dawson Street, Agriculture House on Kildare Street and the Office of the Ombudsman at No. 52 St Stephens Green. The Royal Hibernian Hotel was also sold by the company.

Many well-known auctioneering figures worked in the company in those early years, including Alexis FitzGerald, Dermot Pierce of Earlsfort Developments, Edward Lyons of Mason Owen & Lyons, Des Purcell and Des O'Toole, Denis Bergin, Edward Hammond, Joe O'Riordan, Henry Robinson and many others. In 1966, Denis Keane, Denis Mahony and Des Smith together with Michael Doris all left OKM to found the rival firm of Keane Mahony Smith and, ironically, it was KMS where present Hamilton Osborne King managing director Aidan O'Hogan started out in a summer job during 1966. Subsequently Irwin Druker also left OKM to initially join Keane Mahony Smith and later founded the Druker Fanning practice with Paul Fanning.

OKM continued to expand and a Cork office was opened in 1966, followed by a Galway office in 1970. The Cork office employed Finbar Hill, who later joined Power Securities, while Roger Flack moved to head up the Cork office in 1974.

Prominent auctioneers associated with Hamilton & Hamilton (destined later to merge with OKM under the current Hamilton Osborne King banner) included Corry Buckley and Tommy Keogh of Murphy Buckley Keogh; Tony Morrissey, Morrisseys; Tony Tynan, Battersby and Lambert Smith Hampton. Chubby Williams joined around 1952 and later became a director, staying with the firm until his death in 1986. He was renowned for his knowledge of property and, in particular, fine art. The three other directors of the firm were Gerry Henry who joined around 1977 from Lisney, Tom McCarron who joined in 1956 and Richard Corballis who worked there in the early 1970s. Over the years, Hamilton & Hamilton built up a reputation for selling some of Ireland's most famous country houses and their contents. The firm sold such well known properties as Luttrelstown Castle, Straffan House (now the K Club), Charleville, Enniskerry and Mount Kennedy, County Wicklow. Major furniture auctions conducted included Powerscourt, Birr Castle, County Offaly, Coolatin House, County Wicklow for the Countess of Fitzwilliam,

Adare Manor and Newtownpark House, Blackrock for the late Senator E.A. McGuire.

During the 1960s, the Irish gross national product increased from £676 million to £1,444 million, or about 40 per cent in real terms. Industrial production rose from £443 million to £987 million, or 84 per cent in volume. Industrial exports, which were valued at £51 million in 1960, earned a record £214 million in 1969, or 53 per cent of our total merchandise exports. In 1950, only about 6 per cent of our export earnings had come from the industrial sector. In housing, 98,000 new dwellings were completed during the decade at a cost of £430 million. In the same decade, an estimated 10 million square feet of new factory space was constructed. All the more significantly, this growth was achieved at a time when the British economy was in the doldrums. In the past, a fall in demand in the British market automatically triggered off a recession in Ireland. The Irish experience during the decade demonstrated that this need not necessarily be the case — as was to be clearly demonstrated again by the course of history in the years immediately ahead.

The Dublin office of Jones Lang Wootton was set up in 1964 by Norman Bowie and the late David Bailey. The decision of this expansion-minded multinational operation to locate in Ireland was in itself a testament to Ireland's emergence on the world property scene. The roots of JLW go back as far as 1783 to the practice of Richard Winstanley at No. 10 Paternoster Row, London. Since 1958, the firm has become truly multinational, pioneering the acceptance and understanding of the role of the property professional throughout most parts of the world. The original emphasis of the new Dublin office on largely British-orientated business gradually changed and since the late 1960s the main thrust of the firm's work has been overwhelmingly for Irish clients — a wide range of insurance companies, banks, pension funds, property developers and industrial and commercial concerns. The Dublin partnership, now an independent entity, is an integral part of the global JLW network.

By the end of the decade, Ireland had truly broken out from its cocoon of insularity, ready and willing to play its part on a broader global stage. New cultural priorities swept aside narrow nationalism and a new air of affluence was abroad. O'Reilly's Auction Rooms

staged a coin auction in 1969 — believed to be the first of its kind in
the country.

> I remember with wry amusement the deluge of letters we
> received from all over the country for weeks after the press
> announced "Penny sells for £13" — half the country was
> convinced it had a fortune stashed away in the jug on the
> dresser. The scarce 1943 Irish Floirin realised £250 then, but
> the same coin only six months ago [end 1984] brought
> £1,400. Scarcity or inflation?

Residential values were still tantalisingly inexpensive by our post-
inflationary standards, as shown by this selection of house prices
from January 1961: Palmerston Park, detached two storey, three reception, five bedroom, maid's room and garage — £5,000; Ballsbridge, pre-war semi-detached house with four bedrooms, study, sun
parlour, large kitchen, gardens and four-car garage — £3,600; Clontarf, modern (1935), three reception, four bedrooms — £2,825;
Arklow pre-war brick building, six-apartment house with shop and
store (light grocery business in operation for past twenty years) —
£1,000; Fairview, new three-bedroom house, large kitchen — £1,975;
Greystones, house of character on two acres, three reception, six bedrooms, two bathrooms — £3,750; Lucan, Georgian-style residence on
20 acres, central heating, five bedrooms and maid's, three reception
— £11,500; Newlands Cross, modern semi-detached, two reception,
three bedrooms, fitted kitchen with refrigerator and washing machine, garage — £2,000 (deposit £200); Malahide, freehold Georgian
house, ten rooms and garden in need of repair — £1,100; Bunclody,
County Wexford, cottage-style Georgian residence on 2.5 acres, three
reception rooms, billiard room, four–six bedrooms, fitted kitchen,
secluded gardens — £4,000; Enniscorthy, Georgian residence on 22
acres, three reception rooms, four bedrooms — £5,500; and Howth
Road, detached modern three reception, four bedrooms, garage —
£3,250.

There was little discernible change by the end of the 1960s, but
values were trending upwards as can be seen by the following prices
from December 1969: Phoenix Park, substantial three-storey house,
nine rooms, large kitchen, garage — £7,000; Chelmsford Avenue,
Ranelagh, red-brick, end of terrace, three bedrooms, three reception,
kitchen, bathroom — £4,800; North Strand, two reception, kitchen,

three bedrooms, large rear garden — £3,000; Oakwood Avenue, Ballymun, three bedroom modern house with garage and gardens — £4,000. The 1970s loomed ahead — bringing in its wake the sudden sharp shock of spiralling values and shaking the property sector to its very foundations.

Chapter Six

Brave New World — The Seventies

"It should be remembered that the foundation of the social con-
tract is property; and its first condition, that every one should be
maintained in the peaceful possession of what belongs to him."
— Rousseau, *A Discourse on Political Economy.*

From January 1, 1971, the IAA (then comprising 698 members and 47 students) was renamed The Irish Auctioneers and Valuers Institute. The name change climaxed a lengthy process of internal preparation and development stretching back into the early years of the previous decade. Henceforth, an auctioneer could only be eligible for admission to ordinary membership of the newly styled IAVI who had successfully competed an academic course of instruction recognised by the Institute and:

- had completed a proper period of apprenticeship or served for at least three years as an assistant or clerk with a member of the Institute or

- was a licensed or permit-holding auctioneer or licensed house agent who had been bona-fide practising in Ireland for at least three years or

- was a land or estate agent, a valuer or surveyor who had been bona fide practising in Ireland for at least three years.

The initial membership of the IAVI included several prominent public figures, including politicians Lorcan Allen TD, Gorey; Sylvester Barrett, TD, Ennis; Richard Barry, TD, Cork; Philip Burton, TD, Kanturk; Senator Denis P. Farrelly, Kells; Oliver J. Flanagan, TD, Mountmellick; Patrick Harte, TD, Raphoe; and Patrick Ryan, TD, Newport. Coincidentally, a rival auctioneering body was also founded in 1971 — the Institute of Professional Auctioneers, Valuers and Livestock

Salesmen. Subsequently re-named the Institute of Professional Auctioneers and Valuers (IPAV), this is a corporate body registered under the provisions of the Companies Acts 1963 to 1986. It now claims a membership of approximately 420 (compared with the IAVI's 1,100), drawn mainly from smaller auctioneering firms in rural locations. IAVI members argued that the establishment of the new body at a time when the Institute was closing its doors to unqualified practitioners was indicative of the constituency which the rival organisation sought to represent.

Increasing wage and raw material costs put pressure on firms throughout the country who were soon confronted by a protracted bank strike and general industrial unrest at the start of the new decade. The number of industrial units completed fell by 46 per cent during 1971, signalling a critical slowdown in Ireland's development drive. Paradoxically, the IAVI was at this time entering one of its most progressive phases. The Dublin Congress of the International Real Estate Federation in May 1970 proved one of the most successful held in the entire history of the world real estate body FIABCI. The 21st such event (hence dubbed the "Coming of Age" congress), it was attended by more than 1,000 delegates and their wives from 24 countries worldwide.

The congress was officially launched by Taoiseach Jack Lynch to a fanfare of trumpets by the Army Number One Band in the Royal Dublin Society. The scene then shifted to the ballroom of Dublin's Intercontinental Hotel for the opening ceremony, after which delegates returned to the fourteen hotels throughout the city where they were accommodated. The event generated widespread publicity. Availing of the opportunity, pickets were put on the congress by the Dublin Flat Dwellers' Association to highlight the problem of increasing rents for city flats. An official State reception was later held in Dublin Castle, followed by an active programme of chapter meetings, lectures and social events. A visit to the congress by the President of Ireland Eamon de Valera provided a further highlight, while R.E. Corish, Wexford, Irish FIABCI chapter president, was awarded a medal of honour at the closing session in recognition of his services to the international federation.

Institute president Laurence McCabe declared in his concluding message to the Congress:

We are very conscious in the real estate profession in Ireland that we stand at a crossroads; gone forever are the parochialism and isolationism of the past. Very soon, the Jumbo jets, like villages in the sky, will be putting down at our airports and disembarking passengers by the hundred. If only one in a thousand of the airborne visitors who come to admire, start to buy property, then we in real estate are on the threshold of a property Klondike!

The international goodwill generated by the congress was immense. Tributes were paid throughout the year to its organisers from both at home and abroad. The event firmly placed the IAVI on the map internationally while giving a significant fillip to tourism prospects within the country as a whole. Ireland was, indeed, back in the international limelight once more in 1977, when the Irish FIABCI chapter hosted the FIABCI European Study Days meetings in Dublin attended by delegates from all over Europe.

The Irish Independent wrote in its 1970 FIABCI Congress supplement:

Understandably, and not without justification, the foreigner will think of Ireland as an agricultural country. It would not be a wrong impression, because the time was when we had little else to offer, except our tourist amenities. But the closer observer of the Irish scene, particularly of the last ten to fifteen years, will quickly acknowledge that Ireland today is an industrially developing nation whose potential in this important respect has not yet been fully utilised.

But a small, open economy such as Ireland's is highly vulnerable to external circumstances and international economic pressures were now making themselves felt on the domestic front. Triggered by the Yom Kippur War and severe oil shortages, inflation rose to unprecedented levels in the early 1970s, with house prices soaring by a heady 30 per cent in a single year. Correspondingly, mortgage interest rates spiralled from 9 per cent to over 16 per cent at the end of the decade — but the main saving grace was that the high rate of inflation meant that real interest rates remained negative throughout this period, fuelling demand for home loans. Over the decade, the building societies increased total deposits approximately nine-fold

— about twice the growth of total liquid assets in the financial sector of the economy as a whole.

The 1970s were destined to be an era of notable economic, social and demographic development — all of which gave a new impetus to housing. Rapid population growth was spurred by a heartening new experience for the country: substantial net immigration. The national demographic profile was younger, with increased marriage rates and a growing tendency for young people to set up independent households. Together, these resulted in a rate of household formation exceeding the growth of population.

Estate agents were quick off the mark around the country to make capital out of the spectacular uplift in prices and the escalating demand for residential property. But the halcyon days proved short-lived when auctioneers' fees were brought within the scope of the Prices Acts by the Prices (Amendment) Act 1972. This was to prove merely the first jolt to the *laissez-faire* world which Irish auctioneers and other professionals had inhabited until now. The National Prices Commission informed the IAVI in May 1973 that it was undertaking a review of auctioneers' fees and appointed a consultant to help it with its investigation. Coopers & Lybrand were in turn called upon to advise the institute on the preparation of its evidence and to conduct a pilot study on its behalf. A questionnaire was duly sent by the commission to auctioneers throughout the country, with the IAVI demanding that the format should be revised to suit Irish conditions. An alternative questionnaire was prepared, but the commission found a substantial number of the amendments suggested unacceptable. Following many meetings, a final IAVI submission was drafted by the law agent of the Institute for submission to the Minister. This submission included the Institute's own proposals for restructuring the profession.

These were promptly sidelined by the Auctioneers and House Agents Act of 1973 — introduced without prior consultation with the Institute — which transferred the obligation to pay the auctioneer's fees in the case of a sale of a property from the purchaser to the vendor of the property by making void any contract for the purchaser to pay such fees. The amount of the deposit or insurance bond which had to be maintained in the High Court was raised by both the 1967 Act and the 1973 Act and now stood at £10,000. The object of such a deposit or bond was to permit the indemnifying of clients in the event of default or dishonesty by an auctioneer.

For its part, the IAVI submission to the NPC argued strongly that the years 1970–72 were not really representative and that current market conditions had already resulted in reduced volume/value of business. It argued that this had already produced reductions in earnings and a substantial laying-off of staff. The submission further maintained that the 1973 Act had increased "abortive" work. It went on to contend that the Commission's consultant — Richard Harrington from the Department of Economics, University of Manchester — was unduly influenced by the practice and studies of the profession in Britain. The Institute asserted that a recommended, as opposed to a mandatory, scale of fees would lower efficiency and bring about a weakening of the structure of professional bodies, along with the charging of uneconomic fees by auctioneers. The submission cited the limitation of the Finance Act of 1974 regarding the amount of interest that could be offset against tax; the Kenny Report which led to a virtual suspension of sales of lands suitable for development; and the prospect of new capital gains/wealth taxes. The arguments put forward in the Institute's submission were, however, summarily dismissed by the Commission, and the Report of the National Prices Commission published in November proposed controversial changes to the traditional fee structure operated by the auctioneering profession.

The NPC report was the most comprehensive study of the profession yet completed, but was by its own admission flawed in certain key respects. One of the main flaws of the Commission's report was the inadequate response to the postal survey aimed at reviewing the profession. The Institute of Professional Auctioneers, Valuers and Livestock Salesmen were partly instrumental in bringing this about — requesting· their members not to complete the questionnaire through advertisements in the national press. By the end of 1973, the IPAV had reached the conclusion that no useful purpose would be served by its members engaging in discussions with the NPC consultant and declared that it intended "to oppose this legislation by the use of other methods". The consultant surmised that the Institute had "lumped together" his enquiry and the Auctioneers & House Agents Bill (at the second stage in the Dail, October 1973) and regarded them as "a concerted attack on the profession". In its initial discussions, the different nature of the business of an auctioneer practising in Dublin and in larger cities in Britain had been stressed by the IPAV, which indicated that it wanted a tapered scale where the percentage fee reduced as the value of the property increased. It believed that this would be more equitable than the flat 5 per cent fee currently charged for the sale of property.

"The Commission's study was not initiated because the members of this profession had submitted any proposal to increase any of their charges," the foreword to the report explained.

> The purpose of the study was to provide the background information and analysis that would be needed if the Commission at some later date decided to take the initiative in recommending revised fee scales or were required to examine any proposal for revised scales that might be referred to them. The extension of the Prices Acts to include professional fees and charges for services generally has shown up very clearly the almost total absence in this country of any systematic studies of the "economics" of the profession or major service activities. The Commission therefore commissioned a number of background studies, including reports on building societies, and architects' and quantity surveyors' fees in the summer of 1974.

Setting the scene, the author of the report explained that an announcement regarding the inquiry and inviting submissions had been inserted in the press. Only two letters were received in response — one from an auctioneer and another from a member of the public, both giving reasons why they thought the fees for the sale of property were too high.

A full list of licensed auctioneers was obtained for the purposes of the research from the accountant's office of the Four Courts in March 1973. This revealed that a total of 1,649 auctioneering licences had been granted at that time (139 to auctioneers with licences in Dublin postal districts 1 and 2), plus 11 licensed house agents. This compared with 1,054 licences in 1965–66 and directly reflected the upturn in the economy, as well as the lucrative level of fees charged at the time. Not all licensed auctioneers dealt in property: some were wholly or mainly dealers in livestock or were auctioneers of food-stuffs such as fruit, vegetables or fish.

To obtain an auctioneer's licence, the requirement at the time was to pay an annual excise duty of £10 as well as maintaining an insurance bond. The report highlighted the fact that some licensed auctioneers seldom, if ever, engaged in the profession. Many operated only on a part-time basis. Some felt that holding a licence might be useful in the future: "One man said that he was holding it for his son who, he hoped, would enter one of the large firms of auctioneers when he left school." The report elaborated:

> Almost all firms deal with private dwelling houses and for many auctioneers this is their main business. Of the full-time auctioneers operating in the larger cities, many sell over fifty houses a year and for some the total is over one hundred. The letting of private dwellings is an important business for some firms, but this is variable; many large firms do very little of this business. For auctioneers in rural areas the letting of agricultural land is frequently an important part of their business.

> Most full-time auctioneers deal with commercial and industrial properties. For the firm in a small country town, this will largely consist of selling a few shops during the course of each year, but, for auctioneers in the larger towns, there will be a wide variety of property dealt with including shops, offices, factories, hotels and so forth. This sort of business inevitably involves more skills and more knowledge than does dealing in private dwellings, but the rewards can be considerably higher. One firm estimated that 60 per cent of time was spent on private dwellings, whereas about 80 per cent of the profits were earned on commercial property.

One of the trends highlighted in the report was that the market in modern office space in Dublin was much greater and involved properties of far higher value than could be found anywhere else in Dublin. In 1973, no fewer than 24 new office developments with floorspace of over 10,000 square feet were completed in Dublin. Four of these were of over 50,000 square feet.

These buildings will be let for rents of between £2 and £3 per square foot yielding rental values in some cases of over one hundred thousand pounds. The capital value of many large Dublin office blocks is greater than one million pounds and although such properties do not often change hands, deals running into several hundreds of thousands of pounds are not uncommon. In September 1973 a house on St Stephen's Green, Dublin, with planning permission for the construction of offices to the rear, was sold for three quarters of a million pounds.

Throughout the 1960s, the report pointed out, Dublin in particular and Leinster in general were gaining population, while it was declining or static elsewhere. Dublin boasted far more shops of all sizes than anywhere else and also has a "disproportionate" share of the industrial capital of the country. Author Harrington stated:

All this has meant that the business of auctioneering in Dublin has been transformed over the last decade or so: new skills have had to be learned and there has been a continuing expansion in demand for the services of auctioneers and especially for the highly skilled services of the larger city centre firms. Many of these firms have expanded greatly in size. The main part of this expansion has taken place in Dublin, but several of the large firms have also opened offices in some provincial towns. One firm has announced its intention of setting up a branch in London and I came across one other firm considering such a move. The trends towards larger firms is, I think, likely to continue.

The NPC consultant found evidence that there were economies of scale in auctioneering just as in many industries, While costs were greater for large firms responding to the questionnaire than for smaller firms, they usually rose by less than did income, with the result that profits made per director or partner tended to be larger for the larger firm. Tests were made to see how closely the ranking of a firm by total revenue corresponded to its ranking by profit per director or partner. These tests were conducted separately for 14 firms within the greater Dublin area and for 21 firms outside. "The correlation between the two rankings was not perfect, but it was high in both cases," the report disclosed.

The author forecast that more and more larger properties were in the future likely to be placed with Dublin firms either exclusively or jointly with a local agent, although acknowledging that local knowledge remained a great asset nevertheless. As for part-time auctioneers, the letting of land was their main business with a few sales of farms and maybe the livestock/chattels of farms being sold as well:

> Most sell one or two houses, but few sell many. Commercial premises such as shops are dealt with only rarely. What varies greatly is the expenses of part-time auctioneers. Many work from home and have virtually no expenses apart from the annual licence and bond, plus a small amount of postage and advertising. An extreme example of this is one Munster auctioneer who has average receipts of £10,000 a year over the last three years on expenses averaging about £100 a year. Such a case is untypical in the size of the profit, but there is probably a not inconsiderable number of country auctioneers working part-time for whom 75, 80 or even 90 per cent of revenue is profit. On the other hand, there are many who derive very small revenues and very small profits from auctioneering.

The report explained that there were three main ways of selling property — by auction, by private treaty or by tender. A sale by auction involved the property being advertised for a period of time, often about three to four weeks, then on the appointed day the auction was held and the highest bidder purchased the property subject to a reservation price being reached. Contracts were signed there and then, and the auctioneer received his fee there and then. A sale by private treaty involved advertising the property at a stated price. The first person willing to pay the asking price or such other prices as might be negotiated with the seller became the purchaser of the property. With this method of selling, the legal completion of the purchase might be delayed and with it the payment of the auctioneers' fee. Sale by tender occurred less often than the other two methods, but was sometimes used for commercial properties. With this method, the auctioneer advertised the property for sale and invited interested parties to submit in writing their offers by a certain date. The offers were examined on that date and the highest bid was accepted subject to its being above the reservation price. As in the case of sales by private treaty, the legal completion of the contract might be delayed. The report commented:

> One of the features of the profession of auctioneer in the Republic of Ireland is the prevalence of auction sales. In most countries, there is frequent resort to auction for large and expensive business premises, but the overwhelming majority of private dwellings are sold by private treaty. In Ireland, this is not so. The actual percentage varies from one part of the country to another and from one auctioneer to another within any one part of the country. It is impossible to give any firm overall view of the numbers of houses being sold by auction, but for Dublin and its environs it would appear that about 50 per cent or slightly less of all sales of private dwellings are by auction. This is totally different from the position in Northern Ireland, Britain and, as far as I am aware, in continental countries. Sales of private dwellings by auction are rare in France.

> To a certain extent one can perhaps explain this relatively high amount of auction sales by the fact that the Republic of Ireland is a predominantly rural country and, in consequence, there are less relatively standard suburban terraced houses or semi-detached houses than in neighbouring countries. But it is still the case that many suburban houses in Dublin or in Cork go to auction, when similar properties in Britain or France would be sold by private treaty.

> Many conflicting views were expressed to me about the prevalence of auction sales. Some auctioneers held the view that auctions were the best method of selling and that you got a higher price at an auction. Others took the view that there was too much auctioning of property and that more ought to be sold by private treaty. A frequently held view was that a property should only be sold by auction where there was some reason why its value could not be otherwise assessed. The provincial auctioneers that I met were all but unanimous in their view that too much property was sold by auction in Dublin and that this was a consequence of the special Dublin scale of fees, which gave a higher remuneration to the auctioneer for auction sales than for sales by private treaty.

Dublin auctioneers with whom I have discussed this have denied that reputable firms of auctioneers would allow themselves to be influenced by consideration of fee in deciding whether a property should be auctioned or not. It would seem unlikely, however, that the Dublin scale has had no influence in this matter. Another possible reason for an auctioneer to favour auction sales over private treaty is that a sale by auction is a guarantee of sole agency, that is to say that in the case of an auction only one auctioneer can be involved. A disadvantage of selling by private treaty is that multiple agency may occur, that is to say the same property may be given to several auctioneers. Auctioneers dislike multiple agency. Given that they are only paid a fee if they are instrumental in selling a property, the more that properties are given to several different auctioneers the greater inevitably will be the amount of work done by each which leads to no sale and hence to no remuneration.

Another reproach frequently met by the author of the report against Dublin auctioneers was that they tended to spend far too much money on advertising properties for sale:

Many auctioneers, and this includes some Dublin ones as well as provincial ones, expressed the view that the larger firms of auctioneers used block advertisements of properties for sale as much to advertise their own business as to facilitate the sale of the properties. It is clear that a great amount of money is expended in advertising property in Ireland. This is not unrelated to the relatively high incidence of auction sales. It is necessary to reach as wide a number of people as possible prior to the date of the auction and this results in expenditures often of the order of £100 to £150. Whilst I have no objective measure by which to give a judgement on such sums, they do seem to me to be high. It is worth pointing out that in 1968 the British Monopolies Commission found that average advertising per sale of houses in the North of England was just £7.

It is possible, now that the incidence of fees has been transferred from purchaser to vendor, that vendors will in general be less willing to commit themselves to such large advertising bills. But, if this should not happen and if expenditure on advertising should continue at its present rate, then I think the professional associations should seriously consider whether ways could not be devised of publicising properties for sale in Dublin. During the course of this enquiry, I obtained a copy of the Weekly Realtor, a 104-page weekly paper produced by the Estate Agents Co-Operative Ltd. of New South Wales and which was devoted entirely to advertising properties for sale. The paper is distributed free of charge, through auctioneers, to all intending house purchasers. It would seem worth considering the feasibility of producing something similar in Ireland.

On relations with solicitors, the report found that these were amicable over many parts of the country, but in some areas, notably County Cork, there was "considerable animosity" towards local solicitors along with allegations that they frequently delayed or hindered the payment of the auctioneers' fee.

Auctioneers are far from limited in their work to arranging the selling and letting of property. They are called upon to value property for many purposes and frequently to enter into negotiations concerning the value of a property. This could arise in a case where a rent had to be fixed under the Landlord and Tenant Acts or where a property was being compulsorily acquired by a local authority. At times, an auctioneer may act for a purchaser as opposed to a seller of property. Commercial properties are managed and increasingly advice is given on a whole range of problems relating to property. It is not unusual for fees from property management, valuations etc. to amount to over one quarter of an auctioneer's total revenue.

The report confirmed that the three important statutes governing the regulation of auctioneers were the Auctioneers and House Agents Acts of 1947, 1967 and 1973. Under these Acts, all persons wishing to hold an auction had to be licensed, with the exception of a few categories of persons acting in an official capacity. To obtain a licence, one had first to apply to the District Court for a certificate of qualification. Notice of application had then to be given in the form of an advertisement in a newspaper circulating in the locality where the applicant intended to practice and the superintendent of the Garda

Síochána advised in writing of the application. Where the applicant was renewing an existing licence, an accountant's certificate was required to confirm that he or she had in the past correctly maintained a separate bank account for the receipt of all monies received on behalf of clients. When the application for the certificate was heard, any senior member of the Garda Siochana, or any member of the public having given seven days' prior notice, could object to the grant of a certificate on the grounds that the application was not a fit and proper person. If there was no objection upheld by the Court and if the applicant was not disqualified on any other grounds such as a previous conviction for fraud or similar offence, then the Court would grant a certificate of qualification.

The next requirement was that the intending auctioneer must deposit in the High Court either a sum of £10,000 or an insurance bond giving an indemnity up to this figure. A certificate to confirm that such a deposit or bond had been lodged with the Court was issued by the accountant of the Four Courts. His certificate, together with the certificate of qualification, was required to be forwarded, both within a certain period of time from their date of issue, to the Collector of Customs and Excise together with a payment of £10 excise duty. The Collector of Customs and Excise then issued the licence. Licences were renewable annually when the same procedure had to be followed.

An auctioneer's licence authorised only one person (the licensee or other person named by him or her) to conduct an auction. Where two or more persons were in business together, the holder of the licence might apply for an auction permit for each additional person for whom it was desired that they should be able to conduct an auction. A house agent's licence permitting a person to act as agent in the sale of houses by private treaty, but not by auction, was obtained by a procedure identical to that for obtaining an auctioneer's licence. The excise duty was less expensive, at £2 instead of £10.

On bonding, the report commented:

> For many large auctioneers, a figure of ten thousand pounds is inadequate: deposits held on behalf of clients at any one time could far exceed this figure. On the other hand, this amount is more than sufficient for many small auctioneers, some of whom make it a practice never to take

deposits, preferring to see these paid to their client's solicitor. Since the present cost of the bond, which for present purposes is the relevant cost as few (if any) auctioneers actually make a deposit of ten thousand pounds, is about sixty pounds a year it is clear that raising the value of the bond would bear heavily, and unnecessarily so, on so many small auctioneers.

After extensive debate on the merits of percentage of value fees versus the *quantum meruit* system (charging for work according to the cost involved in each case), the report recommended that all scales of fees should cease to be mandatory forthwith and should become no more than recommended:

> Given the different arguments for and against different methods of charging, it would seem desirable to leave room for individual initiative and experiment rather than continue to accept any imposed uniformity. Auctioneers should have the freedom to respond to market conditions in their area as they see fit and to adopt the method charging for their services that they wish. If such freedom were granted, I doubt that it would lead to any dramatic change from the present system. The scale fee is a known and, to many, a convenient method of charging and would be retained by the majority of auctioneers. Experience in England and Wales where, since the 30 June 1971, the recommending of any scale of fees or method of charging for the sale of private dwellings has been illegal points in this direction. There, some auctioneers have adopted different methods of charging for their services, but they have been relatively few.

Elaborating on current fees for the sale of property, the report confirmed that the fees laid down by the three professional institutes for the sale of property were usually identical; the fees for the sale of fixed property were always identical or virtually so. For residential business and other buildings, there were two different scales of fees, one applying to buildings in Dublin District and one applying throughout the rest of Ireland. Under the Dublin scale, a fee of 5 per cent of the selling price was payable in the case of auction sales and a fee of 2.5 per cent of the selling price is payable in the case of sales by private treaty or by tender. This scale applied throughout an area known as Dublin District. The area was nowhere precisely defined, but was generally accepted to be the built-up area around Dublin and some of the neighbouring towns. It included Malahide to the north, Lucan to the west and Bray to the south. For the rest of Ireland and for all sales of land wherever situated, the fee was 5 per cent of the selling price for all methods of sale. Prior to the Auctioneers and House Agents Act 1973, it was the practice for the purchaser to pay the fees in respect of all sales outside Dublin district and of all sales by auction within it. For sales by private treaty within Dublin district, the vendor paid the fees. In all cases, in addition, the vendor was responsible for the advertising costs.

The report revealed that new house prices increased by 63 per cent from £4,236 to £6,613 over the four-year period 1968/69 to 1972/73, compared with a rise of under 40 per cent in prices generally. No firm figures were available for commercial property values, but these were conservatively estimated to have doubled during the seven years to mid-1973 compared with a 57 per cent rise in consumer prices.

But the crunch issue of the entire report was obviously the super-sensitive matter of fees. In the final analysis, the NPC report recommended that a maximum fee for the selling of all immovable property within Dublin District be fixed at 2.5 per cent. It recommended that this legal maximum should also apply to the selling of all fixed property within Cork, Galway, Limerick and Waterford. Elsewhere, a fee of 3.5 per cent was recommended. No change was suggested for sales of furniture, goods, plant, machinery, livestock, farm implements or timber, while no recommendations were likewise made as regards scales of fees for letting property. A standard fee of 1.5 per cent for acting for a purchaser concerning a named property anywhere in the country was considered appropriate, although the professional associations could, if they so wished, propose a tapering scale that would be greater than 1.5 per cent for properties of low value, but which would give a percentage less than this for higher-valued properties.

"A considerable number of the auctioneers that I met privately were very ready to concede that a fee of 5 per cent was too high," the author commented, pointing out that fees for the sale of property in the Republic compared very unfavourably with those generally charged throughout Britain and Northern Ireland (in the North, the scale of fees provided for 2.5 per cent on the first £5,000 of the value of the property and 1.5 per cent of the balance).

The absolute amounts paid to an auctioneer for the sale of property were contrasted with the sums paid to an auctioneer in the Republic charging 5 per cent as follows:

Value of Property	Auctioneer's Fee — Republic	Auctioneer's Fee — NI
£	£	£
4,000	200	100
8,000	400	170
12,000	600	230
16,000	800	290
20,000	1,000	350
50,000	2,500	800

The NPC report was not convinced either that freedom of entry to auctioneering should be restricted. However, it did agree that there was much to be said for there being a clear and easily recognised distinction between the qualified and the unqualified. This could, it argued, be achieved by restricting the right to use a certain style or title to those who have appropriate qualifications:

> It might be said that the word "auctioneer" should itself be reserved whilst leaving the unqualified free to practise under the title of house agent, real estate dealer or whatever, or it might be found preferable to devise a new form of title for use by those of proven qualifications. I do not feel that this report is called upon formally to recommend any specific scheme or to propose any exact form of title to be reserved. Any change along these lines would need first to be considered and discussed within and between the professional institutes concerned.

So, rather than a complete restriction of entry into the profession, the report advocated some restriction of title as an alternative. This would enable the qualified to indicate this fact to the public and permit the public freedom of choice while still allowing "the innovative to challenge the established". Restriction of entry, after all, to any business creates a monopoly of those currently qualified, it pointed out. The report commented:

> The view of the Irish Auctioneers and Valuers Institute and of the Institute of Professional Auctioneers, Valuers and Livestock Salesmen is that the job of an auctioneer today requires a great amount of expertise and knowledge and that in consequence no one should in future be allowed to commence practice who does not have certain minimum qualifications. In general, there is a willingness to see the auctioneer as a professional and to regard a restriction of entry as in some way bringing auctioneering into line with other professions. Individual auctioneers that I met frequently appeared eager to compare their profession with that of solicitor.
>
> I do not think that such comparisons are particularly helpful. The question of whether a test of competence should be a relevant condition for an auctioneer to obtain a licence must be judged on its own merits. I also feel that there may be some over-estimation of the extent to which other professional groups are regulated legally.
>
> Whilst I accept fully that dealing in commercial and industrial properties is a skilled task and one requiring an amount of knowledge, I am unpersuaded that the degree of skill involved in selling private dwellings is so great that formal qualifications should be imposed by law on those who engage in it, nor in certain cases — notably suburban houses of standard construction — do I feel that the valuation of private dwellings requires such skills that all but those having certain formal qualifications should be barred from performing this service. This is not to say that the professionally qualified man may not make a better job of selling and valuing private dwellings — in general, it is to be expected that he will — but it is to say that there is insufficient presumption that the unqualified will make so bad a job of selling and valuing private dwellings that they should be legally prohibited from offering such services.

Many of the auctioneers to whom I spoke were ready to concede that dealing in private houses, especially in suburban areas, did not require a great amount of skill over and above that which a reasonably intelligent person could soon acquire by practical experience. I did myself meet auctioneers of no professional qualifications and who had not long been in business but who displayed considerable ability and commercial skills such that there could be little doubt of their capability of providing a service.

The report concluded, however, that the arguments for controlled entry as regards the commercial business of the auctioneer were more evenly balanced:

> The skills involved are undeniable: considerable commercial and legal knowledge is required and some formal training seems desirable. But it is not clear that legal enforcement of this is required. In this type of business auctioneers are dealing largely with corporate clients and with people who may be supposed to knew the value of using the services of the qualified. It is evident that in Dublin, for instance, most of the commercial property is dealt with by a relatively small number of well-established firms employing people who are highly qualified, if not in name, then by experience.

> To justify fresh restrictions being imposed on entry to the profession, it is necessary to show that the public interest requires these in that without such restrictions the public will not be able to get the quality of service that it wants. This has not, I believe, been fully demonstrated.

The report did, however, acknowledge that a different view was taken in some countries, as, for example, in New South Wales and Queensland, Australia, as well as in France where under a recently introduced law there was now a comprehensive regulation of the profession of auctioneer. But it noted that, although the French law provided for restrictions on entry, these appeared relatively mild and were actually less onerous than the current requirements to become a member of the IAVI. In America, the American Society of Appraisers had recently been campaigning to achieve statutory control over entry to the profession.

The IAVI duly conceded to the inevitable and adjusted its recommended fee rates in line with the NPC report. But it was soon business pretty much as usual again in the marketplace. Despite the general uptrend in property values, it was still possible to buy a land holding in a scenic Irish location for as little as £50 an acre in the early years of the decade. Bargains of this kind were getting harder to find, however, as more and more overseas visitors came, saw, and bought, despite the legal requirement involving State permission for overseas purchasers seeking a holding of over five acres. Agricultural land was in demand for up to £500 an acre, with stud farms fetching around £800, depending on location and the condition of boxes, fencing and residences. The norm for building land on the outskirts of the capital at the beginning of the decade was from around £10,000 and upwards an acre, with up to £15,000 no longer unusual. New office space in Dublin topped the 30 shillings per square foot level and there was already talk of buildings in the pipeline costing 35 shillings and upwards per square foot. "The magical £2 barrier is closer than most realise," *The Irish Times* declared.

Old values still prevailed in more senses than one — as exemplified by a story related by auctioneer Pat Stephenson regarding Harry and Cecil Lee, two Jewish dentists who practised in O'Connell Street: "The Lees were clients of James H. North & Co. and owned a large property portfolio," the auctioneer related.

> It was not unknown for them to react instinctively and on the spur of the moment rather than undertake detailed research before buying. On one occasion, they were walking down Dawson Street and saw a crowd going into an auction rooms. The two brothers decided that they might as well go in to have a look — and ended up buying a house in flats, without ever having seen the property!

A Dublin Corporation survey revealed that there was some 9 million square feet gross of office space in the capital — at least 5 million square feet of which was either obsolete or obsolescent. Investment in the hotel sector was estimated at about £60 million, with expansion expected to continue at the rate of around £3 million per annum for the next few years. Some 14,000 housing units had been constructed in 1969 and the national home-ownership rate was now in excess of 60 per cent with over 700,000 dwellings in the Republic. House prices rose by over 10 per cent during the previous 12 months, with three- to four- bedroom semis fetching from £3,500 to

£6,000. The IAVI headquarters at Merrion Square was reckoned now to be worth nearly £40,000 — an appreciation of 400 per cent since its purchase 13 years earlier.

Mews houses were beginning to emerge in Dublin around this time, but one segment of the market still not yet filled was the "flats for sale" business. "We are the only city left where the practice of buying flats has not yet become commonplace," Thomas McCarron, Hamilton & Hamilton (Estates), commented. "The self-service flat has a great future in Dublin." In the meantime, the cost of living and houses surged upwards as the decade progressed. Estate agents Sherry FitzGerald have plotted the market value of a typical modern four bedroom two reception semi-detached family house with garage in Clonard Estate, Sandyford, County Dublin over recent decades. In 1973, the southside semi was valued at £8,950; ten years later, its value had soared to £43,500.

In the retail sphere, the 1970s commenced on a high note when developers Power Securities, headed by former Cork dentist Robin Power, purchased Powerscourt House from wholesale drapers Ferrier Pollock and commenced work on a sensitive redevelopment of the historic building , setting a significant conservation headline. The "accidental" purchase of a restaurant in a side street in Cork had brought Power into the property business in 1973. At the height of his property career, the Cork dentist's shareholding in Power Corporation rose to be worth £33 million.

The early years of the decade also saw the construction of numerous new office blocks in the centre of Dublin, together with the gradual spillover of development activity into suburban locations. The first office property boom peaked in 1972, with the oil crisis the following year setting off a dramatic energy cost spiral and forcing interest rates up sharply. Massive inflationary increases were experienced throughout the economy, with house values leading the way. The inevitable slowdown followed, however. The 1970s were characterised by two world recessions — the first sparked by huge energy cost increases in 1973–74 and the latter a more protracted slowdown from 1979. In Ireland, the national growth rate was halved to less than 2 per cent in the mid-1970s and ground to a complete halt by the end of the decade. The oil crisis had a profound effect on the Irish economy. Energy conservation was the order of the day, while decreased cash flow and soaring bank rates put builders under pressure. Between 1974 and 1976, unemployment in the construction industry rose by an alarming 70 per cent.

But building activity was quite frenetic during the boom years when the inflationary bandwagon appeared unstoppable. Architect Sam Stephenson of Stephenson Gibney & Associates won the international competition for the design of the £34 million Civic Offices for Dublin and he described the project as "the greatest architectural opportunity since Gandon took the design of the Custom House off his drawing-board". One of the busiest architects in the country, Stephenson was also responsible for several other noteworthy public buildings in the stages of either planning or execution at this time. These included the new Department of Agriculture building in Kildare Street; a Laing development already fully pre-let by Osborne King & Megran; a Trust House hotel at Dublin Airport; and the £1 million Marlborough development on the Fitzwilliam Lawn Tennis Club site. In addition, Stephenson was responsible for the Ireland Pavilion at Expo 70 in Osaka, Japan. However, his Civic Offices design (only partially completed) was destined to become a major source of controversy, derided as the "concrete bunkers" by detractors of its austere modernist exterior and eventually partly superseded by an alternative design over twenty years later. Developments were, meanwhile, also taking place apace outside Dublin, including Cork where most Irish and British-based insurance firms now had offices in the city, and satellite towns were springing up around the suburbs.

Following the acquisition of No. 24 St Stephen's Green in 1972, leading Dublin-based auctioneering firm Lisney spent many weeks re-planning its existing accommodation. A major step in the development of the firm had been the creation of a partnership in 1970. But it was eventually decided that its prime city site should now be completely redeveloped. The modern purpose-designed building that currently accommodates the firm was designed by architect Ronnie Tallon. Additional offices were established in Cork, Dun Laoghaire and Belfast. The latter has now progressed to a local partnership. A further suburban office was opened in Terenure in 1994.

Outside the capital, the Rural Housing Organisation was founded in 1972 on a voluntary basis as a private limited company without share capital for the purpose of rejuvenating villages in Ireland. RHO pioneer Father Harry Bohan wrote that:

> At the time, I was living in Shannon and had spent some time examining the implications of the industrial pro-gramme being implemented, especially as it related to small villages. I found that industrialisation, although bringing a certain affluence to the country, was also estab-lishing an alarming migratory trend from small towns and villages, thereby endangering a certain aspect of the Irish character and way of life. A major cause of this migration to the urban areas was a lack of housing accommodation for young married couples and I concluded that this trend could only be counteracted by a competent organisation which would undertake to provide this housing.

The RHO began by starting one housing scheme in Feakle, County Clare on an experimental basis. From such humble beginnings, the RHO flourished into a national organisation, constructing over 800 houses in 50 villages spread over eight counties by 1979.

But Dublin was the lodestone attracting the really big property players. One of the most noteworthy developments in the savings and investment market occurred in the early 1970s with the intro-duction of a series of policies linked to the Irish Life Property Mod-ules Fund. For the first time, investment in a wide range of top class properties became available to the general public. The fund accumu-lated over £100 million worth of property held on behalf of policy-holders by 1985, providing excellent returns for investors. A separate property fund for pension funds was introduced in 1973, with simi-lar results. With the continuing success of its investment strategy, staff numbers at the assurance company soon grew to the point where the company's headquarters at Mespil Road became inade-quate.

At that time, auctioneers Osborne King & Megran held a tender for the Brooks Thomas Joinery Works, Lower Abbey Street. Irish Life purchased the property in 1974 and commenced on an elaborate de-velopment programme. By the mid-1980s, the third phase in this gi-ant scheme was completed — by far the largest urban development yet undertaken in Ireland, extending to about 800,000 square feet of offices, shopping centre, car parking for 800 spaces, 70 residential flats together with landscaped gardens and comprehensive all-weather recreation centre. Irish Life also acquired successful phased planning permission for a five-acre site bounded by George's Quay, Moss Street and Townsend Street directly opposite the Custom House. The insurance giant also acquired the former Williams & Woods site at Parnell Street. Both these sites were eventually developed to become cornerstones of the largest property portfolio in the State, valued at £483 million in 1994.

In Belfast, sectarian conflict erupted in 1969 and was destined to dominate the affairs of the province for the following 25 years. Sectarian residential segregation increased sharply as violence flared. Many households of both Catholic and Protestant denominations were forced to relocate or undertook to do so for safety reasons. Abandoned houses were commonplace in neighbourhoods where communities adjoined and so-called "peace walls" had to be constructed. In the city itself, incalculable damage was done to the retail, commercial and residential fabric by terrorist action and town centre bombing campaigns. On the demographic front, there was a net out-flow during the 1970s of some 76,000 people from inner Belfast, while the birth rate of the inner city dropped by 40 per cent. As for the economy, Belfast had an unemployment rate of 5 per cent in the 1960s, rising to 10 per cent by the early 1970s. By the mid-1980s, there was a jobless level of some 20 per cent in the urban area, with pockets of male unemployment of 50 per cent and over.

One of the key contributors to the eventual physical regeneration of Belfast's inner city has been the Northern Ireland Housing Executive, complemented by the work of housing associations and, to a lesser extent, private housebuilders. The first Belfast house condition survey carried out in 1974 showed that 24 per cent of inner city dwellings were unfit. It also revealed that housing conditions in the city were the worst in any major city in Britain. The first half of the 1980s produced almost 8,500 housing completions, three-quarters of which were in the inner city. In 1979, inner city housing unfitness was 15 per cent and this had decreased to 8 per cent by 1991.

For the city of Belfast, the 1970s were a decade of unprecedented trauma. This was a time of intense violence, the worst period being between 1971 and 1976. Of all the explosions recorded, 41 per cent occurred in the Belfast urban area. Almost 70 per cent of bombings aimed at housing were within this area, with targeting of shops, offices, industrial premises, pubs and clubs also disproportionately concentrated in the city. The bombing campaign led to the destruction of some 300 retail outlets and resulted in a loss of almost one quarter of total retail floorspace. Derry suffered similar mayhem. *The Guardian* newspaper reported in May 1974 that:

> In the last three years, more than 5,200 houses have either been destroyed or badly damaged; 124 business premises, mainly offices and shops, have also been destroyed and 1,809 damaged. The city has been so devastated that the entire centre will have to be rebuilt.

The Republic was thankfully spared such violence. Virtually the only onslaught modern property developments had to face was the slings and arrows of outraged architectural critics who mourned the passing of much of the capital's urban fabric and its replacement by a motley lot of purpose-built office blocks. A new property management industry developed alongside the new "glass cages" that sprang up along the city quays and elsewhere. As the commercial property profession developed in Ireland, so too did the statistical and technical tools of valuation. The reverse yield gap (the difference between the high yields on gilts and the low initial yields on property) first became evident for the equity market here about 1958, but it did not become a key indicator for the property market until around ten years later. More specifically, it emerged for the prime office and retail markets around 1968 and for the prime industrial market in 1972.

Ireland joined the European Community on January 1, 1973, having made an initial application in conjunction with Britain 12 years before. The majority in favour of entering the EC in the national referendum preceding entry was a resounding 93 per cent, the anticipated benefits for the agricultural sector being a decisive factor swelling the "Yes" vote. The IAVI yearbook stated:

> January 1973 will mark an occasion of momentous historical importance for Ireland, when she officially becomes a member of that exclusive club or family known as EEC. The consequences flowing from our decision to join are largely a matter of conjecture. Some are still being studied

at this stage and others are quite unforeseeable. For our profession as a whole and the members of our institute in particular, the consequences could be of some significance and it is therefore timely perhaps that we give at least a little thought to what changes might follow this country's entry. As a starting point, it might be appropriate to recall the object of the improvement which is to bring about greater political unity in Europe and as a counterweight to the giant powers, the United States and Russia. We believe that membership will bring us greater prosperity and a higher standard of living.

Capital gains tax was introduced in Ireland in respect of gains accruing after April 6, 1974 and life changed substantially afterwards for all concerned. Income tax had been introduced in the last century and one of its central principles was that it was (and indeed still is) a tax on income. Once it could be demonstrated that a transaction arose on capital account, it was not within the ambit of income tax and, in those pre-capital gains tax days, it escaped tax completely. However, the Capital Gains Tax Act 1974 introduced a tax on capital profits and was part of a substantial reform of capital taxation, which saw the introduction, within a few years, of a series of new taxes including wealth and capital acquisitions tax as well as capital gains tax.

According to the Department of the Environment, some 245,000 new houses (including apartments and conversions) were built in the 1971 to 1981 period, propelling Ireland to the top of the European home-ownership league. By 1971/72, the population of Dublin stood at 619,024, Cork 128,235, Limerick 57,135 and Waterford 31,696. The early 1970s saw new housing construction in Tallaght, with Darndale following in 1975. Between 1971 and 1981, dwellings constructed in the Eastern region represented 41.5 per cent of all new dwellings built in the State (245,000) for this period. Indeed, general housing work cost more in the Eastern region than in the rest of the State at this time. Property values were significantly higher too. The higher level of demand in the region, its greater degree of urbanisation, higher land values and the extent of "one-off" rural housing in other regions were the main reasons for the price differential.

Much new housing activity starts with the provision of serviced land by local authorities. The growth in demand led to a rapid escalation of building-land prices in the early 1970s, due to the scarcity of serviced land. Price inflation was fuelled by intense competition between building firms for the limited supply. Some builders engaged in advance acquisition for future years and there was similar activity by local authorities. The recommendations of the Kenny Report published at this time were to some extent overtaken by events as land prices declined in the recession of 1974/76. In the later 1970s, a recurrence of the 1970/73 experience foreshadowed the setting up of a Joint Oireachtas Committee on Building Land. World trade was back on a growth curve again by 1976. At home, Industrial Development Authority incentives created a climate of optimism, with the volume of manufacturing production accelerating by over 8 per cent per annum between 1976 and 1979.

Housing increased its share of total construction from one third during the 1960s to over two-fifths in the 1970s. Completions doubled from 13,400 in 1970 to 26,900 in 1975 and peaked at almost 29,000 by 1981 — a level that was not bettered until 1995. In the latter part of the 1970s, house sizes increased substantially due to the new "trading up" phenomenon and general income growth, with couples eager to capitalise on low real interest rates and inflationary gains, real or perceived. More than half the houses built were four-bedroom or larger. In urban areas, there was a notable emphasis on infill and town-housing development which diverted later into the apartment sector.

Mounting economic prosperity contrasted sharply with the beginning of the decade. In 1977, an auction of militaria including a collection of Nazi memorabilia at O'Reilly's Auction Rooms on Merchant's Quay in Dublin excited considerable interest — to such an extent indeed, that a repeat auction was organised shortly afterwards. Partner Kathleen Jordan discerned a new trend in pledging evident around this time:

> These were the days of the affluent society, when the country "never had it so good". A new and more valuable type of article was being presented. Gone were the days of shoes and clothes. Instead, cameras, tape recorders, radios, binoculars and expensive jewellery took their place. The general public's awareness of the value to be obtained at auction was increasing and a steady stream of antique

jewellery, silver and plated ware, coins, including sovereigns and Krugerrands flowed in. These were accommodated at our monthly fine art auction.

The IAVI was, meanwhile, gearing up determinedly to meet the demands of a new and more competitive era. The appointment of a part-time public relations officer was under discussion and a newsletter was issued to members in September 1971. IAVI regional committees (Munster, Connacht, Ulster, North and South Leinster, Cork City and County) were formed in 1972 to provide wider communication between practitioners and greater professional training opportunities, in addition to creating greater liaison between all members of the Institute, officers and council. Celebrating the fiftieth anniversary of the auctioneering body, president Brendan Tuohy declared:

> We look at the past with pride at what has been attained. The future we face with confidence, knowing that the young people now being admitted to the Institute have successfully completed the appropriate academic course and have received suitable and adequate practical training. The number of student applicants from the cities and some larger provincial towns is satisfactory, but the number of applicants from the provinces generally is not as great as I would like it to be.

The IAVI found itself unwittingly and dramatically caught up in the turbulence of the "Bloody Sunday" protest in Dublin when angry crowds marched on the British Embassy at No. 39 Merrion Square (next door to the Institute's headquarters). When they left, the embassy building was a charred ruin following a conflagration that blazed throughout the evening and night of January 31/February 1, 1972. This proved a particularly fraught experience for IAVI secretary Joseph Healy who bravely battled throughout the entire night to prevent the fire spreading into the Institute HQ, controlling the draught with a blanket to protect its unique ceilings from smoke damage. In the event, due in no small part to Healy's efforts, the damage was extremely limited. The adjoining embassy building was, however, destroyed and subsequently relocated to Merrion Road in

Ballsbridge — the building (No. 39) was purchased and restored by the ESB.

On the educational front, correspondence courses were made available at this time in association with the College of Estate Management at Reading University to suitable applicants in any part of the country. Interest in the course of studies at the School of Professional Studies in Rathmines leading to membership of the Institute was growing apace. A total of 99 day students attended lectures in 1974, with 31 students taking correspondence courses.

A reciprocal arrangement with the British-based Incorporated Society of Valuers & Auctioneers was agreed in 1974, whereby the president and past presidents of the Institute were offered and accepted fellowship of the Society, and on a reciprocal basis the president/past presidents of the Society were offered membership of the IAVI. It was further agreed that this should be retrospective to 1968 when the society was reconstituted. Additionally, the society decided to offer ISVA membership to any applicant who passed the final examination of the Institute, provided they were prepared to submit a paper on a suitable feasibility study. The liaison between both bodies proved so rewarding that the immediate past president of the society was appointed as a member of the council of the Institute. With administrative assistance from the Institute, a branch of the ISVA was established in Ireland in January 1979 under chairman Raymond Corish of Raymond E. Corish, Wexford, with Desmond Scales, Morgan Scales & Co., vice-chairman; Louis de Courcy, Louis de Courcy, Limerick, secretary; and Anthony Morrissey, Daniel Morrissey & Sons, Dublin, treasurer.

In 1975, it was agreed that the following qualifications other than the passing of the Institute's examinations should be recognised: Royal Institution of Chartered Surveyors — General Practice; Incorporated Society of Valuers & Auctioneers; Diploma in Environmental Economics, College of Technology, Bolton Street; Degrees in Real Estate and Estate Management (a period of one year's practical experience obligatory for applicants in this category). Degrees in Civil Engineering or Architecture were also recognised, provided that the holder, immediately preceding the application, had at least three years practical experience in a recognised office of an auctioneer, estate agent or valuer, or could show sufficient suitable practical experience for the same period. Other degrees or qualifications would be considered provided the holder had at least three years experience in a recognised office or suitable practical experience, and had passed on some or all of the following subjects: valuation; law of landlord & tenant; building construction; and law of planning and competition.

A major tax imposition — stamp duty — was now to prove the auctioneering profession's worst nightmare. This was a bitter enough pill to swallow when first levied, but the tax bill over the years steadily escalated as the Government failed to link thresholds to inflation and stamp duty became an ever more onerous burden on the second-hand house market. According to the IAVI, in the period from 1975 to 1993, yields from stamp duty on residential property sales to which the normal rates applied rose by 848 per cent, while the total capital value of the properties sold only rose by 518 per cent. As a consequence, the average rate of stamp duty paid rose from 3.26 per cent in 1975 to 5 per cent in 1993. In the same period, the percentage of the total capital value to which the top 6 per cent rate of stamp duty applied rose from 9.4 per cent in 1975 to 54.6 per cent in 1993. The reason for this dramatic increase in the average rate of stamp duty paid lies in the absence of any allowance for inflation on the original stamp-duty levels. The only upward movement in the figure at which the top rate of duty becomes payable was not made as an inflationary allowance, but was designed to dissuade tax avoidance at the old level of £50,000 when the old rates of duty jumped from 4 per cent to 6 per cent.

The IAVI has consistently decried the "inequitable" stamp duty in successive pre-Budget statements. If the original top-rate level of £50,000 were index-linked, it calculates that stamp duty would not be payable today at the top rate unless the sale price exceeded £300,000. This is a clear indication, the Institute argues, that the top rate of stamp duty was originally designed to affect only large commercial properties. In the mid-1970s, when the thresholds were established, the best of houses were fetching just 50 per cent of the top-threshold level. The absence of indexation means, however, that the top rate applies now to the sale of most modest second-hand dwellings. A 6 per cent stamp-duty rate results in a total-cost factor in the order of 10 per cent of the higher sale-price when an individual either opts, or is forced through changing jobs or the like, to move home. This duty has thus become a major impediment in the market over the years. So any downward move in the rate or substantial adjustment (to at least £100,000) to the threshold would be welcome and would assist the Exchequer in the longer term, the Institute plausibly contends.

Of course, the other side of the housing coin is that a very effective range of subsidies and incentives have been used to encourage owner-occupation in post-war Ireland. Important subsidies to owner-occupier throughout this period were the non-taxation of residential property (the residential property tax introduced later applied only to a small segment of owner-occupied houses — at least initially), the availability of mortgage interest relief against income tax (£4,800 for married purchasers) and the exclusion from capital gains tax of capital gains from the sale of (principal) residential properties. In addition, cash subsidies were made available to first-time buyers of new homes. A £1,000 cash grant for first-time buyers of new houses was introduced in 1977. Under a special mortgage subsidy scheme, an additional £3,000 was introduced to assist first-time purchasers with the heavy burden of repayments over the first three years. Further subsidies have also been made available to local-authority tenants to purchase their tenanted dwellings or to purchase in the private sector. Grants for the repair and improvement of homes have likewise been made available during certain periods, including a £5,000 "surrender" grant for local-authority tenants who purchased homes in the private sector.

The Local Government (Planning And Development) Act 1976 updated and improved the framework for planning and development based on experience gained with the operation of the 1963 Act — although the latter still formed the principal legislative basis underlying the development-planning process. The main provisions of the 1976 Act related to setting up an independent tribunal — An Bord Pleanála — to determine appeals against decisions of the local planning authorities; withering of planning permissions after five years; strengthened provisions relating to unauthorised development; simplified procedures for amending development plans; and strengthened procedures for the completion of conditions relating to open space attached to approved developments.

With property values fuelled daily by inflation and undaunted by the conclusions of the NPC report, the IAVI took every opportunity to underline the need for a registration system to safeguard the public from "rogue" auctioneers. Citing moves to introduce State registration for architects and insurance brokers, the Institute pointed out that their contact with the public was nowhere as great as that of auctioneers and asserted that the campaign for registration of the auctioneering profession now had the full backing of the Incorporated Law Society as well as the Royal Institution of Chartered Surveyors. The Institute reiterated that the law, as then applied, meant that almost anyone could set up and practise as an auctioneer, house agent and valuer. Many agents were expert practitioners with long experience or good academic qualifications, whereas an "open-house" licensing policy inevitably meant that there were agents practising who were totally lacking in expertise and yet who presumed to advise and influence the public commercially. President Ronan O'Hara wrote in 1975:

> I believe that, in an era of increasing sophistication in all spheres of life, the relevant and unique skills of IAVI members will be called upon to a greater degree than ever before to deal with the great problems of the future. Professional advice on land values should be regarded as essential in the formulation of land acquisition programmes by local authorities and Government Agencies who are acquiring land on any kind of a significant scale so that proper budgets can be drawn which will in turn influence the size and strategy of planning. I feel certain that in the same way as a Town Planner and an Architect are essential to any re-development, so there is a place for the expertise of experienced valuers and estate agents with suitable commercial and professional expertise who can offer constructive criticism on location, lay-out, finance, rental and other factors which arise when comprehensive re-development is undertaken.

The president added on the recession of the mid-1970s:

> Professional services and industry and commerce generally have been adversely affected in varying degrees by the present economic recession. Darkly overshadowed by the

cloud of rising costs and legislation, the profession is suffering and may suffer more. The age-old problem of abortive and consequently unpaid work, and the gratuitous
services which an estate agent provides for clients, prospective or otherwise, needs to be emphasised more than
ever. The high level of inflation resulting in vastly increased overheads of office rent, rates, staff salaries and
other office expenses have still to be met and to be kept at a
proper level to maintain the service which the public
rightly expects. Recent and proposed legislation has meant
a very substantial reduction in the incomes of members. In
this, there is the anomaly that despite the fact that costs are
considerably rising and will continue to do so, the profession
will have to bear these increasing costs without the safety
valve available to industry and commerce of passing them
on to the consumer. This has led to the inevitable result,
which is already well under way, of offices having to cut
overheads resulting in laying-off of staff, the rigid examination of office expenses and consequently and unfortunately a
reduction in the services provided to the general public.

Economic pressures triggered fresh industrial strife. During 1976, the
IAVI was represented on a bank strike committee, organised under
the auspices of the Dublin Chamber of Commerce, by Anthony Leon
and Corry Buckley. During the course of the strike, the committee
met the Minister for Labour and representatives of both parties to
the dispute.

In a landmark development for the profession, a voluntary compensation fund on similar lines to that of the Incorporated Law Society was established by the IAVI in 1977. The fund was established
through mandatory subscriptions from members to provide protection for members of the public. Payments would be made from the
fund where, through the dishonesty of a member acting in a professional capacity as an estate agent or valuer, a member of the general
public suffered loss. The fund was supplementary to the normal requirements of the £10,000 statutory bond and by 1983 covered a total
amount of £600,000. With no action being taken by Government on
the vexed issue of registration, a new general practice committee of
IAVI was also formed in 1979 to ensure the highest levels of professionalism within the Institute.

Sadly, Michael Grey, secretary and stalwart of the Association from 1934 to 1968, died in 1976. As a mark of respect, a portrait was commissioned from leading painter David Hone RHA by council. The following obituary was included in the annual report:

> Michael was a courtly and courteous host and a shrewd and sharp administrator. He was a good companion and an excellent executive. He shaped the Association in its many facets and helped lay the foundations of the Institute as it exists today. He was energetic, volatile in spirit and enthusiastic in many things. He was held in high esteem not alone inside but outside the office. Michael was a man of high integrity, great courtesy, and wide learning. He was a gentleman.

In May, the Institute obtained re-possession of the portion of its headquarters premises occupied by solicitor Hugh Fitzpatrick for a consideration of £8,500. The secretariat was now more properly accommodated in the hall-floor suite of offices, while a new letting was made to fire loss assessors Thomas & Bryan of Nottingham for a period of two years and nine months. A part-time letting of the council and property sales rooms was also made to the Civil Service Bridge Club on a week-to-week basis at £1,000 per annum. In addition, a new lease was negotiated by A.M. Sherry, Dublin with Castle Publications for a 21 year period. During 1977, the interest in a lease of the basement occupied by the Lantern Theatre was purchased by the Institute for around £3,000. The basement was leased to Communique, a firm of public relations consultants for £4,100 per annum for a period of 35 years in 1979.

At the end of 1977, council agreed to send representatives to America and Canada to conduct an investigation into multiple listing systems there, with a view to its possible introduction to Ireland. It was hoped that an American organisation providing such a facility through several real estate boards in the United States could set up a similar facility at low cost in Ireland. Following lengthy discussions and an Irish visit by the executive vice-president of the National Association of Realtors, however, the matter was deferred in 1979.

Two liaison meetings were held with the Incorporated Law Society during the year to discuss a document on co-operation in 1977. A number of solicitors raised objections to the proposed scheme, but a

modified document which sought to improve the working relations
between solicitors and auctioneers was not approved — "a matter of
extreme regret" to the IAVI. The aim of the scheme was to eliminate
the problems that had arisen in various parts of the country where
auctioneers had been presenting clients with initial proposals without giving the benefit of independent legal advice.

Auctioneer Daniel F. Stephenson died in 1977 after narrowly
missing being elected to the Seanad the previous year. The highly
respected auctioneer served on the council of the IAVI for many
years and was elected president for 1957/58. He was largely responsible for the acquisition of the new IAVI headquarters — a skilled
and knowledgeable practitioner who was appointed by the Government to serve on the Landlord and Tenant Commission.
Uniquely, three of his children qualified for membership of the Institute by examination: Patrick, Daniel Jr and Mary. Patrick Stephenson
became president of the IAVI in 1992 and is a director of James H.
North & Sons. He fondly relates the following story regarding his
father's strict code of professionalism:

> One unforgettable day in the early 1970s soon after I
> started working as an agent, I was asked to auction a par-
> ticular house. Before the event, I looked into the auction
> room and to my horror found that there was only one man
> present. I panicked and asked my father what I ought do.
> He replied that we had advertised an auction and an auc-
> tion there would be. So he went to the rostrum in my place
> and, sure enough, there was still only one man present. My
> father read the conditions of sale and opened the bidding
> at £5,000, refusing to sell until he reached £9,000 — and
> then knocking down the property, sold to the lone bidder!

The Landlord & Tenant (Ground Rents) Act 1978 prohibited the
creation of any new residential ground rents. However, residential
ground rents existing immediately prior to the passing of this act
were not affected and tens of thousands of these ground rents remained still in existence despite the fact that ground lessees
(building lessees) had the right since 1967 to buy them out and acquire the freehold (fee simple) interest, subject to the payment of
compensation/costs.

A recommendation by the educational committee that the present IAVI course of studies be restructured was accepted in 1978. It was agreed that a fourth year be introduced for part-time students in 1981. The existing three-year programme was to be telescoped into a one-year full-time course conducted under the auspices of the College of Commerce in Rathmines, Dublin. This was to be followed by a further one-year correspondence course, after which the student would be required to complete a thesis of not less than 5,000 words within a six-month period. For the correspondence course and thesis, the student would have the option of taking subjects orientated to either rural or urban practices. The foundation course in the College of Commerce got off to an excellent start with 34 students participating on a full time basis for the first year of the course. Liam T. Maher of W. Maher & Sons, Roscrea and Patrick Stephenson of James H. North & Co. each donated a substantial sum of money to fund perpetual prizes for the educational course in commemoration of the establishment of their firms in 1879 and 1829 respectively.

Ireland joined the European Monetary System in 1979, breaking the former parity with sterling and ushering in a new epoch of fluctuating currency rates. Notwithstanding such milestones, the decade ended as it had begun with still more industrial turmoil. A postal strike in 1979 disrupted the work of the Institute and most businesses throughout the state. The annual general meeting and the election of a new executive had to be postponed until September. The Institute was forced to operate on overdraft for the entire year as many members failed to respond to repeated telephone requests to submit subscriptions until the strike ended.

The National House Building Guarantee Company was established in 1978, providing a regulatory framework for the private housebuilding sector. The company provided new-home buyers with a six-year guarantee against serious structural defects in privately constructed domestic dwellings. Increasingly, the NHBGS certificate of guarantee was required by lending agencies before they would advance monies for the purchase of new houses. As a result, most houses built for the private housebuilding market were ultimately registered with the company. A Certificates of Reasonable Value system was introduced by the Government in an attempt to control the price of housing. But the device was viewed as "draconian" by the industry, threatening house purchasers with criminal prosecution if a CRV was not obtained and the system was soon axed.

The Irish Times reported in December 1979 that apartments had emerged as "a vital sub-sector of the residential market" during the year. In the Dublin region alone, over 500 flats were sold over the 12 months for an aggregate of just over £20 million. The newspaper reported that:

> In 1970/71, 13,671 new homes were provided (including 700 conversions). But while there was much sectoral back-slapping over the satisfactory rate of housing completions as we entered the Seventies, there was a parallel rumbling of dissatisfaction — because the average price of a new house being bought by Mr & Mrs 1970 had risen to the "impossible level" of £5,424 (this compared with £4,236 in 1968/69 and £2,808 in 1959/60). . . . It is worth recalling that a decade farther back, in 1960, sound new and second-hand houses could be bought in the Dublin area for around £2,000, but people were being forced to adjust to the upward spiral of property prices — and fast. Because, as the decade proceeded, the pace of inflation roared out of control. By 1975, the average price of a small standard semi had risen to £10,428. . . . By the middle of this year (1979), the average semi was costing £23,874 (4.4 times a comparable price in 1970) and by now the figure is somewhere in the region of £25,000.

The decade of the 1970s was clearly a period of major achievement in new housebuilding. Over a quarter of a million houses were built — nearly a third of the current housing stock. The proportion of gross national product devoted to housing increased from under 4 per cent in 1970 to over 7 per cent in 1980. Appropriately, the last year of the period saw an all-time record level of completions — some 27,800 in 1980. New houses were now better equipped in terms of fittings than ever before. They were larger, more of them were detached and had a garage or car port. Major advances in the area of energy consciousness had been made. Whereas few houses as recently as 1976 had 100 mm roof insulation, this was now the norm in 1980. Almost 1,500 housebuilders were already affiliated to the new National House Builders' Guarantee Scheme.

Outside the city, the selling of livestock and bloodstock remained a major preoccupation. Until the 1950s, livestock were sold mostly at local fairs. Property auctioneers frequently did the auctioneering. There were some private marts, but they were few. Since the mid-1950s, there had been a great growth of marts, both private and co-operatively owned. In 1973, about 35 different co-operatives conducted sales from about 65 different centres, no less than ten of them run by Cork Marts, while about 60 different centres were operated by private companies. As a rule, most centres auctioned livestock on one day each week, but this varied with some opening twice a week and others only operating fortnightly. A survey carried out by co-operative marts in 1972 found that on total sales of approximately £150 million commissions earned were approximately £2.25 million or an average of 1.5 per cent.

Bloodstock sales were largely in the hands of one Dublin-based firm — Goff's Bloodstock Sales. Fees charged were 5 per cent on all sales. This business was a unique one, however, with Dublin having to compete directly with Saratoga and Keeneland in America, Deauville in France and Newmarket in England. Thanks to the far-sighted Stallion Income Tax Exemption introduced by Minister for Finance Mr Charles Haughey in the 1969 Finance Act, the Irish breeding industry had embarked upon its greatest expansion phase ever and was well on the way to establishing an enviable track record as Europe's premier bloodstock nursery. A direct corollary of this was a new demand for stud farms in Ireland's lush, limestone-base pastures and fresh fields for auctioneers specialising in this lucrative market.

There were 723 members of the IAVI and 60 students at the end of the decade, by which time the Irish property industry was again on an upward cycle. A resurgence in world trade accompanied by a series of expansionary budgets had lifted the economy by 1978. Building employment grew from about 75,000 to over 100,000 by the end of the decade. But this was to prove merely a temporary respite. In September 1979, Construction Industry Federation managing director Tom Reynolds warned prophetically in a speech to a Rotary Club meeting in Bray:

> Ireland is presently an economic cloud-cuckoo land. If the issues are not faced up to we will have a deep and painful

recession which also will have a long-term effect on our monetary position in line with our change in the relationship with sterling.

CHAPTER SEVEN

HIGHS AND LOWS — THE EIGHTIES

"The newer people of this modern age, are more eager to amass than to realise." — Tagore, *The Cycle of Spring.*

It was the best of times, it was the worst of times — the 1980s, when the property market plumbed new lows before ultimately scaling fresh heights. The decade was in some respects like the proverbial curate's egg — good in parts. There was certainly little to commend the early years of the decade when a harsh dose of economic reality brought many who had been riding high on the inflationary gains of the 1970s down to earth with a vengeance. A relentless downward slide into recession in 1981 plunged the construction market into its deepest-ever slump, with commercial property reaching its nadir in 1985. The eventual recovery was tentative at best and really only began to manifest itself in 1988, the improvement rippling slowly outwards at the close of the decade. It was all a sudden, sharp shock to the inflation-led profits of the 1970s. Those whose credo was the divine right of property values to move upwards only had a rude awakening.

The population of the eastern region of the Republic stood at 1.29 million in 1981, representing 37.5 per cent of the national population. There were 896,000 private dwellings recorded countrywide in the census of that year, including flats, apartments and bedsitters. The majority of permanent housing units — 481,000 — were in urban areas compared with 395,000 in rural locations. About half of the national housing stock was detached, one-quarter terraced and one-fifth semi-detached. Virtually all houses were either single- or two-storey, with nearly all detached "one-off" houses in rural areas single storey. Overall housing density was low by European standards. Eight-to-the-acre was typical of suburban estates, while new rural houses (other than farm dwellings) were usually on sites of one-third to half an acre. Almost 90 per cent of housing stock was in private hands and around 74 per cent of dwellings were owner-occupied. The total value of new housing was estimated to be in the order of £700 million, while the total finance involved in both the new and second-hand markets exceeded £1,000 million.

Things began propitiously enough in the marketplace, with little hint of the turmoil to come and plenty of high rollers around, ready and eager to ride on the inflationary tiger. Housing completions set a new peak of just under 29,000 new dwellings in 1981. O'Reilly's Auction Rooms on Merchants Quay in Dublin made front-page headlines the same year when selling a semi-detached house in Rathgar for £125,000. The pioneering "Section 23" tax incentives introduced the same year for investors in designated areas proved an immediate success, auguring well for the future. But the euphoria proved misplaced as the property industry suddenly hurtled into its worst-ever recession — triggered by the crash of the country's leading private developer. The spectacular failure of the Gallagher Group dealt a hammer blow to the entire property sector, its consequences reverberating from the lowliest sub-contractors through to the heavyweight financial institutions who pulled the plug with devastating effect.

The Gallagher Group was originally founded by legendary builder Matt Gallagher from Tubbercurry in County Sligo who made his fortune in the building trade in England after the war. By 1970, the group had grown to become one of the biggest builders in the capital, with a construction programme totalling 4,000 houses. Following the death of his astute father in 1974, the youthful Patrick Gallagher took over the reins at the head of the group, quickly establishing himself as the prime speculative force on the Dublin commercial property scene with a succession of increasingly daring, quick-fire deals. These were heady times indeed, climaxing in April 1979 when the larger-than-life tycoon bought Sean Lemass House (formerly St Vincent's Hospital) on Dublin's St Stephen's Green for £5.4 million and then proceeded to sell it a month later to the Irish Permanent Building Society for £7.5 million — netting a profit of £2.1m in just thirty days. Other deals followed at an even more hectic pace, with the banks apparently prepared to advance any sum to the man with the Midas touch — Straffan House, a mansion on 300 acres in County Kildare; No. 16 St Stephen's Green (claimed to be the largest semi-detached house in Ireland); and the former Jury's Hotel in College Green.

In November 1981, Gallagher parcelled three of his properties into one package — the Jury's block, No. 16 St Stephen's Green and an earlier scheme in Clare Street — and sold the lot for £11m to a pension fund managed by Allied Irish Investment Bank. The brash young developer enjoyed an ever more lavish lifestyle, splashing out huge sums for dud racehorses, pouring £2 million into the ailing Phoenix Park Racecourse and circling the city in his Rolls Royce in search of further properties to bag. In loquacious mood, he reportedly boasted that his group had multiplied twenty-fold since he took over from his father and predicted that its turnover would soon top £160 million. There seemed to be no stopping the property speculator's gallop.

Growing more expansion-minded, Patrick Gallagher agreed to purchase the 4.5 acre Slazenger site on the west side of St Stephen's Green for £10.5 million, a prime slice of Dublin property deemed by other developers as simply too large to be viable. Moreover, the deal was done by acquiring shares in the vendor Slazenger company — a ruse aimed at avoiding tax. Although the nominal share capital was £0.5 million, only £2 is claimed to have been paid up and Gallagher reputedly gained control of the largest development site to come on the market in Dublin's city centre for a down-payment of just £50,000 — roughly the price of a modest estate-type house. Next in this dizzy spending frenzy came a £9.5 million deal to acquire a major development site at Earlsfort Terrace — assembled by his uncles for less than £1 million — and a sudden bid for the H. Williams supermarket chain. Such frenetic over-trading eventually proved Gallagher's undoing. The supermarket gambit sparked rumours that the group was severely strapped for cash and that his reason for bidding for the grocery chain was to gain control of its £50 million turnover.

The end came as abruptly as the most precipitous of the developer's deals. Amid mounting speculation that Gallagher was in serious financial straits, the offer for H. Williams was withdrawn. Two days later, the group was put into receivership by its bankers and liquidation veteran Laurence Crowley moved into its corporate headquarters. The news that the Gallagher Group owed the banks almost £30 million dealt a hammer blow to the entire property industry — a stunning bombshell to confidence, the reverberations of which spread with domino-like effect. In the final analysis, it would take the industry the rest of the decade to recover its equilibrium (indeed, proceedings in court were not ultimately terminated until 1996). As for Patrick Gallagher, the once all-mighty property tycoon was now the subject of intensive fraud investigations, eventually serving twelve months of a two-year sentence in Magilligan Prison, County Derry on foot of the collapse of his Merchant Banking Ltd. in April 1982 with losses of £3 million and debts of over £30 million (including £1.3 million to some 590 small investors).

The ensuing recession was deepened by the recurrence of emigration, adding to the supply of second-hand houses on the market and seriously diminishing demand for new housing. Although 1983 was a peak year for mortgage finance, a much larger proportion of loans went to second-hand houses. The private-estate housebuilding sector had to adjust to providing modestly priced houses under severe competition from the second-hand market. The main saving grace for the troubled property sectors remained the Section 23 concession, which not only stimulated output and employment in the construction and allied industries, but also had far-reaching social implications in that, for the first time in decades, a steady stream of good quality rental accommodation was provided for tenants. The concession allowed landlords to claim relief on their existing and new rental income, normally averaging 80 per cent of the cost of a new house or apartment. Even this tax break, however, proved inadequate to withstand the deepening recession. Then, with the worst possible timing, the Government axed the Section 23 incentive in 1984 and replaced it with Section 29. A very much watered-down version of Section 23, this proved to be a damp squib as far as investors were concerned, attracting much less attention at precisely the time when reflationary measures were desperately required.

Overall commercial property activity was, meanwhile, in serious decline. Industrial property was badly hit, with 4.6 million square feet of IDA space vacant in 1983. By 1984, 17 per cent of the Irish workforce in the Republic was out of work, compared with 10 per cent for the rest of the EC. Irish unemployment soared to over

200,000, an unprecedented level — much higher even than during the early 1930s. Moreover, the rate of joblessness among construction workers was twice the average. But business life went on nonetheless. One of the stalwarts of the local retail scene, Brown Thomas, returned to "family ownership" when taken over by Galen and Hilary Weston. Dublin still had four great department stores remaining: Clerys, Arnotts, Switzers and Brown Thomas — each still maintaining its own distinctive individual identity, characterised by Dublin wits as "Clerys for the Yobs, Arnotts for the Dubs, Switzers for the Prods and Brown Thomas for the Snobs".

The period 1975 to 1980 had seen a steady increase in the value of farmland from £1,000 an acre to over £4,000 in certain cases. By 1985, prices dipped to a new low and farmers who had bought farmland at peak prices with borrowed funds were soon under severe pressure from bankers who had been only too keen to put up funds in the first place only a short time before. The banks' policy of lending, having regard largely to a single criterion — security — and paying little attention to ability to repay, came in subsequently for severe criticism. In the meantime, the share of national output accounted for by agriculture continued its relentless decline — from 53 per cent of the workforce in 1926, to 36 per cent in 1961 and 16 per cent in 1984. Auctioneering firms were among the first to feel the pinch as the recession tightened its grip, with many practices cutting back significantly on staff numbers and some even forced to put up the shutters completely. A changing society ushered in major challenges for the auctioneering profession. Those firms who could adapt and discern opportunities in the altered circumstances fared best; less flexible concerns were soon under pressure.

In September 1981, a new player entered the Dublin estate agency picture. Founded in Monaghan thirty years before, P.B. Gunne commenced operations as a successful cattle market business and expanded into Carrickmacross in 1956. Widening its horizons into estate agency, the firm opened a branch in Dundalk in 1964. The Monaghan office was rebuilt on a new and still more diversified basis after the death of its founder Patrick Gunne, setting its sights on the lucrative auctioneering scene in the capital some years later.

Most of the established professionals were initially disdainful of the threat posed to the Dublin "first division" by the expansion-minded new Gunne team from the provinces. They soon changed their tune, however, as the Gunne combine expanded rapidly in the capital, branching into residential and commercial property with equal proficiency and defying the prevailing recession. Through perseverance, hard work and attention to customer service, Gunne not only stayed in business, but grew in size. Others, with more established reputations, were not as resourceful. Some firms floundered and collapsed like Murphy Buckley Keogh, despite earlier having been built dynamically into a major business by the late Corry Buckley. It took five years for the new Gunne Ballsbridge office to demonstrate any worthwhile profits, but by 1987 the firm had established itself firmly as a force to be reckoned with on the national estate agency scene. Headed by Fintan Gunne, it now ranks among the top four estate agencies in the country, with a network of offices in the capital and elsewhere.

In July 1982, Anthony M. Sherry merged his Dublin practice with FitzGerald & Partners, formed ten years before as a break-away from Osborne King & Megran by Alexis FitzGerald, Denis Bergin, John de Vere White and later Barry Smyth. A young Mark FitzGerald — destined to spearhead the development of the newly amalgamated Sherry FitzGerald as managing partner from the 1980s — joined the firm from school in September 1975, subsequently completing the Rathmines auctioneering course. Based at No. 13 Merrion Row, Sherry FitzGerald lost no time in making an impact, employing sophisticated marketing techniques and introducing a new dynamic into the property sales process. Among its many accomplishments, the firm provided an important catalyst for the entire profession by bringing women to the fore (currently, Sherry FitzGerald has five women equity shareholders holding 17 per cent of the company).

The firm achieved a major breakthrough in the residential sales sphere by targeting the middle market and successfully selling houses to teachers, nurses, civil servants and small business people on a scale never previously achieved. In 1985, the fast-growing Dublin auctioneers successfully completed the £3.5 million Clover Meats liquidation, further consolidating its position in the commercial property sphere by clinching the sale of the Irish Cement building at Nos. 19–20 Pembroke Street, Dublin 2 for £5.2 million in December 1988 (joint agents Lisney). In September 1987, the agency grabbed the residential headlines by selling "Clancool" on Shrewsbury Road, Dublin 4 for £460,000. A decade of further expansion followed, with branch offices established in Dun Laoghaire, Drumcondra, Dundrum, Sutton and Terenure. Sherry Fitzgerald now employs some 110 staff and claims residential sales in excess of £250 million per annum.

In 1983, the Government added insult to injury to an aggrieved property industry by introducing the controversial residential property tax, charged on all properties priced above £65,000 with an income threshold in excess of £20,000. An IAVI survey carried out between June and December 1984 found that the average price of a three-bedroom semi-detached house in the Greater Dublin area was £30,500, a four- or five-bed semi £40,000 and detached £52,000. By contrast, corresponding figures for provincial cities (Cork, Limerick, Galway, Waterford) for each of these three categories were respectively £25,750, £31,500 and £37,500.

In October 1985, the Government announced a package of economic measures to stimulate the building industry, including grants of up to £2,000 for householders for home improvements and up to £5,000 for the rehabilitation of older houses. The new measures also included 100 per cent capital allowances for commercial development, a new Section 23-style concession to encourage the use of vacant space above shops and rates reliefs in designated city-centre areas of Cork, Dublin and Limerick. While the lower end of the housing market benefited, however, the measures only made it more difficult to sell well-priced second-hand houses in established areas. The IAVI formally welcomed the Government response. But the Institute felt that the proposals were "as usual" selective both in their extent and their geographic spread. A more broad-based relief, by a simple elimination of the VAT liability on developed property, would, it felt, have benefited the economy to a greater extent and avoided the high administrative costs involved in implementing the new package.

The Local Government (Financial Provisions) Acts of 1978 and 1983 relieved householders from paying domestic rates and obliged the Minister for the Environment to pay to the local authorities a grant "not exceeding" the lost rates. However, in 1984, the Supreme Court decided that the collection of rates on agricultural land on the basis of the existing valuation system was unconstitutional and therefore invalid. Thus, businesses were made the only local rate payer — a burden that was to grow steadily over the following decade.

Under the Housing (Private Rented Dwellings) Act 1982, the District Court set the terms of tenancy of formerly controlled dwellings. The principal effect of the 1983 (Amendment) Act was to substitute the Rent Tribunal for the District Court in determining the terms of tenancy. The District Court continued to deal with the other matters assigned to it under the 1982 Act.

Membership of the IAVI had grown to 795 members and 68 students by the end of December 1980. The Irish Auctioneers & Valuers Institute battled vigorously to shrug off the recession, concentrating on professional development and improved educational standards. In 1980, the College of Commerce course for auctioneers at Rathmines in Dublin was established on a full-time basis for the first year, followed by a correspondence course of two years duration, with students completing the course by producing a thesis on a named subject within the six-month period. The importance of education was further recognised in 1981 by the appointment of an IAVI education officer, since which date the course was still further developed and extended. In 1985, the educational programme was transferred from the College of Commerce in Rathmines to the College of Technology, Bolton Street, Dublin on a three-year, whole-time diploma basis.

The opportunity was taken to suitably upgrade the programme at the time of transfer. Auctioneering, valuation and estate agency courses were also commenced at both Limerick and Galway Regional Technical Colleges and the University of Ulster at Jordanstown. The Institute also provided its own educational programme for students in approved employment. The latter's exams were administered under the supervision of an independent examinations board including representatives of third-level colleges, tutors, examiners and other appropriate specialists. In addition to the Institute's direct final examinations, a new course in residential estate agency was established in 1991 leading to associate membership of the Institute.

To help promote both the Institute and the profession, a series of information leaflets entitled "Buying a House," "Selling a House" and "The Services of a Property Valuer" were produced by the IAVI during 1982. The diamond jubilee conference of the Institute took place in April at Killiney Castle Hotel, where addresses were delivered on "Professionalism" by Alexis FitzGerald Snr, solicitor; "Building Societies" by Joseph Treacy, president-elect of the Building Societies Association; and "Solicitors & Estate Agents" by Rory O'Donnell, chairman of the conveyancing committee of the Incorporated Law Society. A charity auction organised in November on behalf of the Simon Community in the Fine Art Salesrooms of Keane Mahony Smith, Molesworth Street realised £6,000.

In September 1982, the Institute had reached an agreement with the Incorporated Law Society on recommended procedures for members on property sales, excluding new houses. "It would appear that where the procedures have been adopted by members they have and are working well," the annual report stated. "However," it went on,

> it has come to notice that a number of members in various areas have neglected to implement the recommendations, mainly through intention. There is no excuse for this where such an important document is concerned. Members in general are reminded that the strength of the agreement is in proportion to the numbers of members adopting it. Members are advised again that the greatest care must be exercised in completing the format of instruction which must be sent to the vendor's solicitor, preferably on the day instructions are taken, if not certainly on the day following.

The IAVI was, meanwhile, trying to come to terms with the impact of the brave new world of "high-tech" now making itself felt in business procedures throughout the globe. Lengthy discussions took place the same year on the possibility of the Institute establishing a computerised information system, culminating in the running of a mini-programme in November. The format originally proposed for the new IAVI databank was similar to that of a highly successful system operating in France, but this proposal did not find favour with all Institute members. A computer installation in Crawley, Surrey, was subsequently viewed and the Institute finally agreed to establish a multiple listing system along these lines. In 1986, the LINK property retrieval system was introduced by the IAVI in conjunction with Cara Data Processing. It was described as a "low-cost marketing system by which participating members can match the requirements of vendors and purchasers of property in a suitably efficient manner, thereby reducing costs and facilitating sales".

By year end, the system was "on-line" in Dublin, Kerry, Wexford, Kilkenny and Offaly, with other areas poised to join in the immediate future. It was originally anticipated that 100 firms would enter the LINK network by the end of 1987. But members proved reluctant to pool their information. A year later, the Institute had reluctantly to concede that LINK had not received the required backing from members. "In the light of pending changes in the profession generally, this is to be very much regretted," the annual report stated. "The prognosis for the effective continuation of the system at the year end was not optimistic." And so it proved, with the ambitious venture being quietly terminated shortly afterwards. For once, the Institute may have been too far ahead of its own members.

During a busy period, submissions were made by the Institute to Government on the Urban Development Areas Bill 1982; Local Government (Planning & Development) Bill 1982; Local Government (Building Land) Bill 1982; inner city development; and the proposed Property Tax. The legislation committee held many additional meetings to discuss the contents of a submission to the Joint Committee on Building Land. A controversial Government white paper on land policy was issued in December 1980 and closely examined by a specialist IAVI committee under the chairmanship of vice-president Dermot McMahon. Around this time too, the Electricity Supply Board applied for planning permission for a "massive" development at the rear of their premises adjoining the Institute's HQ. The IAVI architect lodged an objection to the application which was subsequently turned down and ultimately shelved by the electricity body. Permission for a three-storey office premises was later sought in 1984. Outline planning permission was refused by the planning office on one ground only (a residential accommodation requirement), with permission ultimately granted on appeal by An Bord Pleanála. This permission was not acted upon and has since lapsed.

Another noteworthy event at this time was the election of IAVI candidate Alexis FitzGerald on the industrial and administrative panel in the 1983 Seanad General Election. The inaugural edition of *The Property Valuer*, the official journal of the Institute, was launched on October 19, 1983 following the appointment of new IAVI information officer Cliodhna O'Donoghue (ultimately to become an award-winning journalist with *The Irish Independent*). The publication included a comprehensive property survey reflecting members' views on the state of the property market nationwide, together with a wide range of feature articles and Institute news. The new IAVI journal generated widespread publicity and has continued to comment authoritatively on the Irish real estate scene on a quarterly basis in the intervening years.

The journal's comments on Government efforts to reflate the ailing building industry are an example of its forthright approach when occasion merited:

> The property market has been in a state of almost permanent confusion in recent years, caused by a combination of recessionary pressures, roller-coaster interest rates and Government meddling with the mechanism of a free market — all compounded by the traditional role of construction as the "football" of the economy,

it fulminated in the winter 1985 issue. It continued:

> No Government, of the many in recent decades, stands blameless. It is perhaps inevitable that our present political leaders come most immediately to mind in terms of the problems within the property sector generally, the residential marketplace in particular, and also in the dependent area of construction. It was our present government which gave us the iniquitous and ludicrously unsuccessful residential property tax; that doubled the VAT rate on all construction activity (adding some £1,500 to the price of the average new house); in the process dropped the highly successful Section 23 investment incentive and replaced it with a watered-down version which has not worked; restricted mortgage interest relief and assailed the building sector with many technical disincentives.

The outspoken article concluded: "Progress always has a price and if we are to maintain progress in the residential sector, the bedrock must be a deliberate new policy encapsulated in the words — HANDS OFF PRIVATE PROPERTY!"

The Institute had its own regulatory headaches to contend with, however. One such example (discussed by the planning and policy committee in October 1983) related to publicity regarding property contracts "being signed for a lower price than the real one, with the purpose of the balance of the purchase money being paid in cash in order to avoid tax and stamp duty". The Institute declared that a serious view should be taken if a complaint was lodged concerning any member involved in such a transaction. "It should be made known, however, that there is no knowledge of any breach of discipline in this regard," the annual report stated. "The practice is without doubt fraudulent and members should be on their guard against any approaches in the matter."

Considerable publicity was given to the subject of land leasing in 1983, a great deal of it generated through Minister of State at the Department of Agriculture Paul Connaughton. Draft master leases were produced by Allied Irish Banks in conjunction with the Irish Farmers' Association and by the Irish Co-Operative Organisation Society. The Institute took the view that these documents would not achieve the objective of extending land leasing except in a minor manner. It consequently drew up a much simpler lease to provide for a maximum five-year leasing period. The Land Act was passed on December 16, 1984 to pave the way for the introduction of land leasing on a wide scale throughout the country. Reflecting the views of his colleagues, IAVI president Thomas Gavigan argued that leases must be for five years with provisions for reviews during the terms of the lease. He contended that tax incentives must be realistic and should include special provisions for widows, especially those with dependent children. Mr Gavigan stated:

> Of the lands currently let on the eleven months system, the vast majority of them are handled by the members of the Irish Auctioneers & Valuers Institute, who are in an excellent position to administer extensions to any new system. Already established and trusted in the local community, they are experts in the area of land transactions and

valuations and capable of advising on both the legal and administrative aspects of leasing agreements. They are trusted by the farming community and can create a viable framework for change, while still preserving continuity.

The IAVI president further pointed out that financial institutions, insurance companies and pension funds in Britain are permitted to purchase agricultural land which is on lease to farmers. He said that this is an added dimension to leasing, which can make available large areas of land and is worth consideration by farming organisations and government alike. "The policy of long-term leasing of farm property, if properly handled, has every chance of success," Mr Gavigan concluded. "In summary, it can increase agricultural efficiency, encourage greater use of our land resources and must prove of benefit to owners, tenants and the economy."

In June 1983, the presidents of leading professional bodies were invited by the IAVI to a luncheon, together with members of the planning and policy committee of the Institute. The object of the exercise was to try to create a new channel of communication through which the professions could bring a stronger voice to bear in influencing public opinion and legislation generally. The gathering proved highly successful and it was agreed that further meetings should be held on an informal basis, at least initially. These meetings duly followed at the offices of the Incorporated Law Society, the Society of Chartered Surveyors and the Construction Industry Federation — at which point it was decided to formalise proceedings. Senior IAVI members, vice-president Desmond Scales and secretary Joseph Healy, were elected chairman and honorary secretary respectively of the resultant Inter-Professional Group — one of whose first initiatives was to publish a co-ordinated statement on the forthcoming January Budget. Meetings of the group normally convened at the offices of the Institute. The group duly became a member of SEPLIS (European Secretariat for the Liberal Professions) in 1990.

From January 1, 1983, IAVI members were covered by way of cash and bond for over £1.1 million. A claim on the fund arose in April when the Board of Works sought compensation of approximately £14,000 on foot of the alleged dishonesty of a member in practice in Dublin. Following notification of the claim, the council accepted the resignation of the member in question and placed a notice in the national daily newspapers to that effect on April 18. "It is a matter of considerable regret that this default has arisen, particularly as there has been no claim against a member of the Institute on grounds of dishonesty since 1959," the annual report stated. The sum of £14,442 was paid to the board in settlement in September 1984.

The apparently interminable discussions regarding registration of auctioneers continued with the Department of Justice from the beginning of the decade. The pace of the talks appeared to quicken following a meeting with the Minister of State at the Department Sean Doherty, in 1980. At the request of the Minister, the IAVI convened a meeting of representatives of the IPAV, the ISVA and the RICS with a view to making a joint submission to government. A memorandum was agreed between all parties, subject to the views of the representative bodies being obtained. Hopes of a united front were, however, dashed when the IPAV indicated in a letter to the Institute dated December 1, 1980 that, while they were pleased to co-operate with the Institute in any development to further the interests of auctioneers, they would make their own submissions to the Minister in order to maintain their own identity and independence. It was, however, agreed that the case for a revision of legislation would be made by the other bodies to the Minister early the following year. A joint submission was duly made by these to the Minister for Justice in 1981, while discussions continued in the meantime with Minister Doherty and his successor Mr J. Mitchell. The results of these discussions were deemed encouraging, as evidenced in the speech of the Minister at the annual dinner in November.

True to form, however, the matter lapsed for some time after this, until Minister for Justice Mr Noonan received a deputation from the Institute on November 13, 1984. The Minister "very readily" accepted the logic of amendments proposed by the Institute to the Auctioneers & House Agents Acts 1947/67/73 and set the machinery in motion for consideration of these amendments. This process included reference to the Department of Industry, Commerce & Tourism to "ascertain the applicability of restrictive practices legislation" to the proposed reforms. At the annual dinner in November, the Taoiseach was most positive when, proposing the toast to the Institute, he stated:

I was interested to hear that a delegation led by your president met with the Minister for Justice this morning. . . . With the plethora of complicated property legislation, the need for increasing professionalism has never been greater. There can be no doubt that the principle of change has been established; what remains to be done is to determine the specifics. Incorporated in such changes should be a requirement for professional experience before the granting of an auctioneering licence and the raising of the bond to give members of the public greater protection. I would hope that the Minister, within the next few months, will be able to come to the Government with the proposals that reflect the needs of the consumer and that from these proposals, legislation will ensue.

At the 1985 annual dinner in Cork (held for the first time outside the capital to mark the city's 800th anniversary celebrations), the president of the High Court — current Chief Justice Liam Hamilton — took the unusual step of implying criticism of current attitudes towards licensing of auctioneers and "intimated that there was a veritable obligation on district justices to grant such licences in the absence of proper legislation". His comments drew enthusiastic applause from the IAVI audience. But action was deferred pending the completion of a study of all professions by the Restrictive Practices Commission. IAVI council members Alan Cooke and Pat Stephenson provided oral evidence before the commission in June 1987.

"Nineteen-eighty-five will be remembered by the Irish people and the farming community as the year without a summer, but in Cork it will go down on record as the year of the total collapse of the construction industry," wrote Joe McCarthy in *The Property Valuer*. He added that 18 builders had been wiped out of the market in Cork City alone. The number of private houses built in Cork City for the first nine months of 1985 showed a dramatic drop of no less than 47 per cent over the same period in the previous year. Unemployment in the industry had doubled during this time. McCarthy went on to say that

Some of these builders have gone to the wall through no fault of their own and have left behind them unfinished estates and partly built houses — some of which were sold and monies paid — purchasers, many of them first time buyers, now facing financial ruin, alas all victims of this deepening recession. There is no doubt but that the demise of the construction industry, both nationally as well as in Cork, has been expedited by the imposition of 10 per cent VAT on all new houses.

The re-formation of a Northern Ireland branch of the IAVI was approved by council in May 1986. Michael McArdle of Crossmaglen, County Armagh contributed a revealing article to the IAVI journal in Spring 1985 on how the Northern Ireland property scene compared with the Republic:

> Travelling along the main Dundalk–Castleblaney Road, a distance of approximately 14 miles, one crosses the invisible line that separates North from South. The only way you could tell that you were in the North is the marked improvement in road surface and the steady business on the three petrol station forecourts along this two-mile stretch of road. Better road surfaces and cheaper petrol are only two of the differences between North and South.

The Northern Ireland Housing Executive were at that time offering their houses for sale to their tenants at a reduced price — 30 per cent discounts allowed after the first year of tenancy and 1 per cent for each year afterwards. Some tenants were purchasing their houses at the maximum 60 per cent discount on the price set out by the NIHE. In 1976, a general valuation had been carried out and as a result the net annual valuation in the North was much higher than in the South. To allow for the high NAV, there was a lower rate in the pound. "The recession has hit this part of the country like everywhere else with farm prices coming down to £1,000–£1,200 per acre," the auctioneer commented.

The Northern Ireland Property Market Analysis Project (a research unit established within the University of Ulster) found that the mean house sale price in the six counties was £26,836 in summer 1985 — the cheapest house in the survey cost £3,000, the most expensive £89,000. The mean sale price of all properties in the Belfast sample (£23,222) was below the average value computed for the whole of Northern Ireland (£26,836). The University of Ulster team commented:

> Initially such an observation may seem rather curious as normally it would be expected that property values in a capital or major city should outstrip the rest of a region or province. Clearly this is not the case here and indeed only in the detached property sector do Belfast property values significantly exceed the Northern Ireland mean values. A number of factors are operating to depress the overall average sale price of residential property in Belfast, in particular the age profile of housing which for Belfast, on the basis of this survey, is significantly older than for the rest of the province. Indeed, over 50 per cent of the Belfast sample are pre-War properties compared to a province-wide figure of 26 per cent. In addition, much of this older property is terraced housing which traditionally is the cheapest sector of the housing market. The survey also highlights the small percentage (13 per cent) of the Belfast sample taken up by new developments relative to the overall Northern Ireland picture.

There was significant unemployment among auctioneering students nationwide in Spring 1985, with many who left college the previous summer still without a job. As regards remuneration, it was accepted that salaries for beginners could not be particularly large at that time. A starting figure of around £50 per week was considered reasonable. The IAVI property survey in spring 1985 indicated a dramatic fall in values of houses between £50,000 and £80,000, citing residential property tax as a major depressant — a contention firmly denied by Minister for Finance Alan Dukes who argued that only around £300 or £400 extra was being levied when the various reliefs were taken into account and this "would not be a major factor in a house like that".

The Property Valuer reported in summer 1985:

> Based on the results published in the national press for the six-week period to June 7, two-thirds of residential properties offered were sold at, or immediately after auction. But the auction is fast becoming a selling method of the past. Purchasers gamble on properties being unsold at auction

and deal afterwards on a private treaty basis, thereby saving the expense of a building society survey until they are
in a contractual situation. They are also in a stronger position to bargain after an abortive auction.

The picture was not entirely black, even at the depth of the recession. The ill winds that hit other auctioneers, for example, blew good
for those specialising in the bloodstock business. Since its move in
1975 to the ultra-modern Kildare Sales Paddocks in Kill, Goffs
Bloodstock Sales recorded a phenomenal increase of 691 per cent in
turnover from 5 million guineas to just over 40 million guineas in
1984. The rapid growth of the Irish thoroughbred industry was accelerated by the introduction of favourable tax concessions, luring
Arab and other overseas interests to Ireland; these were soon to
emerge among the biggest landowners in the country.

While the bloodstock trade proved a reverse image of the rest of
the economy, the fine-art sector was, however, under pressure like
most segments of the market. A Government committee concerned
about the outflow of works of art from Ireland was appointed by the
Minister of State for Arts & Culture Ted Nealon, and reported its
findings to the Minister in December 1985. Among the bodies who
made submissions to the committee was the IAVI which urged that a
central board should be created for the prevention of export of such
works of art.

By the latter half of the decade, the tide of economic growth was
finally on the turn. The recessionary cycle had run its course and
Government policies were at last beginning to make an impact.
Around 20,000 lots a year passed through the hands of O'Reilly's
Auction Rooms in Dublin during this period. Resident auctioneer
"Jackie" Long could get through 700 lots in an afternoon. New initiatives played a key role in changing sentiment in the broader marketplace. The establishment in November 1986 of the Custom House
Docks Development Authority under the Urban Renewal Act 1986
marked a major turning point. Redevelopment of the largely redun-
dant dockland area proved slower than originally scheduled, but the
resultant International Financial Services Centre was destined to add
an exciting new multinational dimension to the fabric of the city over
the following decade.

A State urban renewal programme was initiated to revitalise central areas of Dublin and other specified towns and cities which had fallen into decline. The programme aimed to stimulate investment in new building and development work on the basis that the construction industry had the capacity to expand output and employment in the short-term. The Urban Renewal Act 1986 designated parts of Dublin, Cork, Limerick and Waterford for redevelopment. The scheme was further extended throughout Ireland in subsequent years. Industrial capital allowances were extended to commercial buildings in designated areas. Double rent relief was allowed for qualifying tenants against taxable profits, while rates relief was also provided. Section 23 incentives were also made available for residential owner-occupiers and investors.

Section 23 apartments indeed could be said to have become the new residential building form of the 1980s, although the main thrust of the new urban renewal package in the period 1986–92 was primarily in the offices sphere (up to 70 per cent of all space developed in Dublin's designated areas). Innovative housing schemes like Oak Apple Green and Morehampton Mews showed that there was an alternative to the serried rows of box-like houses that repeated themselves endlessly throughout suburbia in monotonous housing estates. American-style shopping malls came to Ireland too, although the Powerscourt Townhouse Centre managed to resolve the conflicting pressures of commerce and conservation in a tasteful development by Power Securities just off Grafton Street.

But the two greatest landmarks on the urban renewal horizon were undoubtedly the International Financial Services Centre in Dublin's docklands and Temple Bar further along the Liffeyside. Within a year of the appointment of the new dockland development authority, a comprehensive planning scheme had been issued and a prime developer appointed for the biggest commercial property development ever undertaken in the capital. The Custom House Docks site — 27 acres of dock basins, warehouses and quays — was ready for building work to begin at the end of 1987. Flagship of the new project was the International Financial Services Centre with a special corporation tax rate of 10 per cent. In addition to the ambitious IFSC complex, the development blueprint encompassed residential buildings, shops, restaurants and bars. Leisure centres, community facilities, museum and exhibition areas were also included in the grand design, but the latter have yet to come to fruition. The consortium appointed to turn these plans into bricks and mortar was a combination of two Irish companies and one British — Hardwicke, McInerney Properties and British Land — who combined forces as the Custom House Docks Development Company. In 1988, a second order was made, extending the area in an easterly direction and increasing the total area designated within the Custom House Docks area to approximately 54 acres.

House prices recovered in 1985 and 1986, increasing by 10 per cent and 14 per cent respectively. A report on the Irish property market by Price Waterhouse in October 1988 revealed that the number of residential properties sold each year in the Republic had been fluctuating around 36,000 since 1982. The report concluded that there had been very little growth in the market during the period under review when the value of residential properties sold averaged £1.36 billion. The figures tallied with national newspaper advertising which averaged about 700 individual properties offered for sale each week. For the purposes of comparison, the combined English and Welsh residential property market was estimated at £60 billion. Because of the higher value of property in Dublin, the mobility of its inhabitants and its large share of the national population, the accountants concluded that Dublin accounted for 40 per cent of the total residential property market. The overall average price of new properties only changed from £35,500 in 1983 to £39,500 in 1987. The breakdown of new houses sold by type was: semi-detached, 32.8 per cent; detached bungalow, 27.5 per cent; terraced house, 15.3 per cent; detached house, 14.5 per cent; semi-detached bungalow, 5.7 per cent; and flat/apartment, 4 per cent.

While speculative development stopped in its tracks for much of the 1980s, a welcome spin-off was that conservation of our existing built fabric began to come into its own. From 1980 to 1984, a massive restoration was undertaken at The Royal Hospital, Kilmainham — one of Dublin's most historic landmark buildings — at a cost of £20 million by the Office of Public Works. The building was given a new lease of life and is now used for state functions, exhibitions and selected entertainments as well as housing the Irish Museum of Modern Art. The scale and success of the preservation works were acknowledged when the Royal Hospital was awarded a gold medal by Europa Nostra. Major repair and conservation works costing over £6 million were undertaken to the fabric of James Gandon's Custom House from 1984. Commencing in 1986, remedial action was carried out at Leinster House and the beautiful plastered ceiling of the nation's parliament building was saved and refurbished at a cost of £1.1m. In 1985, the Minister of State at the Office of Public Works gave formal recognition to the new trend by signing the Convention for the Protection of the Architectural Heritage of Europe on behalf of Ireland.

In a highly significant move for the re-emerging Irish property market, The Green Property Company was successfully floated on the stock market at the end of June 1985. To mark the event, Green lodged a detailed application to carry out a development of 540,000 square feet of retail and civic space on an 88-acre site at Blanchardstown. Blanchardstown Town Centre was not, however, destined to be developed until more than a decade later.

By the middle of the decade, despite earlier promotional efforts, members of the public relations committee and the council of the IAVI were openly expressing concern that the public could not differentiate between auctioneers in general and members of the Irish Auctioneers & Valuers Institute. The committee commented:

> Our own market research has shown that the public is not well informed about the advantages of dealing with a member of the Institute. It is critical that the public is made aware that: (1) Members have a compensation fund in excess of £1,000,000; (2) Strict educational requirements guarantee professional service; (3) 1,000 members practise nationwide.

FIABCI World President Clive Lewis declared during a visit to Dublin that, in marketing national institutions, those in Ireland and Britain "tend to be very far behind the United States, Canada and Australia". He said that this was the case with the United States, in particular, because the enormous resources of the National Association of Realtors are used to sustain an office in Washington and provide top level administration to influence legislation and voting patterns in the Senate. He stressed that he was not, however, suggesting that the Institute should operate at the same level, but that certainly there should be greater efforts made to enhance the image of estate agents. Mr Lewis indicated that one of his prime concerns as president of the Federation was the low level of credibility of the profession throughout the world and instanced the fact that major companies have a board of directors on which there may be lawyers, or financiers, or accountants, but no estate agent despite the fact that property is the bedrock of many of these companies.

To improve the IAVI image, the Institute crest was re-designed, allowing built-in flexibility for display by members on every possible occasion, including headed stationery and the like. Members were requested to use the letters MIAVI as regularly as possible and on all advertisements, signs, headed stationery and business cards. A brass plaque — bearing the wording "MIAVI, Member of The Irish Auctioneers & Valuers Institute" — was likewise launched in summer 1985. The plaques were 12"x 8", with countersunk holes and screws mounted on a flush timber block base. They were for external use and placed outside the offices of members with the name of the firm engraved thereon. "Consistency of the use of this plaque by members is highly desirable as it emphasises the corporate identity of members and distinguishes them as professionals," the Institute commented.

Conscious of its public image, a statement to members declared in Summer 1985:

> It has been noticed in recent months that a plethora of sign boards of members have appeared attached to ESB poles and other poles of a convenient nature which are obviously not the property of clients or the agents. This activity is particularly noticeable in Dublin and members are reminded that the council has issued a directive that this practice be discontinued. How, for example, would you react if the ESB or some other local authority placed its logo without sanction on your sign boards as a method of extending its corporate image? Will you please take note of this matter and advise your staff and/or the sign erectors accordingly.

At the instigation of FIABCI, the United Nations designated 1987 as "The Year of Shelter". The theme for the second FIABCI European Study Days Congress held in Dublin in October of that year and

nnual Dinner held at the Gresham Hotel, Dublin, on Wednesday, 12th April 1939.

Iow a provincial Member solved the Petrol Problem during the "Emergency".

The Late Mr. Harry Lisney

Guests at Annual Dinner, held at the Clarence Hotel, Dublin, on Wednesday, 14th March 1945: Alderman, Martin A. O'Sullivan, T.D., Lord Mayor of Dublin; Mr. Arthur Bennett, F.S.I., President; Mr. Gerald Boland, Minister for Justice.

CLEARANCE SALE OF
CATTLE, HORSES

Poultry, Fowl-Farming Equipment, Farm Implements, Harness and Saddlery, Agricultural Effects and Residue of

HOUSEHOLD FURNITURE

Having Sold her Residence and Land, we are instructed by Mrs. G. Reddy

TO SELL BY AUCTION

AT ST. WOLSTAN'S, CELBRIDGE

On Thursday, April 8th, 1943

At 12.30 o'clock

To hold a Clearance Sale by Auction, which will include:—Three Milch Cows (1 freshly calved and 2 due to calve), 1 in-calf Heifer, 5 S.H. Heifer Calves, 1 Suck Calf, 3 Farm Horses, 1 Six-year-old Half-bred, doing farm work; 1 Sow (in young), 75 head R.I.R. and W.W. Hens, Pullets and Cockerels (in lots), 3 Poultry Houses, 8ft. x 6ft.; 1 do. (glass fronted), with nests and perches, 30ft. x 14; 1 do. with trap nests, 47ft. x 12ft.; 1 Night Ark, 6 Wooden Hoppers, 2 Zinc do., on wheels; 1 Glevum Incubator (150 egg), 1 Hoover, "Buckie" (300 chicks); 1 do. (150 chicks), Poultry Feeding Troughs and Fowl Farming Equipment, Scotch Cart, Hay Bogie, Star No. 2 Chill Plough (new), 3-part Iron Harrow, Set of Swings, Root Pulper, Stone Roller, Wheelbarrow, Rubber-tyred Inside Trap, to fit 15 16 hands (in new condition); Set of Silver-mounted Trap Harness, 2 Sets Cart Harness, Hunting Saddle, Bridles and Tackling, 20 Rolls Wire Netting, 60 Sheets Galvanised Iron, 2 Metal Boilers, quantity Iron Posts, Piping and Trestles, Barbed Wire, Pair Carriage Lamps, 4 Slate Slabs, 6ft. x 3ft.; 4 Iron Gratings, quantity of Lead and Scrap Iron, Flower Pots, Iron and Wooden Barrels, Oak Doors, Gent's Bicycle (as new), 2 heaps Farmyard Manure (approximately 70 tons), Rick of Oaten Straw, about 14 tons (in field on roadside at Moortown, Celbridge); and numerous lots of Agricultural and Farmyard Effects.

Residue of Household Furniture and Domestic Effects, including:—Wireless Set, complete with new battery; Large Packing Table, 14ft. x 3ft.; Iron Fire Grate, Table, Chairs, Pictures, Ornaments, etc.

E. A. COONAN & SON, M.I.A.A.

Auctioneers, MAYNOOTH

LEINSTER LEADER, NAAS

Delegates en route to FIABCI Congress in 1968.

Former Secretary Mr. Michael H. Grey and his successor Joe Healy at the 1970 FIABCI Congress in Dublin.

Speakers at the World Real Estate Congress, Dublin 1970 include the FIABCI World President Mr. John Tysen, USA, An Taoiseach Mr. Jack Lynch T.D., Mr. Laurence McCabe, Mr. Michael Kileen and Mr. Raymond Corish.

At the Students' Annual Dinner and Dance in the Gresham Hotel in 1972 were, (back row): Mr. Alan Cooke, Morgan Scales & Co., President S.R.C.; Miss Ann Finn, Committee; and Mr. Nigel Bennett, A.F. Bennett & Co. Ltd., Sec. S.R.C. (Front row): Mr. Maurice Pearse, Lisney & Son; Miss Mary Twohig, Lisney & Son, Council Member; Mr. Brendan Tuohy, Pres. I.A.V.I. and Miss Carol Manahan, Committee.

At the Graduation and Prize-giving Dinner in Powers Royal Hotel, Dublin, in October 1973 were (left to right): Mr. Ronan O'Hara, Vice President; The President , Mr. Anthony Morrissey; Mr. Brian Coyle, Hon. Treasurer; and Mr. Joseph Healy, Secretary.

Past Presidents' Dinner at the Gresham Hotel, 14th December 1996, to mark the 75th Anniversary of a meeting held at the same venue on 14th December 1921 at which a decision was made to form a limited company which ultimately became the IAVI.

Left to right standing – Gerry Slattery (2nd Vice President), Paul McDowell (Senior Vice President), Brendan Donohue (1995), John Corish (1989), Patrick Stephenson (1992), Joseph McCarthy (1993), B. Dermot McMahon (1981), Anthony O'Loughlin (1994), Brian Coyle (1971), Laurence McCabe (1970), Alan Cooke (1986)
Left to right seated – Anthony Morrissey (1973), Frank Aherne (1976), Noel Judd (1955), Cormac J. Meehan (1996), James Adam (1961), Frank Meldon (1966), Tom Gavigan (1985).

THE PROPERTY VALUER

SPRING 199

Published by
Irish Auctioneers and Valuers Instit

CELEBRATING 50 ISSUES

attended by delegates from throughout Europe was — appropriately
— "Urban Renewal in the Year of Shelter". IAVI president Alan
Cooke commented:

> Despite the economic difficulties facing Ireland and their
> effect on the activities of the property profession, it is im-
> portant that we consider the serious plight of the homeless
> both at home and abroad. Home ownership remains one of
> the primary aims of most family units, affording an unri-
> valled sense of security and achievement. Our members
> have a worthy record in facilitating and encouraging the
> realisation of this ambition in the community.

The objective of housing policy as stated by the Department of the
Environment during the 1980s was

> to ensure that, as far as the resources of the economy per-
> mit, every family can obtain for their own occupation a
> house of good standard at a price or rent they can afford
> located in an acceptable environment. A secondary aim of
> housing policy is the encouragement of owner-occupation
> as the widely preferred form of tenure.

As the NESC Review of Housing Policy pointed out in 1988, the outstanding feature of the Irish housing system is the prevalence of
owner-occupation: 74 per cent of the dwelling stock was owner-
occupied in 1981, compared with 69 per cent in 1971 — the highest
proportion among EEC countries. The Review stated:

> In noting Ireland's very high level of owner-occupation, it
> should be realised that the relatively generous subsidisa-
> tion of owner-occupation has made owner-occupation
> possible for many groups in the struggle for land owner-
> ship, the existence of a significant "self-build" sector in ru-
> ral areas, and the role played by building on the entire
> population, including those on average and below-average
> incomes. Another factor which has contributed to the high
> level of owner-occupation is the historical importance of
> the building societies in tapping personal and household
> savings. In addition, high family size relative to other
> countries, the general preference for semi-detached or de-
> tached dwellings with gardens, and a relatively abundant

supply of land outside major urban areas have all sustained the high level of owner-occupation.

The decline in housing output evident throughout most of the
1980s was finally halted in 1988 with a significant increase in output
the following year. The commercial property market, meanwhile,
remained in the doldrums, with around 5 million square feet of industrial space vacant in 1986 — around 40 per cent of which was
prime accommodation. Offices were still under a cloud too, with
demand from the public sector (which had taken around 60 per cent
of the leased space coming onto the office market during the previous two decades) evaporating as a result of new restraints on public
sector recruitment.

A survey in 1986 showed that location was easily the single most
important factor in assessing the investment potential of a house in
Dublin. Picking the right location can result in extra capital gains of
several thousand pounds, even in very cheap houses. The results of
the survey — by Lisney Research Association prize-winner Martin
Nolan — were as follows:

- Only three areas out of 29 surveyed showed any real increases in
  price since 1974

- Prices in eight areas fell in real terms by over 30 per cent since
  1974

- Second-hand houses represent better value than new ones

- Current house prices do not determine future capital appreciation

- The rise in unemployment has had a severe effect on house prices,
  particularly in the west of Dublin

- Proximity to local authority estates only affects prices when the
  housing was built before the local authority development

- Areas with good access to Dublin 2 and Dublin 4 have risen in
  price at above average rates since 1974

- Proximity of major amenities has an improving effect on prices

- House purchase on the southside is a better investment generally
  than on the northside, but both are considerably better than the
  west. However, there were wide variations within each area.

Two of the estates surveyed were Willow Park, Finglas and Woodbine, Raheny. Houses in these areas cost between £31,000 and £35,000. Both areas are close to local authority and industrial estates and have amenities close by. However, Woodbine increased in price by 500 per cent since 1974, whereas Willow Park only increased by 341 per cent. When inflation is taken into account, Woodbine registered a real increase in price, but Willow Park dropped in price by over 30 per cent. Why should there be such a wide variation in price rises? According to the researcher, the answer to this question lies in the fact that Raheny has easy access to the city centre and to office employment through the new DART electric rail system and the local authority estates close by were beginning to settle down. On the other hand, Willow Park has no such easy access and the social problems of Ballymun flats continue unabated.

But the housing market had undoubtedly taken off once again. *The Property Valuer* was already commenting in Autumn 1987 that

> In recent years, a practice known as "gazumping" in relation to sales of property has caused a lot of dissatisfaction to intending purchasers of property and it has exposed auctioneers and house agents to some criticism. Thus a note on the subject may be helpful. Gazumping occurs when a vendor has agreed to sell a property at a stated price to an intending purchaser and then (before the legal formalities can be completed) reneges on his agreement and deals with some other interested party who offers a higher price. The first intending purchaser naturally feels very aggrieved after he had negotiated in good faith and has been told the property would be sold to him at the agreed price. So far as an intending purchaser is concerned, a commitment binding on the vendor only comes into existence when a contract for sale is signed in the fullest legal sense or there is in existence a note or memorandum of a verbal agreement to sell, signed by the vendor or his authorised agent, which is a sufficient record of the verbal agreement to sell to satisfy the Statute of Frauds.

Legislative proposals on building societies announced by Minister for the Environment Padraig Flynn in November 1987 constituted the most far-reaching reform of the building society movement since its inception in Ireland over a century ago. The new Building

Societies Act was designed to bring building societies into the main-stream of the financial services industry, while retaining their pri-mary role in the financing of houses. One of the proposals impinging directly on the auctioneering profession was carefully noted by members of the Institute. The following extract taken from the pub-licity material released by the Minister's office explains the reason for their apprehension:

> Conveyancing and estate agency are two services closely related to the principal activity of building societies, viz. house purchase, and the Minister is not convinced that there is any good reason why, in principle, societies should not be able to compete in the provision of these services. He thinks that it would ultimately benefit house purchas-ers if societies were permitted to offer these services. He is aware of the potential for conflict of interest, but considers that suitable safeguards may be devised.

The IAVI declared that it was not opposed to the extension of com-petition, but the Government must ensure that adequate safeguards are devised to prevent conflicts of interest. Indeed, it maintained that the idea of a building society offering as estate agency, conveyancing and structural survey services "raises problems which may be inca-pable of solution". A clear conflict of interest arises when a building society acting as agent for the sale of a property is also offering fi-nancial and related services to an intending purchaser, the Institute asserted.

Despite all the promotional effort, the decade ended on some-thing of a downbeat note for the Institute. A survey of Irish attitudes to estate agents revealed that 25 per cent of the 600 respondents in-terviewed would not use the services of an auctioneer in the sale of their house. The reasons expressed for this negative view were var-ied, but included remarks like: "It's just money for old rope"; "they are too dear for the type of service they provide"; "I could do just as well myself "; and "they are a bad experience".

"When over a quarter of the population will not use the services of an estate agent/auctioneer to sell their house, it is startlingly ob-vious that this service sector has a serious image problem," *The Pro-perty Valuer* declaimed in Spring 1989.

This is a shocking reflection of the public's regard for the work and service of estate agents and auctioneers. Blame for it lies entirely within the profession itself. Visitors to the country are amazed at the "let's sit back and wait for the business to walk in the door" attitude that has been evident in some instances. The Irish consumer is also becoming more choosy and demanding, expecting value for the money it pays. In addition, the "old boy" network is disintegrating and critical comments are becoming more widespread than ever before.

The Institute, conscious of this growing public discontent, set specific targets to counteract this emerging image. It concentrated on improving the educational status within the profession and succeeded. It spent huge funds on publications for the public such as "Buying & Selling a House" and "The Services of an Auctioneer & Valuer." These were gratefully received. The Institute established a voluntary compensation fund for the public who might suffer through the dishonesty of one of its members and launched an expensive nationwide advertising campaign to publicise this. It distributed brass nameplates to members so that the public would recognise that a firm was a part of the Institute. It acts as a watchdog for the public by lobbying the Government on items such as stamp duty and any other legislation detrimental to property owners. The Institute advised and continues to advise members on professional practice by holding regular seminars. It represents members at home and abroad on a wide range of issues. But it cannot change public opinion — only members themselves can do this. Practices are not only beginning to realise the benefits of a "good" public image. The Irish public's reluctance to complain has now been replaced by a justified expectation and demand for value for money.

Writing in a subsequent issue of the IAVI journal, auctioneer John Harrington articulated the sentiments of many of his colleagues on the key issue of standards. He acknowledged that greater professionalism, coupled with high-end marketing and a good corporate image would go some way to restoring the public confidence. He commented:

However, one of the major complaints by property professionals over the years has been the freedom enjoyed by unqualified people to "set up shop". Despite the efforts of
IAVI to convince the paying public to deal with qualified
firms only, the term auctioneer and "cowboy" are often
synonymous to the public. Why has the onus fallen on
IAVI? For years we have heard successive ministers promise legislation to tighten entrance standards and qualifications; we still wait.

I do not decry self-regulation, indeed the members of IAVI
have a high standard of competence and the entry system
via college courses ensures its future outside the recognised professional bodies that invariably create the problem. The creation of the IAVI plaque and the important
compensation fund whilst laudable in their own right are
symptomatic proof that successive legislators have "passed
the buck". It is unrealistic to allow people who are investing their money in what is globally referred to as "the most
important transaction of their lives" to make contact with
auctioneers whose only claim to professionalism was a ten-
minute court hearing, possession a £10,000 bond
(sponsored by an insurance company) and no known
criminal record. Whilst many of you may smile at the low
standard minimum entry requirement to practice elsewhere, think of the Irish minimum — none.

In 1989, the rivalry between solicitors and auctioneers surfaced
again when a group of solicitors in the Dublin area disclosed that
they were investigating the possibility of setting up an estate agency
closely linked to solicitors' practices, with a view to providing clients
with an "all-in" service — incorporating that is, estate agency allied
with legal conveyancing. The move came at a time when there was
great mobility in the market. In Britain, for example, estate agencies
were being purchased by building societies and banks, primarily
with a view to selling those institutions' products, such as endow-
ment mortgages, loans and insurances.

Over the summer, some 220 firms of solicitors came together to
organise the project. Staff were trained and five offices opened under
the "Solicitors Property Service" (SPS) banner, with some qualified
estate agents running the agency. Initially, SPS traded from premises

in Dundrum and Dorset Street and then took over an existing agency in Lucan, County Dublin. It later opened a new office at Walkinstown Cross and a further premises in Georges Street, Dun Laoghaire. Subsequently, the agency set up its headquarters at College Green in the heart of the city business district, complete with elaborate auction room and all the latest technical backup.

At an early stage, SPS had over 400 properties on its books, successfully selling on 60 per cent of its portfolio. The new agency proceeded to develop a computerised system whereby all properties would be linked, giving immediate access to each of the offices through "on-line" connections. With such rapid expansion in such a short space of time, however, it abruptly ran into a major cash-flow problem. Due to its structure (the trading company having as its shareholders a number of regional companies controlled by local solicitors), the necessary funds did not become available and SPS ceased trading in April 1991, to ill-concealed glee on the part of estate agents.

While the launch of such an agency initially sent shock waves through the auctioneering industry, it also ultimately had the effect of changing the perceptions of a number of financial institutions, causing them to recoil from investing or purchasing estate agencies and also, no doubt, caused large estate-agency firms to drop any intention on their part to provide a legal "in-house" service through their own firms. Indeed, the experience to date in Britain in this regard has shown such developments to be universally unsuccessful.

Two of Dublin's biggest auctioneering concerns — Hamilton & Hamilton and Osborne King & Megran — merged in 1987 to form Hamilton Osborne King (OKM having enlarged its presence in Cork by taking over the Cork operation of Aston Deller in 1980, with Peter Deller becoming a new partner). By the time of the merger, John McFarlane had stepped down as senior partner and Hugh Hamilton became chairman of the new company, with Ian French as managing director. Since 1988, the company has gone from strength to strength, with turnover multiplying fivefold during the period.

Over the years, its residential section has disposed of many prime properties, including its near neighbour, the Masonic Girls' School, the Johnston Mooney & O'Brien/Telecom site in Ballsbridge and the Sweepstakes site in Ballsbridge (auctioned jointly with Lisney) for

£6.6 million — the highest price ever paid at auction for a commercial property in this country. Under chairman Ian French and managing director Aidan O'Hogan, HOK now has a formal asso-ciation with Hillier Parker in Britain and is working throughout the Americas via its link with Oncor.

By the end of the 1980s, the stakes being played for in the sector were now higher than ever before. A report on advertising expenditure in Ireland showed that the total promotional expenditure for the property business in Ireland stood at around £15 million in 1988. "By any standards, this is a huge volume of advertising," Stephen Stynes, account director, Peter Owens Advertising & Marketing commented. "Yet for such a sizeable investment, the overall standard of presentation and execution of this advertising is low by comparison with other industries."

House values, like all other property prices, had been badly stalled in the aftermath of the Gallagher collapse. Mortgages peaked at around 16 per cent in 1982, remaining in double digits until 1986. Sherry FitzGerald record that the market value of a typical modern four-bedroom semi in Clonard Estate, Sandyford, County Dublin marked time at £43,500 during the period 1983–88. By the end of the decade, however, the market had at last moved into gear, with residential values suddenly and dramatically making up for lost ground. The collapse of the British property market was the major factor propelling this recovery, with cross-Channel buyers turning to Ireland instead. The year 1989 saw residential property achieve unprecedented auction results, with confidence on the part of agents, developers and buyers in the area of new homes firmly placed at the top end of the market. Existing residential values in Dublin increased by more than 50 per cent in some locations on the previous year. A 10 per cent increase in house prices for the same period in Tallaght, until then traditionally one of the weakest spots on the Dublin market, highlighted the overall resurgence of confidence amongst buyers across the whole range of available existing housing stock.

The Section 23 tax incentive for investors had been re-introduced in the 1988 Budget. An allowance of 100 per cent of construction expenditure (including development costs, but excluding site cost) incurred on that period on the provision of certain residential accommodation could be set against all rental income in computing liability of tax under Case V of Schedule D. Between 1981 and 1984, this measure was credited with creating, directly or indirectly, up to 8,000 jobs within a three-year period and the measure had a similarly stimulating impact this time around.

Auction rooms experienced frenetic activity — fuelled in part by a bottleneck caused by a relatively limited number of available properties, lower interest rates and a race to "catch up" on values stalled for some years. Within a few weeks of each other, two record residential auctions were transacted when No. 85 Ailesbury Road was sold under the hammer for £515,000 at the end of September 1989 by Lisney and No. 12 Ailesbury Road fetched a record £560,000 for Bergin's in October 1989. By 1991, Sherry FitzGerald recorded that the semi in Sandyford was now valued at £71,000.

The Dublin investment market increased from £45 million to £220 million between 1987 and 1989, helped by a stabilisation of interest rates. There were overseas forays too. Floated on the stock exchange in October 1987, Power Corporation formed a joint-venture company with AMEC and Brent Walker to purchase the Trocadero Centre and adjoining island site in London for £105 million. The Irish company increased its interest in Trocadero to 50 per cent the following year, increasing its British holdings and expanding into the American market in April 1989, where its acquisitions included the San Francisco Centre for $130 million, and other interests. The 1989–90 boom represented the apex for the Irish concern, however, soon to run into major financial difficulties in the decade ahead.

Confidence returned in the provinces too, with prices in Cork shrugging off previous job worries and rising by up to 30 per cent at the upper end of the market. New apartment developments along the city quays achieved prices of £45,000 to £65,000 and the opening of the Merchant's Quay Centre with Dunnes Stores and Marks & Spencer as anchor tenants provided a commercial property highlight. A new State decentralisation programme was a further plus factor. But the greatest boost of all was provided by EC agreement to double structural funds available to Ireland between 1988 and the end of 1998 — providing scope for increased expenditure on roads, tourism and sanitary services.

Signalling a general economic recovery, increases were also experienced at this time in all categories of fine art from Victorian iron gates and garden gnomes to the highest price yet paid in Ireland when *Harvest Moon* by Jack B. Yeats sold for £308,000 in September 1989. Bloodstock values boomed too, with Goffs transplanting "The Million" concept from its native Australia to Europe and a new record set for a yearling sold at public auction — 3.1 million guineas, paid by Sheikh Mohammed for subsequent Irish St Leger winner Authall (by Shergar, the former dual Derby winner sensationally kidnapped by the IRA). A rival £4 million sales complex was, in the meantime, launched opposite Fairyhouse Racecourse by Tattersalls Ireland in 1988.

Miss Adeline (Della) Weir passed away in November 1989, approaching her 93rd birthday. She served the Institute as assistant to former secretary Frank Warner, who retired in 1934 and continued as assistant to his successor Michael Grey until both retired in 1968. Despite the physical handicap of having only one leg, she travelled on the regular bus routes until well into her eighties and, in her younger days (around 60), one had to walk at a brisk pace to keep up with her on her crutches. Up to a few weeks before her final illness, all that was troubling her was the entry of solicitors into estate agency, advancing the view that those involved were greedy and it would not have happened in the old days!

In 1989, the IAVI regional structure was changed. Each of the six regions are now particularly concerned with local matters and hold both professional and social meetings on a regular basis. There were 829 qualified auctioneers on the IAVI register on December 31, 1989.

CHAPTER EIGHT

FIN DE SIÈCLE — THE NINETIES

"Who buys a house ready wrought
Gets many a screw and nail for nought."
— Battersby & Co., *100 Years & More A-Growing.*

The Irish property market has been spared the turmoil and depression that has hung like a pall over its cross-Channel counterpart throughout most of the nineties. This is as much a tribute to
the increasing sophistication of the local market as a measure of the
extent to which membership of the wider European Union and other
international influences have broadened Irish horizons. The Irish
economy is no longer dictated solely by British interest rate or currency fluctuations — the main benefit for the property market being
historically low mortgage rates coupled with a correspondingly
modest inflation rate in line with continental norms. The advent of
the Single European Market in 1993 climaxed this trend, offering
Irish real-estate professionals the additional prospect of plying their
wares in a community of 320 million "Euro-citizens".

To its credit, the Irish Auctioneers & Valuers Institute has capital-
ised to the full on the new opportunities afforded by this brave new
multinational world. In 1990, the Institute joined the European Property Agents Group, the largest pan-European estate-agency body
with a permanent Brussels-based secretariat, to represent Irish interests on aspects of property harmonisation. The IAVI has also become
a member of the TEGOVOFA (the European Group of Valuers of
Fixed Assets — recognised by EU stock exchanges).

At the start of the decade, the construction industry in the Republic accounted for approximately 12 per cent of gross domestic
product and employed over 100,000 workers either directly or indirectly. The average second-hand house in Dublin cost £56,058 at end
March 1990, while the price of a new house was £61,642. A total of

£982 million was paid out by the main Irish lending agencies the same year for home loans (split 2:1 in favour of existing housing). Building societies accounted for just over half of all loans paid, but the banks were now challenging the traditional dominance of the societies by lending 34 per cent of mortgage funds. The upturn in property activity which commenced in 1989 proved ephemeral, however, and values marked time again after eighteen hectic months. But the housebuilding sector continued to make headway behind the scenes, with the introduction of National Building Regulations in June 1992 and the launch of the HomeBond ten-year house warranty scheme in 1995 representing major landmarks.

Over four-fifths of Irish households now live in owner-occupied accommodation — one of the highest percentages of owner-occupation in the world. "Social Housing — The Way Ahead" launched by the Government in May 1995 was a further milestone, introducing the broadest range of social-housing schemes ever operated by the local authorities or voluntary housing agencies and promising a better national housing service with a more client-centred approach.

There has been only limited research on the wealth of Irish households. However, such analysis as there has been indicates that housing and farm land are the dominant asset types, accounting for 80 per cent of reported wealth in 1991. Residential property represents the principal asset owned by the average Irish person, with only a small percentage owning stocks and shares directly. A corollary of our high home-ownership ratio has been that interest in property-related matters is intense — large newspaper supplements are devoted to what it now seems scarcely an exaggeration to call the subject closest to just about everyone's heart. House-hunting could indeed be said to verge on being a national sport, with thousands thronging through new house/apartment developments every weekend and auction news more avidly read than the racing results. A near obsessive interest in property ownership is, in fact, deeply rooted in the national psyche — linked to folk memories of expropriation by colonists and exploitation by absentee landlords. An Irishman's 1,000 square feet semi-detached house (or 600 square feet apartment) may not exactly qualify as his castle, but it is most assuredly his prize possession — with the rights of property firmly enshrined in the national Constitution. A grand total of 30,575 new homes were completed during 1995 — almost double the 1988 level and the highest number of completions ever recorded in any year since the foundation of the State. The previous record of 29,000 was set in 1981, while 26,863 new dwellings were completed in 1994.

Dublin residential property soared to new heights in 1996, with agents experiencing their busiest period since the 1989/90 boom. Buoyed by a booming economy, more than seventeen properties sold for prices ranging from £1 million to £3.5 million, with suburban houses in fashionable areas regularly realising six figure sums. The highest price paid — in a reputed £3.5 million deal — saw business-man Tony Ryan purchase the Lyons Estate on 600 acres from fellow tycoon Michael Smurfit. "Bartra", a marine period residence in Dalkey, attracted £1.95 million at auction when the 10,000 square feet property on 2.5 acres was acquired by the family interests of Inde-pendent Newspapers chairman Tony O'Reilly. "Pitcairn", a seven-bedroom house on three-quarters of an acre in Shrewsbury Road, Dublin 4 in need of renovation, topped the auction list in the first half of the year at £1.55 million.

Other major sales included Bushy Park, Enniskerry, County Wicklow (eight-bedroom Georgian house on 22 acres) £1.525 million; Auburn House, Malahide (eleven-bedroom Georgian house on 26 acres) £1.4 million; Drumleck, Baily, Howth (Victorian house on nine acres) £1 million-plus prior to auction; Seafield House, Donabate (period house on 82 acres) £1 million-plus before auction; Glandaart House, Coliemore Road, Dalkey (Victorian house overlooking the sea) around £1.13 million before auction; and "Undercliff", Strath-more Road, Killiney (five-bedroom house on 1.6 acres) around £980,000 after auction.

In the first six months of 1995, the eleven top selling houses in *The Irish Times* auctions list sold for between £380,000 to £590,0000. Twelve months later, the least expensive of the top eleven houses — "Cooldrinagh" on Brighton Road in Foxrock (birthplace of Samuel Beckett) — sold for £850,000; the property last came on the market in 1989 when it changed hands for £400,000. Most, if not all of these sales were achieved by IAVI members.

Irish agricultural land values soared by 17 per cent to £3,161 per acre in 1994, with prices of up to £6,000 an acre achieved for choice

small parcels of land close to major conurbations. The Irish country-
house market is currently at its strongest since 1989 when the collapse of the British property market dealt a body blow to sales. The
Jackson-Stops McCabe diamond-anniversary review noted that local
values have multiplied a hundredfold over the past sixty years, yet
prevailing prices still compare favourably with markets elsewhere.
The increasing affluence of domestic buyers has been an obvious factor in this progression, but Ireland's constant appeal for overseas
purchasers has been equally apparent. A Georgian period house on a
few acres close to the capital can command over £500,000 with a
waiting list of ready buyers for the few such properties that come to
the market. To help put the value-for-money equation into perspective, an Irish bloodstock farm can still be acquired for around £5,000
per acre against £12,000 an acre in Newmarket.

According to a survey by Marcus Magnier, partner in JSMcC's
country department, around 35 per cent of properties sold in the
£200,000 to £400,000 category are acquired by foreign purchasers,
with the remaining 65 per cent taken up by the Irish market. A remarkable 50 per cent of properties in the £400,000-plus category are
sold to non-Irish purchasers. To further emphasise the importance of
the international market, if one excludes country houses within easy
commuting distance of Dublin in this higher category, non-Irish purchasers account for no less than 70 per cent of total sales. Noteworthy deals successfully conducted by the Dublin-based firm included
the sale of Ashford Castle in County Mayo (1935); Russborough
House, County Wicklow (1953); Castletown House, County Kildare
(1971); Headfort estate, County Meath (1982) and Athgarvan Stud in
1994.

The new-homes sector enjoyed strong demand during the first
half of the decade, helped by a re-focusing of the Section 23 tax incentive scheme in favour of residential rather than commercial development. A major expansion of the National House Building
Guarantee Scheme was announced by chairman Joe Tiernan of Tiernan Homes in January 1995, extending the warranty from its previous six-year term to ten years. Now called "HomeBond," the scheme
— administered by managing director Michael Greene — is one of
the most progressive warranty packages in the world and over 2,000
builders have enrolled.

A record 8,500 new houses and apartments sold in Dublin during 1995, with a sales value of over £600 million — up 17 per cent on the previous year. The new roads network in the capital has had a significant effect on demand, with the west of the city emerging as an increasingly popular residential location (around 5,000 houses constructed in a two-year period) and huge demand for commercial sites located beside the new ring road system. The outstanding phenomenon of the new-homes scene has, however, been the apartments boom, capturing an increasing slice of first-time purchases and attracting a whole new generation back into the city centre. Approximately 40 per cent of all new homes built in greater Dublin during 1995 were apartments. For the Dublin city area alone, the figure was 70 per cent.

Whereas the population of Dublin's city centre fell from 131,503 in 1971 to 76,558 in 1991 as whole communities re-located in the suburbs, the 1990s have seen a partial reversal of this trend. Over 15,000 people have moved in to live in the city centre since 1991 and this is forecast to rise to over 25,000 by the end of the decade. The apartment vogue has played a key role in reviving hitherto largely derelict areas of the city, including the "cathedral precinct" around Christchurch, Gardiner Street, Francis Street, Aungier Street and the North and South Quays — now transformed into living, vibrant neighbourhoods. The capital city has seen an investment of no less than £1 billion of private money alone in less than a decade, including a £200 million investment in hotels on foot of a 10 per cent annual growth in tourist receipts. Massive public funds have also been ploughed into the city centre. The development of a rapid rail system will be a further major step forward, while other proposed transport improvements include the Dublin Port Tunnel. The 1995 Hooke & MacDonald review states:

> One of the key factors in the residential upsurge in Dublin's city centre is that most of the new units have been available at very affordable prices. These are unrelated to tax incentives and are in themselves a powerful attraction for buyers. One-bedroom apartments have been available mainly from £40,000 to £50,000, with two-bedroom units mainly from £55,000 to £70,000. The affordable prices

prevailing are also a factor in the strong sales of new homes, some in non-designated areas of the city centre.

Convenience to places of work and leisure has also been another important factor. Once a trend has been established and a large number of people move into the city, their friends tend to follow them and this has certainly been the case in the Dublin residential market. Apartment living is catching on and is contributing to the objective of making Dublin a living city. Young first time buyers locating in the city centre are achieving significant savings in time and money by being adjacent to their places of work and leisure.

Headed by auctioneer Ken MacDonald, Hooke & MacDonald was the first estate agency to specialise in apartment sales, carving out a lucrative niche in this rapidly growing market and making major inroads into the new housing market also. The Merrion Square-based estate agency has sold over 7,000 new homes in the past five years, during which period it claims to have been the leading auctioneering firm involved in the sale of new houses and apartments in Dublin.

New housing has been expanding rapidly outside the capital also. Indeed, according to the official Department of the Environment statistics, Galway was actually the most expensive place to buy a new house in 1995 with an average price of £69,379 compared to £68,416 for Dublin. The average price for Cork was £64,343; Limerick £57,248; and Waterford £54,734. Second-hand averages were Dublin £69,901; Galway £61,511; Cork £54,904; Limerick £47,571; and Waterford £46,888. The national figures, of course, mask significant locational variations and do not distinguish between apartment/house prices. Sherry FitzGerald has, for example, revealingly charted the market value of a typical modern four-bedroom two-reception semi-detached family house with garage in Clonard Estate, Sandyford, County Dublin, rising from £8,950 in 1973 to £100,000 in 1996. At the other end of the scale, houses in remote rural locations often only command around half the prices prevailing in urban areas.

A survey conducted by Sherry FitzGerald at the close of 1995 showed that the reasons why Irish people sell their homes are quite varied. Owners wishing to "trade-up" to better properties make up over one-third of all sellers at 35 per cent, although this figure has been steadily declining from a high of 38 per cent in 1991. The next principal reason for sales is that the owners of the properties in question have passed away. Executor sales represent 16 per cent of the market. One in twenty house sales in Dublin are now as a result of marital separations, a figure that has almost doubled since 1989. Another of the most interesting changes since that time has been a marked drop in sales due to emigration, which has likewise more than halved since 1991. In 1989, 14 per cent of all house sales were due to emigration, while six years later this figure has diminished to just 5 per cent. There has also been a significant downturn in the number of houses purchased in order to be renovated for quick re-sale.

The Irish commercial property market was, by comparison, subdued during the first half of the 1990s for a variety of reasons, ranging from the Gulf War and world currency crisis to local over-supply and other factors. Over the period 1967–1988, property offered a relatively attractive long-term return in relation to gilts and equities allied to a very low exposure to risk. Yet, despite these impressive statistics, the proportion of the average institutional-investment portfolio in property has been declining rapidly since the 1970s, from 20 per cent to approximately 8 per cent. Then, without any fundamental change in underlying economic circumstances, institutions suddenly decided from 1988 to 1990 that they required property investments and this influenced other non-institutional investors to follow their lead. Conversely, when property fell out of favour with the institutions, turnover in the market dropped dramatically from £220 million in 1989 to £30 million in 1991. The concentration on office development resulting from the bias towards commercial schemes then prevailing in the urban renewal scheme exacerbated the problem still further.

There has been a significant upturn, however, since 1994 and the market has been much more stable than in Britain, all things considered. The momentum has gradually built up throughout the decade, spearheaded by showcase schemes such as the renewal of the Custom House Docks area in Dublin and the development of the International Financial Services Centre there. The revitalisation of this long unexploited wasteland to a thriving business complex has been quite remarkable. The IFSC has, in fact, already been acclaimed as the fastest-growing offshore-fund centre in Europe. Some 400 companies had located there by mid-1996 and job numbers are now set to rise from a current complement of 3,000 to 5,000 within the next two years. In order to accommodate IFSC-approved companies, seven major office blocks have been constructed at the time of writing and largely occupied, with work under way on a further six. Another building has been adapted to house FINEX Europe, a division of the New York Cotton Exchange. Four retail outlets have also opened for business — one of them achieving a sub-5 per cent yield, representing the lowest yield ever for a tax incentive property. A residential development of 333 apartments has been completed and fully sold, while a new Jurys Hotel and a multi-storey car park have been constructed there.

The £200 million redevelopment programme initiated by the Temple Bar Area Renewal and Development Act 1991 has likewise been one of the mainstays of development activity in the city. The Government singled out the renewal of this historic precinct beside the banks of the Liffey as its flagship project marking Dublin's year as European City of Culture in 1991. A special development agency — Temple Bar Properties — was established to oversee the development, while a comprehensive framework design blueprint was prepared by Group 91 Architects. From a down-at-heel centre of dereliction once earmarked for a bus station, the area has been transformed into Dublin's own "Left Bank", already widely lauded as a model for architecturally-led EU-funded development and featuring a broad array of cultural and tourist facilities.

After a period in the doldrums, office property has recently staged a welcome recovery, together with the retail and industrial sectors. A key factor in this recovery has been the return of the State to the office market after an absence of twelve years following the decentralisation phase commenced during the mid-1980s. The total take-up of Dublin office space in 1995 was 1.1 million square feet — the highest annual level ever recorded in the city. A report by Hamilton Osborne King and the Centre for Urban & Retail Studies at Trinity College Dublin found that only 775,000 square feet of space remained unoccupied at the end of 1995 — of which only 224,000 square feet was of "third-generation" quality.

Irish Estates (Management) celebrated its fiftieth anniversary in 1996 — a measure of the growth of the sector is that Ireland's largest property management company now manages the largest office buildings in the country, collecting £60 million annually from six million square feet of property.

The strength of the Irish economy, low interest rates and low levels of inflation continue to maintain a high degree of confidence within the business sector, in turn generating an expansion of business services and a growing demand for office accommodation. A large part of this demand has been from companies attracted to Ireland by the Industrial Development Authority in the teleservices, computer software and financial services. A record amount of office space was again taken up in Dublin during the first half of 1996, amounting to 884,415 square feet — substantially higher than the annual level of take-up recorded during eight of the previous ten years. Significantly, the vacancy rate has fallen below 5 per cent for the first time since December 1989 — a crucial point in the development cycle which signalled the start of the most recent development boom. Tax-based yields were expected to hit record low levels of around 6 per cent in 1996 and perhaps even drop below this level.

There has been a steady drift towards shorter leases and break options over the past decade, sparked by the influx of overseas organisations demanding a more flexible approach. The market has also become tiered with a demand for different categories of accommodation at corresponding rental levels. Technology and changing patterns of work practice have also begun to make an impact. "Hot desking" and "hoteling" have spread across the Atlantic, while the market as a whole has become more complex and competitive with an increasing demand for research based on professional advice.

Business parks, retail warehousing and other innovations are now part of the Irish scene, most of them located within easy reach of new motorways largely financed by European Structural Funds. Leading international retailers have joined the many industrial giants who have chosen Ireland as a location and currently vie with local operators in an increasingly sophisticated marketplace. Shopping-centre floorspace nationally totalled around four million square feet in 1983, with some 2.3 million located in the Greater Dublin area. By 1995, this had risen to slightly in excess of seven million square feet, divided equally between Dublin and the rest of the country. In 1996, a massive 900,000 square feet of new shopping space was scheduled to open for trading (the largest area of retail floorspace released in any one year), with a further 600,000 square feet coming on stream in 1997.

The first regional scale development in the country — The Square in Tallaght, launched by developers Monarch Properties and GRE Properties — opened in November 1990, providing 700,000 square feet gross floorspace. Other schemes included the Ilac Centre in Henry Street; Nutgrove Shopping Centre; St Stephen's Green Shopping Centre; Omni Park; Blackrock Shopping Centre and Frascati Centre in Blackrock; Janelle Shopping Centre, Finglas; The Swan Centre, Rathmines; and Artane Castle. At the end of 1996, both the long-awaited Blanchardstown Centre (Green Property) and Jervis Centre (Stamshaw Ltd.) opened for trade, while O'Callaghan Properties has commenced sitework at Quarryvale (with funding from the Duke of Westminster's Grosvenor Estate) — heralding the most competitive era yet seen in this sector.

At the other end of the scale, the high-flying Power Corporation era came firmly to ground in November 1996 when a syndicate of banks led by Irish Intercontinental Bank appointed a receiver to Power Corporation following a request by the company. A management buy-out team, led by former chairman and managing director Tony Leonard, acquired the Irish properties. The share listing of the group had been cancelled the previous month following the failure of the heavily indebted corporation to negotiate a deal. At the height of his career, founder Robin Power (who resigned from the group in 1995) had clinched deals with high-profile US property developer Donald Trump and British boxer-turned-developer George Walker. At the end of 1996, the financial deficit was understood to be in excess of £70 million and the bulk of the group's portfolio was in the United States.

Shopping centres have emerged over the last decade wherever there has been sufficient population to sustain such development. In fact, roughly half of the shopping-centre floorspace brought to the market in that period has been located outside Dublin. The most notable provincial developments have included Merchants Quay and Douglas Court in Cork, City Square in Waterford, Eyre Square in

Galway, Parkway, Arthur's Quay and Cruise's Street in Limerick, Dundalk Shopping Centre, Navan Shopping Centre and Market Cross in Kilkenny. An estimated 3.5 million square feet of shopping centre floorspace has now been provided outside the capital.

The investment market has seen a shift towards retail investment outside Dublin and a substantial withdrawal of funds from offices, according to the 1995 Investment Property Databank commercial property survey. In terms of investment flows, the survey confirms that the institutions have been consistent net investors in the Irish market. Over the last twelve years, they have spent £530 million through purchases, development and improvement (£373 million net). But, on balance, the IPD analysis shows that investors put their money in 1995 in much the same places as in the previous year — reinforcing patterns that have been steadily emerging over the past decade. The latest statistics show that investment flows have been running against offices in eight out of the last eleven years. Since 1986, the annualised performance of Irish property has, however, been on a par with that of Irish equities and gilts.

Solid property returns in 1995 marked the third year of recovery from the recession of the early 1990s. The market return on capital employed in property investment was 12.9 per cent in 1995, according to the IPD survey. The return averaged 8.9 per cent per year from December 1983 to December 1995. Over the 12 years, market returns have consisted mainly of income return (at 7.6 per cent per annum); capital growth has been low (1.3 per cent), amounting to a cumulative rise of 17 per cent since 1983. Industrial property generated returns well ahead of the other two sectors — 3.3 per cent a year above retail, which in turn showed returns 2.2 per cent a year ahead of offices. Industrials were the best performing sector in 1995 for the seventh consecutive year, registering a 10.5 per cent rate of income return, underpinning an industrial total return of 15.1 per cent. Retail and office total returns stood at 14.1 per cent and 11.8 per cent respectively.

An important difference in commercial property trends over the past decade has been the "downsizing" of institutional property allocations. In the 1970s and 1980s, insurance companies often invested a quarter of their funds in property. This has now been reduced to somewhere in the region of 5 per cent to 15 per cent. The slack in institutional investment has, however, been more than made up by private investors, mostly operating in the tax-based investment market. The volume of transactions is now much higher at around £250 million a year compared with only £30–£50 million in the mid-1980s.

Building-land prices continue to escalate. Recent sales of infill residential sites have soared to new heights: 1.6 acres at Dartry sold for £1.9 million and 2.5 acres at Radcliff Hall, Sandymount for £3.75 million (or £1.5 million an acre, a record for a Dublin 4 property). At Ashbourne, County Meath, a 31.5 acre site sold for £3.25 million, equating to £17,000 per site. Industrial land in well-located sites close to the motorway network now commands prices of around £200,000 an acre. Farmland is now approaching between £2,500 and £3,000 an acre for small holdings in sought after areas, with, of course, wide regional variations and the north-eastern region leading the way.

The rising economic tide has lifted all boats. The fine art business has, for example, enjoyed an upturn also — most spectacularly underlined by £730,000 sterling paid for the oil painting *A Farewell To Mayo* by Jack B. Yeats (formerly owned by the late actress Vivien Leigh who had been given the picture by her then husband Laurence Olivier) at auction.

The Dublin metropolitan area currently has a total population in excess of one million people, of whom 996,000 occupied 311,000 private households in 1991. The overall population of the Dublin sub-region has risen by 298,000 from 852,000 in 1971 to 1,150,200 in 1991 or by 35 per cent of its 1971 population, representing an annual average rate of growth of 14,895 people. Almost two-thirds of the Republic's population now lives in urban or suburban areas, with Dublin accounting for two-fifths of the urbanised total. "During this century, Dublin has changed from a well-defined, compact city to a more populous, more dispersed city region," a Department of the Environment report to the second United Nations Conference on Human Settlements — Habitat II— commented. While there has been considerable progress, the report redresses the balance by pointing out that many Irish people are still living in "poverty blackspots" characterised by crime, vandalism, drug addiction, poor environmental conditions and a lack of community structures.

Urban renewal has been under way outside the capital too, with the availability of State tax incentives triggering many schemes that would never otherwise have been undertaken. Limerick is a case in point — around £100 million plus has been invested there in river-front schemes like Arthur's Quay and the civic offices, while the inner core of the city has been revived by the new Cruise's Street precinct and other projects. Galway and Cork have likewise seen major urban improvements, as also have other provincial centres. As in the capital, the main areas of investment opportunity include tax-based opportunities in designated or enterprise areas and multi-storey car parks.

Since 1986, over £1.7 billion of private-sector investment has been generated in designated areas under the urban renewal schemes. The investment breakdown has been as follows: residential 28 per cent; offices 32 per cent; commercial 26 per cent; and other 14 per cent. Of projects completed and in progress at the end of 1995, 42 per cent of investment took place in the county boroughs and towns outside Dublin City. A total of £334 million was invested in Cork, Galway, Limerick and Waterford.

Tourism and leisure schemes have also experienced rapid growth, buoyed by a 58 per cent rise in revenue from overseas tourists since 1988. Dublin has, however, nevertheless cornered most of the hotel development action, with 25 hotels worth an estimated £200 million planned for the capital alone in mid-1996.

One of the highlights of the Irish property scene in the 1990s prior to the latest outbreak of sectarian violence has been the renaissance of Belfast, long a centre of declining prices and neglect. Interestingly, the abortive peace process was not the sole factor in this resurgence. The flagship Laganside development traces its origins back long before the recent ceasefire. Property prices right across the North have been inching upwards for some time, but to what extent this process can continue obviously depends upon future political events. The Real Estate Studies Unit at the University of Ulster pointed out that house prices rose faster in Northern Ireland during 1994 than most of mainland Britain, where the market has remained clouded by negative equity and other concerns. Average NI prices rose by almost 7.5 per cent in 1995 and by the end of the year were accelerating towards an annual rate of increase of over 9 per cent. A semi-detached bungalow in Carrickfergus, valued in 1993 at £33,000, sold in 1994 for £40,000; a three-bedroomed terraced house at Ulsterville Avenue, valued at £42,000 in 1993, made £58,000 two years later.

The most crucial property development for Belfast is undoubtedly the Laganside project. Representing a partnership between the Laganside Corporation and the private sector, this major scheme is blueprinted to take fifteen years to complete at a cost of around £750 million. The Laganside Corporation was set up in 1989 under the chairmanship of the Duke of Abercorn with a brief to develop a site of about 340 acres along a half-mile stretch of the river from the Abercorn Basin to the Ormeau Bridge. The original site included some of the most run-down, desolate and polluted areas anywhere in the city or indeed in the country. The first major highlight of the hugely ambitious development programme came in 1994 with the opening of the Lagan Weir project. Central to the whole concept, it has improved the river corridor by maintaining a semi-tidal stretch of water upstream of the weir. The weir is aimed at regenerating the very heart of the city along Donegall and Queen's Quays and now even boasts its own visitors' centre. New housing schemes at Ravenhill Reach and Bridge End have bolstered the list of improvements, culminating in the opening of the new bridge.

The most ambitious project outside the weir and the new bridge itself is the Laganbank site beside the city centre. Here fourteen acres have been chosen as the site for a combined concert hall and conference centre, which will seat close to 2,700 people. The centre will comprise some 40,000 square metres of office space, 6,000 square metres of shopping area, a 187-bedroom hotel and 1,400 car parking spaces. Altogether, developing Laganbank will cost around £140 million or roughly £10 million an acre.

As early as 1981, housing in Belfast had been identified as a prime social priority and the necessary resources to tackle the problems were earmarked. During the decade, the Northern Ireland Housing Executive is estimated to have spent over £700 million on urban renewal. This massive public-sector new-build programme made a dramatic impact on the physical fabric of inner Belfast. Joseph Cowan, Under-Secretary for Urban Affairs at the Department of the Environment for Northern Ireland, told the first IAVI annual conference to be held in Northern Ireland during March 1996 that:

All this was achieved in a highly unfavourable environment with violent community conflict and a complete unwillingness by people to move outside the perceived safety of their own community. It was also achieved despite the involvement of paramilitaries in intimidating contractors, organising protection rackets and orchestrating squatting. The provision of public sector housing in Belfast has been quite revolutionary in its impact on housing quality and on the general visual amenity of the city.

In terms of environmental improvement, over one million trees have been planted on the streets and parks of Belfast over the past decade, while city-centre streets have been paved to high standards and embellished with award-winning street furniture. Retail development has been a major contributor to revitalisation. A net retail floorspace of 1.1 million feet in 1975 increased to 1.3 million in 1985 with a further 0.5 million square feet added in the early 1990s including a large enclosed shopping complex known as Castle Court. The latter comprises 250,000 square feet of retail floorspace, 20,900 square feet of office accommodation and parking for 1,600 cars. The development was completed in 1990. This scheme was funded by a syndicated loan of £40 million sterling, developer's funds of some stg£15 million and urban development grant of stg£10 million.

By 1994, the retail vacancy rate in Belfast had dropped to 2 per cent compared to a 21 per cent vacancy rate in 1980. Many leading multiples have now become established on prime city-centre sites and the city was recently singled out as the ninth best performing retail location in the UK. Hopefully, this trend will not be marred by further senseless violence.

Urban development grants in Belfast since the mid-1980s have generated an estimated £176 million of private sector investment. The peace process climaxed the process of reconstruction in 1995–96, although the Drumcree Orange Parade and the bombing of the Killyhevlin Hotel in Enniskillen provided a chilling reminder that sectarian hatred still lurks just beneath the surface on both sides of the religious divide.

Elsewhere, the physical revival of Derry got under way at the beginning of the 1980s, with the building of the Richmond Shopping Centre and offices on a four-acre site at the Diamond in the heart of the "Walled City". More recently, the £65 million Foyleside Centre in Derry has been one of the largest developments ever constructed in Northern Ireland. Occupying a 5.5 acre site in the city centre, it provides approximately 200,000 square feet of retail floorspace on four levels. The projected catchment population for the centre is estimated at 225,000 people, including a major portion of County Donegal. When the centre opened for trading in September 1995, it was virtually fully let. In addition to anchor tenants Marks & Spencer and Dunnes Stores, many other well-known names such as Dixon's, Iceland, Café Kylemore and Argos have taken units there.

The process of cross-border redevelopment has been facilitated by the allocation of over £263 million by the International Fund for Ireland in the period 1987–94. The fund's intervention helped finance the formation of 37 local enterprise agencies, each under the direction of cross-community boards, while a total of 441 organisations were assisted to promote social and economic development in these years. Overall, IFI claimed to have provided leverage of over £450 million of other funds, leading to a total investment of over £700 million — much of it targeted at specially disadvantaged areas in the region.

The population of the Republic has increased by almost 100,000 since 1991, bringing the total to more than 3.6 million for the first time in the history of the State. The preliminary report on the 1996 census reflects a steadily falling birth rate, offset by a high level of inward immigration. Overall, the value of construction activity in the Republic was approximately £4.5 billion in 1995, exceeding 13 per cent of gross national product. Employment in the construction sector has been expanding rapidly in recent years and approaching 115,000 people — almost 10 per cent of the total employed in the State. Lending on new homes is estimated to have increased in value by 25 per cent in 1995 and now accounts for 40 per cent of all residential lending. The number of mortgages paid on second-hand properties is estimated to have dropped by 5 per cent to 28,788, while the major banks have made strong inroads into the building society share of the overall mortgage market. Helped by the demutualisation of our biggest lender, Irish Permanent (now classified as a bank), the banks accounted for no less than 67 per cent of the £1.8 billion mortgage market by value in 1995. Responding in kind,

Irish building societies provided £183 million worth of commercial mortgages during 1995 — in turn challenging the traditional hegemony of the banks in this lucrative area.

But the acceleration in the building tempo has by no means been universally applauded, with dissenting voices heard even within the industry itself apart altogether from conservationists, environmentalists and others. A major policy document "Europe & Architecture Tomorrow" — compiled by Irish architect Eoin Ó Cofaigh on behalf of the Architects' Council of Europe (ACE) — argues that the development of an unrestricted free market in the European construction industry has largely put the interests of building users and the environment to one side in the name of economic efficiency. The ACE "White Paper" sets out specific proposals for the radical reform of the construction process — such as legal restrictions on land use — so that imbalances can be redressed.

"The open economy is the current European norm, involving a drive for profit maximisation and cost reduction," Ó Cofaigh states in the ACE document.

> It has brought many benefits such as broader freedoms in market access, competition and consumer choice and higher levels of consumer protection. The free market concept dominates State economic thinking, with the effect that more people now have access to greater quantities of goods and commercially available services than ever before. We have to ask ourselves, however, has the working of the market economy improved the built environment in recent decades? In general, the answer is no. What it has given us is suburban and rural sprawl, the destruction of the inner cities, declining housing space standards, increased urban noise, energy consumption and pollution. All of these stem from an inadequately regulated market economy.

> The free market views construction as a merely economic process. The impetus is towards growth or to avoid stagnation, profit maximisation, price-based selection and externalisation of all environmental costs. The promoters (i.e. the people who commission the building) are central to the free market construction sector and their interests focus on the procurement of the desired accommodation at the

appropriate level of quality — not always the highest attainable — within an agreed timescale, for an agreed budget and as cheaply as possible. These interests differ from, and permanently risk contradicting, those of the building user and society.

The architect argues that we must regulate the process by which buildings come into existence, in order to balance the public need for the best quality built environment with the private interests of all building promoters, particularly inexperienced ones:

> We need good building. The planet demands it, people need it. In the name of the building user, public policy must shift to strengthen the voice of the building user and citizen.

On the home front, the Consumer Credit Act 1995 provided a very welcome additional measure of consumer legislation — ushering in a new era for borrowers and lenders alike. The new act provides for the regulation of mortgage intermediaries, imposes specific obligations on mortgage agents, demands disclosure of "tied" status, prohibits linked services, and requires detailed disclosure of information.

While its members have been busily fighting their own particular corner in the property marketplace, conservation has been high on the IAVI agenda for the 1990s. The designation of Dublin as the 1991 European City of Culture provided the perfect platform for the IAVI to progress long-standing plans for restoration work on its historic Merrion Square premises — generally regarded as one of the finest buildings in Georgian Dublin. Refurbishment work on the principal rooms commenced the previous year and the project duly proved an unqualified success.

Chief executive Joseph Healy was responsible for the day-to-day administration of the refurbishment programme. An exacting task, this involved restoring the rooms back to their pristine condition complete with original features, plus much painstaking work with plasterwork, wiring, skirting, floors, walls, ceilings and the like. The old-established firm of J.F. Keatinge & Sons was engaged to undertake the principal work of restoration and redecoration. The work was meticulously carried out and scrupulously faithful to the eighteenth-century pedigree of this splendid building. According to expert opinion, the plasterwork at No. 38 is today at least equal to anything of its kind in Dublin.

This work dates originally from an even earlier period than the more famous and more flamboyant stucco work of such masters as Michael Stapleton, but marks something of a transition between the techniques of rococo plasterwork where the designs were executed *in situ* and the later technique of casting the designs on a bench and setting them into the plaster undercoat. The glory of the restoration can be seen at its best in the two interconnecting main rooms on the first floor — the front room which was once a drawing room and is now the IAVI principal auction room, and the boardroom. Here the subtle blending of soft pastel colours has enlarged and enriched the impact of the delicate yet strong plasterwork to perfection, set off by outstanding woodwork. The chief executive's impressive office has also been restored, as has the intriguing barrel-vaulted ceiling at the top of the house. The annual report stated:

> Taken as a whole, the refurbishment has exceeded expecta-
> tions and the magnificent rooms have been enriched, in the
> main by soft pastel colours which have shown off the rich
> and delicate plasterwork to perfection. The members can
> view with pride their headquarters, reflecting their status
> in the profession.

Still more recent changes in HQ facilities and auction rooms have included the complete refurbishment of the basement area to pro-vide state-of-the-art conference/auction space. No. 38 thus now combines the elegance of Georgian Dublin with the comfort and the amenities of an up-to-date conference centre. Large or small units can be made available complete with audio-visual and public ad-dress systems, while catering services may also be provided as re-quired. The functions hall has been completely refurbished, includ-ing comfortable seating, and will accommodate up to 100 people in a theatre configuration which can also be divided for smaller groups.

Never content to rest upon its laurels, the IAVI has continued to give top priority to professional development throughout the 1990s, determinedly expanding its sphere of influence and refining its services both at home and abroad. The Institute continues to estab-lish new member benefits, including group bond/licence schemes and the establishment of a professional-indemnity scheme with Lloyds, specifically written for Institute members and thereby resulting in significant savings. Most recently, at the end of 1996, the IAVI was finalising a sophisticated Internet and e-mail service for its members in conjunction with Trinity Group who have developed customised electronic commerce services for a number of leading organisations. A multiple-listing system (MLS) may well form part of the finished product.

An in-depth analysis of the strengths and weaknesses of Institute operations was embarked upon in 1991. Over the following three years, the executive committee reviewed strategic areas such as membership benefits, education, public relations and continuing professional development. President Joseph E. McCarthy commented in 1994 that:

> The results of that analysis are positive and encouraging. One can see that members have benefited from the group bond/licence schemes and in particular the professional indemnity insurance scheme. These benefits have been particularly welcome this year when the property market was slow to recover from the devaluation of the punt and the high interest rates that enveloped the market until April.

The Single European Market brought with it many new challenges and opportunities for Irish auctioneers. The unexpected downside of the new monetary union was an initial sudden sharp increase in interest rates, but this proved a temporary phenomenon and the cost of money soon found a new level alongside cheaper European rates. From the outset, the IAVI fully recognised the desirability of taking an active role in European affairs and accepted an invitation to join the European Group of Valuers of Fixed Assets (TEGOVOFA), in addition to its commitments to EPAG. On a world-wide scale, the Irish chapter of FIABCI (the International Real Estate Federation) was successful in its bid at the World Congress of the Federation in Montreux to host the Bank of Ireland sponsored 1997 World Congress — a testament to the high esteem in which the Irish Institute is held by auctioneers and realtors throughout the world. It is expected that about 1,200 delegates will attend the FIABCI Congress in

Dublin — aptly coinciding with the 75th anniversary of the foundation of the IAVI who will co-host the event with FIABCI-Ireland.

A bi-lateral co-operation agreement has been made with the National Association of Realtors, a 750,000-strong US professional body,
whereby IAVI members can take advantage of a still wider variety of
international services. Overseas affiliate membership of NAR is now
available to IAVI members.

The Institute has been no less active on the home front, engaging
in a wide variety of activities which reflect its increasingly diverse
nature. IAVI has been the most vociferous opponent of the controversial residential property tax, highlighting in particular its dis-
criminatory effect on property in Dublin. The wide differential between capital and rural prices has meant that 29 per cent of the
population resident in Dublin paid an estimated 77 per cent of residential property tax in 1995 compared to Munster with a similar
population which paid just 12 per cent of all RPT. In January 1994,
the IAVI was again to the fore in publicly denouncing changes announced in the Budget. Its opposition proved effective on this occasion, when 1993 thresholds were adjusted to 1995 levels allowing for
inflation as requested in the IAVI pre-Budget submission to the
Minister for Finance. The Institute again led its 1997 Budget submission with a strong demand for the abolition of RPT. Its glee at the
abolition of RPT in the January 1997 Budget was, however, damp-
ened by the hiking of stamp duty, up to 9 per cent on housing costing over £170,000.

The IAVI has also been vociferous in its condemnation of the increasingly anachronistic Irish stamp-duty regime. This has seen
thresholds remain effectively static throughout a twenty-year period
during which property prices have risen dramatically. At a conser-
vative estimate, the IAVI argues that linking stamp-duty thresholds
to the Consumer Price Index would have ensured that only properties worth over £300,000 should now be liable for the 6 per cent rate
of stamp duty. Instead, this rate actually now applies to all second-
hand sales between £60,000 and £150,000 (with even higher rates
above this level), and has proven a major hindrance to trading-
up/second-hand sales (and latterly expensive new-house sales). If
indexation is regarded as equitable in some other areas of taxation
thresholds, the IAVI asks, why is it not applied to stamp duty?

Despite its anti-stamp duty campaign, the Institute has, however, never encouraged members to shirk their legal responsibility in this regard. *The Property Valuer* declared in Spring 1995:

> Stamp duty evasion through the deliberate understatement of consideration (or market value where no monetary consideration is involved) carries very severe penalties for those concerned. On occasion, professionals involved in property sales may come under pressure to facilitate such understatement. Professionals, whether solicitors or auctioneers, are themselves tax compliant and should not risk their own professional career or reputation to facilitate a questionable and marginal benefit to another party in this manner.

In the commercial property sphere, the business sector continues to be burdened with annual increases in commercial rates which are substantially in excess of inflation. Opponents of the system argue that such increases have an adverse economic impact on business cost structures, hindering prospects for growth/employment. Together with the Chambers of Commerce in Ireland, members of the IAVI have hit out at every opportunity against the lack of uniformity in the amount of rates being paid in different parts of the country, the lack of transparency in how effectively money collected as rates is spent by local authorities and the absence of any apparent understanding on behalf of either the Government or local authorities regarding the need for restraint in commercial rates increases.

According to a Chambers of Commerce report, the yield from commercial rates has been increased from £164 million a decade before to £322 million in 1995, an increase of 96 per cent. Inflation totalled only 32 per cent in the same period. The average rate in the pound struck by local authorities increased 55 per cent, while the valuation base also expanded greatly. The CCI has urged the Government to commission a national revaluation of all properties and argues that this revaluation be repeated every five years (possibly on a rolling basis). Assuming that the valuation base would increase substantially as a result, the chambers stress that rates in the pound must be lowered accordingly. The CCI report states:

> The government continues to ignore the fundamental problem facing local authority funding. Despite paying lip service to the need for more effective, dynamic, relevant local authorities in Ireland, the Government continues to prevaricate over how they should be funded. . . . It is clear that the business sector is seen as an "easy option" when it comes to local financing. Councillors can vote for sizeable rates increases without directly affecting the majority of the electorate.

An IAVI signboard competition was initiated in 1994, aimed at improving the appearance of Georgian Dublin by minimising the visual impact of unsightly auctioneering signs. In the on-going IAVI awareness campaign, some 5,500 membership list booklets were circulated to all legal and accountancy practices and bank/building society branch managers in the country during 1995 and again in January 1997. Meetings were likewise held and agreement reached with the Irish Farmers Association on fee structures for long term land   lettings.

December 1993 was a black month for the Institute when chief executive Joseph Healy passed on after a short illness — the huge turnout at his funeral attended by members and kindred professionals from throughout the country testifying to the tremendous esteem in which he was held. The quiet-spoken Corkman was for many years the prime mover of Institute affairs behind the scenes, shunning personal publicity and administering the affairs of the Institute with great efficiency. His wife Nancy recalls that he was so committed to his work that he stayed overnight at his offices in No. 38 Merrion Square on two occasions (once at real personal risk when a break-in had earlier occurred), sleeping in a fold-up bed. Friend and colleague John Doyle recalled the late CEO's ever-friendly and courteous manner, remembering how he "loved to hear the latest news from all parts of the country, especially any news of any member's good fortune". Journalist Cliodhna O'Donoghue, who worked as information officer alongside the former CEO, concluded her obituary by saying that he was a "hard-working professional with a great love of sports and fine art; that he was very much a family man who leaves behind him Nancy and his five children of whom he was very proud and loved dearly".

Alan Cooke, who served as IAVI president in 1986 (and of the Young Members' Association during his student years), was appointed chief executive of the Institute in January 1994, bringing a wealth of practical experience of the auctioneering profession to his new appointment. He successfully completed the Rathmines course in 1973 while apprenticed to dual IAVI president Desmond Scales, after which the young Dublin estate agent devoted the following 12 years to learning his trade with the firm of Finnegan Menton where he was appointed a director. He was a partner in the firm of Cumisky & Cooke and subsequently Cumisky Cooke Scales in the 1985–93 period. Since taking up the reins at the Institute, the new chief executive has lost no time in progressing one of the busiest programmes ever initiated by the IAVI.

In February 1996, the IAVI Practice Handbook was launched at the Merrion Square headquarters by Minister for the Environment, Brendan Howlin. The publication of the manual represents yet another significant landmark in the ongoing IAVI commitment to improving auctioneering standards. Five years in gestation and published with the assistance of the ICS Building Society, it is the most definitive document of its kind, covering all aspects of estate-agency practice in Ireland. The manual is divided into a total of 27 separate sections, ranging from agency through to valuation and even including such highly practical topics as personal-safety guidelines for auctioneers. The main emphasis of the manual to date is on agency practice in the Republic. The manual has, however, been produced in loose-leaf binder format to facilitate regular updating and subsequent additions will cater more fully for Northern Ireland practice.

Chief executive Cooke writes in a preface to the manual that:

> In this litigious age, one of the golden rules is that a practitioner should only undertake work within his/her area of competence. Professional work must not be delegated without supervision to subordinates who do not have the expertise to undertake same.

Reference to the personal safety factor is a reminder that auctioneering can sometimes be a hazardous business. Repossessions or bank sales can be particularly tricky. A case in point is that told by Patrick Stephenson of James H. North & Co. who had a gruelling experience when selling a farm on the instructions of the High Court on behalf of the Northern Bank. The auction was preceded by a number of threatening phone calls to the auctioneer who was consequently obliged to apply to the court for an injunction to stop the owners "watching and besetting". Before the auction, the auctioneer even received a mass card through the post. The auction was ultimately held with two detectives at the back of the room concealing Uzi machine guns beneath their coats to protect the auctioneer in the event of an attempt on his life. Happily, there was no incident on the day and the farm was subsequently sold. Other auctioneers have had similar hair-raising experiences (some involving threats from terrorists/criminals), but were unwilling to relate them on the record.

As the new millennium approaches, IAVI members can justifiably pride themselves on having acquired a degree of expertise and efficiency that compares very favourably with their counterparts anywhere in the world. Leading agencies have reached out to embrace the brave new world of computer technology — the first property "hit" or home sold on the Internet in this country being claimed by Hamilton Osborne King in January 1996, when an Irishman working in the US reportedly bought "Stonehaven" in Monkstown after viewing the property details on the Internet from his office. A visit home over the Christmas holidays secured the deal with the Dublin-based agents who were quoting £149,500 for the property. "There is no doubt that the Internet is set to become the marketing tool of the future for selling residential and commercial property to the foreign and indeed Irish buyer," HOK chairman Ian French enthused.

With over 30 million users connected worldwide and growing fast, the IAVI is likewise determined to harness the unprecedented potential of the World Wide Web. Building upon the success of LAWLINK, a secure electronic commerce service for the Incorporated Law Society of Ireland, the Trinity Group has proposed a similar electronic commerce service to the IAVI and its members. The customised IAVI service will comprise:

- Integration with LAWLINK for Land Registry and Companies Office searches

- Internet sites for all IAVI members

- A database of Irish properties accessible worldwide

- Electronic mail for all IAVI members and the IAVI headquarters

- Transaction security at all levels.

At the end of 1996, there was a grand total of 1,389 on the IAVI membership register — 1,041 members, 73 associate members, plus 205 students and 70 honorary fellows/retired members. Deposit Cover by the IAVI compensation fund stood at £1 million (with inner limits of £50,000 per claim and £150,000 per firm). The fund operates in connection with real property transactions in Ireland only; thus chattels, livestock, plant and/or machinery including motor vehicles, fine art and rents/service charges (other than rental deposits) are outside the scope of cover.

The activities of auctioneers are more diverse than ever, with firms ranging from local agencies with only one member and per-haps a building-society agency to a staff of over 100 employees in the largest Dublin firms. Members offer some or all of the following services:

- Valuation for sale, purchase, estate duty, compulsory acquisition, mortgage, rating, insurance and other purposes

- Sale by auction, tender or private treaty of residential, industrial, agricultural or investment property

- Property acquisitions

- Management of land and property of every description

- Agricultural land lettings

- Town and country planning applications/appeals and represen-tations at public enquiries against planning schemes

- Sale and valuation of chattels, works of art, plant and machinery

- Acting as arbitrators and experts for rent review purposes

- Representing clients at rent review hearings

- Lease renewals under landlord and tenant legislation.

Persons intending to apply for full membership of the Institute must currently satisfy one of the following conditions:

1. They must have completed a recognised course of education and have approved professional experience, or

2. Passed all required subjects of the direct final examination and have appropriate practical experience, or

3. Hold a professional qualification recognised by the Institute and have appropriate practical experience.

The principal full-time third-level courses which the Institute recognises are:

- the three-year certificate/diploma courses held in the Dublin Institute of Technology, Bolton Street, Dublin 1 and in Galway Regional Technical College

- the four-year property degree courses in Limerick RTC; Dublin Institute of Technology, Bolton Street; and University of Ulster, Jordanstown, Newtownabbey.

Under the appropriate EU directive, the Institute will also recognise appropriate overseas degree and diploma courses. The DIT and Galway RTC diploma courses are grant-aided from the EU Social Fund. Persons intending to apply for associate membership of the Institute must have passed the one-year residential and land agency course administered by the IAVI or its equivalent. To be eligible to apply to enter the direct final examination part-time courses, a candidate must have a minimum of seven years approved professional experience, hold a university degree, a national diploma or equivalent qualification or have passed all subjects on the residential and land agency course.

Among the objectives of the Institute remains the provision of a central organisation for licensed auctioneers, estate agents and valuers in Ireland; the promotion and protection of the general interest of members of the profession; the maintenance and extension of its usefulness for the general public; and the provision of a better definition and protection of the profession and the education of its members by a system of examination.

Compulsory continuing professional development courses for IAVI members have been introduced since January 1, 1995. Chief executive Cooke comments:

Knowledge cannot remain static in the modern business environment. Today's practitioners must stay abreast of changing legislation and practices. New practice trends are emerging, as are new laws and difficulties never before addressed. Any professional body worthy of that title will insist on keeping up to date and the Institute, through the continuing professional development programmes, the yearbook, *The Property Valuer* and the Practice Handbook, endeavours to ensure that members are provided with as much information as possible. The Institute is not a club but a professional body. Setting standards for the intake of new members is not enough. We must set goals and standards for experienced practitioners which will enable us to justifiably claim that auctioneers who are IAVI members are more knowledgeable than those outside our fold.

While individuals within a practice have been members of the IAVI, individual practices themselves have until now not been registered as member firms. However, in a move described by chief executive Alan Cooke as "one of the most radical and fundamental since the Institute was established," IAVI member firm status has been established for the first time. A letter circulated to members by the chief executive explains that:

From January 1st 1997, only IAVI Member Firms will benefit from a range of existing services provided by the Institute. Many of these services are of major financial benefit to practices and IAVI Member Firm status will be of immense importance. A sizeable budget has been set aside to promote the use by the public of the services of IAVI Member Firms using the new IAVI Logo — only Member Firms may use this logo.

IAVI member firms will henceforth be entitled to:

- Cover by the Institute's compensation fund
- Use the Institute's collective licensing scheme, where available
- Benefit from the Institute's collective bond for licensing purposes
- Solely represent themselves as an IAVI member firm
- Use the facilities at headquarters for auctions, etc.

- Cover under the Institute's professional indemnity insurance scheme.

The IAVI chief comments:

> Collectively, our members are their own best advertise-ment. By promoting the quality of IAVI Member Firms, our members will benefit by further improving their already dominant collective share of the market. The Institute is prepared to take the all important lead and to undertake the necessary work on your behalf to achieve this aim. We will, of course, need the proactive support of all firms to succeed.

CHAPTER NINE

TOWARDS THE MILLENNIUM

The globalisation of property affairs has brought Irish practice steadily into line with larger and more developed markets. The availability of reliable statistics on the Irish property industry has, however, been limited over the years, with firms in this sector notoriously backward in coming forward with data — particularly on the scale of their own operations. An economic analysis of the property services industry (PSI) in the Republic by David McKenna, however, suggests that total fee income in this sector is now in excess of £80 million. McKenna is presently with the Dublin office of Lambert Smith Hampton, who in March 1996 became the first firm of surveyors/estate agents practising in Ireland to obtain a Stock Exchange listing, having taken over Battersby in 1994 — once the predominant firm in Ireland, Battersby was at its peak between the Wars, but went into a period of decline before being given a new lease of life in the 1970s by Anthony Dwyer (who died suddenly in 1996), Des Ringrose and Fred Devlin.

Based on an estimated PSI output of £74 million in 1993, the study concluded that the actual value of transactions undertaken is "in the order of several billions". The study (dated January 1994) reported that there were a total of 469 auctioneering and surveying firms in the Republic — 157 Dublin and 312 non-Dublin. The two main PSI classifications are agency and professional services, the latter being sub-divided into five separate categories — valuations, compulsory purchase work, rating work, rent review negotiations and property management.

For the purposes of the study, the property services industry was defined as consisting of the member firms of the IAVI and the general practice/valuation division of the Society of Chartered Surveyors practising in the Republic where the business is wholly or partly providing property services to clients. The member firms under this umbrella principally describe themselves as being estate agents, auctioneers, valuers, surveyors, chartered (valuation) surveyors, property consultants or a combination of these titles. Explaining the decision to limit the definition of the property services industry to these two bodies, McKenna commented:

> The IAVI and SCS are the two oldest and largest, in individual membership terms, property services organisations in this country. The SCS had 205 (general practice alone) members in 1992 and the IAVI had 788 members in the Republic of Ireland in the same year. In addition to full members, there were approximately 200 persons in 1992 working within the industry who were studying to achieve membership of either organisation.

The author noted that figures are available from the Central Statistics Office Statistical Abstracts on the number of auctioneers' licences granted annually, but no further information or further analysis of these figures (such as the spatial distribution of licences throughout the country or names of licence-holders) is provided. As a result, such figures were deemed unsuitable to be used as a basis for the definition of the industry. The Institute of Professional Auctioneers & Valuers was also excluded as it did not provide a list of members.

A total of 1,406 auctioneering licences were issued by the Revenue Commissioners in the year to July 5, 1996, together with 13 house agents' licences. At present, the following conditions of application apply for those seeking an auctioneering licence:

- Certification of qualification stating that the candidate is of sound character from a District Justice

- Lodgement of a £10,000 deposit with the High Court

- A tax clearance certificate from the Collector General's Office

- The licence must be taken up within 28 days of receipt of deposit from the High Court.

In ownership terms, the McKenna study concluded that the industry is a mix of partnerships, limited companies and sole traders. Of these firms, less than two per cent originated or were set up outside the Republic. Approximately 2,500 people are employed in Irish property services. The study revealed that the majority of firms have only one outlet, less than ten staff and output of less than £100,000 per annum. Around 87 per cent earned less than £250,000 in fee income. Only a handful earned in excess of £1 million. *Business & Finance* magazine calculated that the top five firms — (in alphabetical order) Gunne, Hamilton Osborne King, Jones Lang Wootton, Lisney, and Sherry FitzGerald — collectively accounted for an estimated £19 million in 1991; McKenna reckoned that 7.5 per cent of Dublin firms earned between £3 million to £5 million.

According to *The Irish Times*, the four biggest Dublin residential sales agencies handled 71 per cent of the 1,221 auctions held in 1996 (a 20 per cent increase on the previous year). Sherry FitzGerald maintained its position as the biggest auction house, holding 342 auctions (28 per cent of the total); Lisney held 19 per cent of all auctions; Gunne 14 per cent; and Hamilton Osborne King 10 per cent. Jackson-Stops & McCabe handled around 4 per cent of auction sales, putting them in fifth place in the auction league followed by Douglas Newman Good with 3.6 per cent of total sales.

Each of these firms also operate substantial commercial property operations. Jones Lang Wootton claims to be currently the only specialist firm in Ireland involved exclusively in business property and employs over 100 people including outdoor staff. In keeping with JLW practice, control of the Dublin firm is in Irish hands with six partners looking after the following aspects of the business: valuation and investment practice (Alan Bradley and John Mulcahy); industrial agency (William Tuite); office agency (Anthony O'Loughlin); and retail agency (Stephen Murray). The managing partner of the firm is Patrick McCaffrey, who is also responsible for the firm's extensive property management operation.

The McKenna study makes the point that the importance of the PSI in Ireland should not be measured solely in terms of output and employment. Property, whether as an investment, factor of production or home is a crucial and integral part of any modern economy. McKenna states:

> The wide and diverse range of property (and non-property) services undertaken by PSI firms underlines the fact that the industry has a significant role within the function of the economy. The industry cannot be regarded

simply as a selling agent for the products of the construction industry.

The Irish market is nevertheless small in international terms with limited growth potential:

> Changes in nominal PSI fee income from year to year are due to inflation and cyclical factors. The PSI by its nature does not have the export market to exploit in contrast to manufacturing industry and some service industries. Limited potential for growth in real terms has obvious implications for employment in the industry. In an ideal world, the number of graduates coming out of valuation surveying and estate agency courses in third-level institutions should equate approximately to the number of graduate vacancies in PSI firms. However, the number of students graduating from the various courses (usually) far exceeds the employment opportunities available.

In principle, a firm can charge whatever rate of fee it wishes for its property services. Prior to 1990, however, both the IAVI and the SCS issued recommended scales of professional fees. The 1991 Competition Act, however, altered the playing pitch by prohibiting any anti-competitive agreements, decisions or attempts to fix prices. Section Four of the 1991 Act specifically prohibited all anti-competitive agreements, decisions or concerned parties including all attempts to fix prices or other trading conditions, sharing markets, controlling markets etc. Sections Three and Four of the 1991 Act were interpreted to mean that professional associations, such as the IAVI and SCS, can no longer issue fee guidelines to their members.

The McKenna study reveals that the majority of firms still quote standard fee rates in line with the former recommended scales of the IAVI and the Society of Chartered Surveyors in the aftermath of the 1991 Act. However, its questionnaire survey revealed that, in order to attract and to retain business, there must be a degree of flexibility in terms of fees charged, particularly in respect of larger transactions.

All firms which responded to the questionnaire included with the survey based their agency fee rates on a percentage of either capital value for sale and acquisition or rental value for letting. For each of the property sectors, the most common fee rate for sale of property was 2.5 per cent of capital value with 3.5 per cent being the second most commonly quoted fee rates. The range for all sectors went from as low as 1 per cent to 3.5 per cent. In the new residential sector, 2.5 per cent was adopted by just 26.6 per cent of firms (which was the lowest for all sectors) with 19 per cent using 1.5 per cent. The rate of fee rates adopted for acquisition work was from 0.2 per cent up to 3 per cent. The most commonly quoted rate in all sectors was 1 per cent of capital value with 35 per cent of firms quoting this rate, with almost as many firms quoting 1.5 per cent. Letting fee rates ranged from 2 per cent up to 15 per cent of rental value. In all sectors, with the exception of agriculture, 10 per cent was the most commonly quoted rate for lettings, with 5 per cent being the second most used rate.

The survey concludes that fee rates can vary considerably between firms for the same property services. Agency output represents the largest proportion of total PSI output. Residential agency is the most important source of agency output by a considerable margin, with valuations dominating professional services output in a similar manner. Very few firms in the industry chose to specialise or concentrate on only one or two property services, opting instead to have a wide and diverse income base.

A comparative EU study published in *The Property Valuer* in Spring 1990 revealed that Irish estate agents' fees were generally lower than in the other countries examined. The minimum and maximum rates respectively in France were 5 per cent and 7 per cent payable by the vendor. In Italy, the minimum was 4 per cent, the maximum 8 per cent of which payment was divided between the vendor and purchaser. Spanish vendors and purchasers also split the payment of estate agents' fees, of which the minimum rate was 3 per cent and the maximum 5 per cent. FIABCI figures published in 1991 likewise showed that Irish estate agency fees are quite low in world terms. In a survey of over 30 countries, in which minimum and maximum levels of fees paid in residential property transactions were examined, Ireland figured quite modestly in all respects. According to this study, the highest minimum estate agency fees in the world are paid by buyers in France, Mexico and the United States (all 5 per cent — Ireland 2.5 per cent), while the highest maximum fees are charged to buyers in Korea (9 per cent — Ireland 3.5 per cent). The survey also showed wide variations as to when estate agents are paid their fees for a transaction, although Ireland is in line with most countries in that the fees are paid at the conclusion of a sale.

For the majority of firms in the Irish industry, specialisation in one or two property services is not an option they can consider. David McKenna comments:

> Smaller firms in particular need to offer as wide a range of services as possible (given the limitations of each individual firm) to generate sufficient income to remain in profit. This applies especially to firms outside Dublin. Non-property services, such as sale/valuation of machinery, fine art, antiques, livestock etc., and acting as a general financial broker are an important source of income to many PSI firms. Approximately 85 per cent of firms earn fees from non-property services.

> Agency output is derived from two sources: the occupation market and the investment market, which between them span the various property sectors. Agency accounts for approximately 75 per cent of total property services output with the residential sector being the most important source of agency income.

> Professional services output is derived from five different property services: valuations, rent reviews, property management, rating and compulsory purchase. Professional services earn approximately 25 per cent of total property services output with valuations representing the most significant source of work within the professional services classification.

McKenna adds:

> Property, both in volume and value terms, is disproportionately concentrated in the Dublin region. Small practices outside Dublin, would find it virtually impossible to compete for instructions for property services within Dublin. Many of the larger Dublin-based firms are appointed sole or joint agents for many of the larger property developments and transactions outside Dublin, making inroads into the local firms' potential market. Many PSI firms have

to undertake related work such as insurance and mortgage brokerage thus acting as general financial services advisers. Agriculture is a more important economic activity outside Dublin and consequently some PSI firms act as livestock auctioneers.

Over the years, the IAVI has played a particularly important role in ensuring that the status of women has changed for the better in all aspects of property , with increased involvement in professional and market activity generally. Around a third (32 per cent) of the total intake into IAVI membership in 1995 was female, as compared with 10 per cent in 1986. At present, attendance at college courses is split roughly 50/50 male/female.

What can the female professional auctioneer of tomorrow expect to face, *The Property Valuer* asked?

The general feeling expressed by some of the prominent women involved in property today is that the situation has changed dramatically over the past years. Expressions of shock, or outright disbelief, from male and female vendors or purchasers thinking that a woman would lack the necessary knowledge to assess, value or manage property are now no longer the rule but the exception.

For Dublin auctioneers, life has certainly changed quite a lot in the fourteen years since *The Property Valuer* was launched. A special issue celebrating the fiftieth issue of the IAVI journal, comparing 1983 to 1996, stated:

In agency terms, the market has undoubtedly become more competitive, though the names of the key players have changed little. Some medium-sized firms may be finding it more difficult to prosper in an environment where specialisation is the norm for both small niche firms as well as the larger firms — all of whom have become somewhat typecast in market terms despite their best endeavours to be otherwise. Some smaller niche firms prominent in 1983 are no longer operating.

The profession remains one of great stimulus but also of great challenge and, while competition has increased, standards have remained high and indeed have risen.

There still remains a sense of collegiality in the profession despite the best efforts of competition and that is something the Institute must nurture in the future.

As the profession has changed, so has the market. In 1983, our economy was experiencing great difficulty in coming to terms with high inflation and crippling borrowing resulting from over-expansion in the late Seventies. Consequently, the house market was feeling the pinch. For those who bought then, great value was available:

In Ranelagh, for example, a house in Hollybank Avenue sold in 1983 for £41,000 which in today's (1996) money represents £70,000 (though most owners of houses on this road would probably require another £50,000 on top of this to tempt them to sell). In Churchtown, a four-bedroomed bungalow sold for £46,000 (£77,500 in today's money). Today such a bungalow would probably achieve £140,000.

On Brewery Road, the then relatively new development of Woodford saw a four-bedroomed house sell for £51,000 (£86,000 in today's money). Such a house would probably now sell for £110,000.

On the northside, a four-bedroomed two-reception redbrick house on Upper Drumcondra Road sold for £35,000 (£59,000 in today's money). Such a house would probably sell now for £130,000.

Taking these houses with others sold throughout the city in 1983, it would appear that investment in bricks and mortar has paid good dividends, with Dublin house prices having on average risen by 150 per cent against a corresponding rise in inflation of 68 per cent.

The process of legislative change continues to evolve as the millennium approaches. Radical changes in the right to private property have recently been proposed by the Constitution Review Group in its final report to Government. The review group agrees that the Irish Constitution should continue to protect the right of property, but it should expressly provide that such rights may be "qualified, restricted or even extinguished by legislation where there are clear social justice or other public policy reasons for doing so". The wording recommended by a new article on property rights by the review group reads:

> Every natural person shall have the right to peaceable possession of his or her own possessions or property. The State guarantees to pass no law attempting to abolish the right of private ownership or the general right to transfer, bequeath and inherit property.

The review, chaired by Dr T.K. Whitaker, proposes a new qualifying clause imposing legal restrictions on property rights in relation to the raising of taxation and revenue, proper land use and planning controls, protection of the environment and the conservation of objects or archaeological and historical importance. However, doubts persist about the extent to which the legislature can limit such a fundamental right.

Property thus continues to play an even more pivotal role than ever in both the Irish economy and society in general as the twentieth century draws to a close. It is involved in some way in virtually every type of commercial activity, whether as a form of investment, an essential input in the process of production or as a place for people to live. As for future prospects, if Mark Twain's axiom still holds that land is the best investment because they stopped making it, Ireland is (literally) sitting pretty, with the unique appeal of the Emerald Isle more alluring than ever. Where Ireland is concerned, a fourth "L" can indeed be added to the accepted trinity governing successful property selling (Location, Location and Location). The magic extra ingredient here is the Irish Lifestyle: overseas buyers are drawn to these shores in ever-increasing numbers by the leisurely pace of a country where hunting, shooting, fishing and other recreational pursuits have been elevated to an art form. The peace process has accelerated this trend significantly.

Environmental quality has been conserved throughout the country despite its rapid transformation from a predominantly agricultural community into a highly developed modern economy. Ireland today is, for example, the second largest exporter of software outside the United States and its economy is currently experiencing unprecedented growth, outstripping other European countries. The rising tide has lifted all boats — not least the auctioneering confraternity where activity across the board has seldom been greater. The rate of growth is likely to decline somewhat in the immediate future, but demographic and other indicators suggest that construction demand will remain strong for a further decade at least (the threat to the Northern Ireland peace talks being one of the few clouds on the horizon at this vantage point).

As has been the case consistently over the past 75 years, the IAVI continues to press for a review of licensing policy in relation to auctioneers and house agents. Institute president Cormac Meehan took up the refrain yet again at the annual dinner on November 1, 1996. The minister to whom the refrain was addressed had changed (Justice Minister Nora Owen on this occasion), but the message was the same. The IAVI president stated:

> The Irish Auctioneers & Valuers Institute is the largest and, we believe, the leading property organisation in Ireland with a professionally qualified and accredited membership, a highly developed education system and a progressive and vital national and regional programme of professional seminars and conferences which affords our members the opportunity of keeping abreast of the most recent trends and legislative and practice changes that impinge on the property sector.

> In September, we launched the Member Firm Status of the Institute. Member firms must now comply with a number of regulations including control by individual IAVI members, mandatory professional indemnity insurance, the submission as appropriate of an annual auctioneer's licence to the Institute and an acceptance of the desirability of solely employing qualified staff. The IAVI has not, and does not, seek a "closed shop" — with 1,100 individual qualified members, how could we? We are, however, openly in favour of a fully qualified profession to better serve the public. We are also in favour of accessibility to qualifications so that anyone with ability can qualify and practice as a property professional.

> Third level colleges are not in the habit of wasting resources and energy in creating needless courses. College students at DIT Bolton Street, RTC Galway and RTC Limerick study in depth, over a three or four year period such

subjects as The Valuation of Property, The Law of Property, The Law of Landlord and Tenant, The Law of Contract and Tort, Town Planning, Building Construction, Economics, Agency and Marketing. When one considers the plethora of legislation and regulations with which the modern auctioneer, estate agent and valuer must be conversant to properly serve his clients needs, it is readily evident that existing legislation controlling the issue of auctioneers and house agents licences is grossly deficient.

You will forgive me Minister, but this Institute has been asking the Government for regulation since its establishment in 1922. In the intervening years, we have quite deliberately grown as a self-regulatory body without State support or legislative recognition. Despite a vast investment in educating the profession, Government still fails to recognise in its licensing requirements the need for practitioners to be educated to better serve and protect the public.

The IAVI president's answer, he said, was simple:

The purchase or sale of property is undoubtedly the largest single transaction in which most individuals will be involved. Surely it is appropriate that this transaction is dealt with solely by properly qualified individuals? We are all aware of the shock waves that have run through the public as a result of difficulties in other professions. There is always a flurry of activity after the horse has bolted. I want to go on record to say that we want action now. There is an urgent need for new legislation appropriate to the Nineties that will take our profession and the property-dealing public into the next millennium with security and peace of mind.

Giving an example of the complexity of the auctioneering business, he pointed out that, in addition to 12 European Union Directives, there are over 80 principal Acts that impinge on the profession relating to aspects of property such as the licensed trade, landlord and tenant and the compulsory purchase of property. Calling upon the Department of Justice to allocate resources to a comprehensive review and reform of the Auctioneers & House Agents Acts, the IAVI president called for comprehensive licensing legislation that is firmly linked to the maintenance of educational and professional competence in the auctioneering business. Mr Meehan concluded:

> I recently had the opportunity to visit Eastern Europe with a view to assisting professional property organisations in Hungary, Poland, Slovakia, Russia and Romania develop professional property structures. The Governments in those important emerging economies are committed to the development of licensing systems hand in hand with professional and educational qualifications in an effort to stamp out the Black Economy in property. At the moment, those operating in the Black Economy are called Black Brokers or Mucklers. I'm sure my colleagues would agree that we are not without the odd "Muckler" in Ireland!

> It is important to protect the public and preserve the integrity of the property transaction whether it is a sale, purchase, letting or valuation. Ireland and the UK are grouped with Greece as the only EU countries where Government does not insist on professional experience and qualifications to practice in property. To paraphrase the British Chancellor of the Exchequer, Kenneth Clarke, at the recent Conservative Party Conference: "We have business to do and we must therefore play a powerful part in determining how that business is to be done".

In the marketplace, improved professional standards have already brought benefits for both client and auctioneer. Sales and marketing techniques have improved immensely. Valuation techniques have likewise been refined, while sophisticated computer technologies are now commonplace. The Information Superhighway and the Internet have opened up exciting new horizons — a quantum leap into the future. But old methods die hard. At the 100th annual bull show and sale held by Mahers of Tipperary Town, it was noted that bullocks fetched £4 to £6 each at the first-ever sale conducted by the livestock auctioneers — the same price as an acre of land. Things haven't changed, the auctioneers pointed out: today, in line with the old adage that an acre of land is not worth any more than the price of one good beast, the cost of buying either is about the same. *Tempora mutant et nos mutamur in illis.*

BIBLIOGRAPHY

Books

150 Years of Architecture in Ireland — RIAI 1839-1989, Dublin, 1989.

Bannon, Michael J. (Ed.), *Planning: The Irish Experience 1920-1988*, Dublin, 1989.

Bohan, Harry, *Ireland Green — Social Planning and Rural Development*, Dublin, 1979.

Cleeve, Brian, *1938 A World Vanishing*, London, 1982

Cullen, L. M., *Princes & Pirates: The Dublin Chamber of Commerce 1783-1983*, Dublin, 1983.

Farmar, Tony, *Ordinary Lives: Three Generations of Irish Middle Class Experience 1907, 1932, 1963*, Dublin, 1991.

Gillmore, David, *Economic Activities in the Republic of Ireland — A Geographical Perspective*, Dublin, 1985.

Griffin, David and Simon Lincoln, *Drawings From the Irish Architectural Archive*, Dublin, 1993.

Haverty, Anne, *Elegant Times — A Dublin Story*, Dublin, 1995.

Land Registry Centenary 1892-1992, Dublin, 1992.

Liddy, Pat, *Dublin Stolen From Time — Perspectives of Dublin 1790s-1990s*, Dublin, 1990.

Mahon, Alan P., *Auctioneering & Estate Agency Law in Ireland*, Irish Law Log, Dublin, 1990.

McDonald, Frank, *The Destruction of Dublin*, Dublin, 1985.

Nolan, Brian, *The Wealth of Irish Households*, Dublin, 1991.

Rothery, Sean, *Ireland & The New Architecture*, Dublin, 1991.

Scott, Michael, *Michael Scott, Architect, in (casual) conversation with Dorothy Walker, Dublin, 1995*, Kinsale, 1995.

Shaffrey, Patrick & Maura, *Buildings of Irish Towns*, Dublin, 1983.

The Architecture of The Office of Public Works 1831-1985, Architectural Association of Ireland, Dublin, 1987.

Reports/Theses/Journals

An Economic Analysis of the Property Services Industry in the Republic of Ireland, David McKenna, Master of Business Studies Degree, Dublin City University, January, 1994

Commercial Rates — The Inflationary Tax, Chambers of Commerce of Ireland Briefing Document for All Affiliated Chambers, September, 1994.

Construction Industry Development Board Final Report, 1990.

Construction, 50th Anniversary Issue, 1935-85.

Dublin Shopping Centres: Statistical Digest , UCD, 1990

Dublin: A City In Crisis, Dublin Urban Study, RIAI, 1975.

Housing In Ireland — A Review, Paper to National Housing Conference 1981, Robert Jennings Research Office, An Foras Forbartha.

Irish Property Market, Price Waterhouse, 1988.

National Prices Commission Occasional Paper No 15, A Report on the Services Provided by Auctioneers by Richard Harrington, April 1974, Dublin, Published by Stationery Office.

NESC Review of Housing Policy, Dublin, December 1988.

Office Development in Dublin 1960-83, Plymouth Polytechnic School of Architecture, Patrick Malone, 1983.

Office Survey, Hamilton Osborne King, 1960-1989.

Planning For Good Environmental Residential Environments — Address by Fionnuala Hayes, Architectural Inspector, Department of the Environment, to the National Housing Conference 1996.

Practice Handbook, Irish Auctioneers & Valuers Institute, Dublin, 1996

Property Cycles in Dublin: The Anatomy of Boom and Slump in the Office and Industrial Property Sectors, Andrew MacLaran, Moran MacLaran and Patrick Malone, TCD, 1986.

Property Valuer, The, Official Journal of The Irish Auctioneers & Valuers Institute, issued quarterly from Autumn 1983.

Restrictive Practices Commission Report of Enquiry into the Policies of Building Societies in regard to Insurance Related to Mortgage Properties and Valuation Reports on Properties, 1985, Stationery Office, Dublin.

Study on the Urban Renewal Schemes, KPMG in association with Murray O'Laoire Associates and Northern Ireland Economic Research Centre, Department of the Environment, 1996.

Survival in a Nuclear War — Advice on Protection in the Home and on the Farm, Cosaint Síbhialta, 1971.

Booklets

100 Years And More A-Growing, Battersby & Company, Dublin.

Irish Country Property, Jackson-Stops McCabe, 1995.

Irish Industry, Con Power — No 46, Folens Environmental Library Series.

Newspapers

Irish Independent

Irish Press

Irish Times.

IAVI Past Presidents

BRENDAN DONOHOE 1995
ANTHONY J. O'LOUGHLIN 1994
JOSEPH E. MCCARTHY 1993
PATRICK J. STEPHENSON 1992
PATRICK J. QUINN 1991
ANTHONY G. O'DWYER 1990
JOHN CORISH..1989
JOHN G. DOYLE..1988
PATRICK F. QUIRKE 1987
ALAN A. COOKE 1986
THOMAS P. GAVIGAN 1985
DESMOND G. SCALES................................1984
SEAN NAUGHTON 1983
KENNETH A. GREGORY........................... 1982
B DERMOT MCMAHON 1981
THOMAS A. LOMBARD..............................1980
JOSEPH P. GALVIN 1979
P. LOUIS DE COURCY 1978
ANTHONY D. LEON 1977
J. FRANCIS AHERNE 1976
CORRY A. BUCKLEY 1975
RONAN O'HARA 1974
ANTHONY M. MORRISSEY 1973
BRENDAN TUOHY................................... 1972
BRIAN COYLE 1971
LAURENCE J. MCCABE...............................1970
SEAN MEEHAN 1969
DESMOND G. SCALES................................1968
OLIVER J. FLANAGAN 1967
FRANK W. MELDON..................................1966
RAYMOND E. CORISH................................1965

ARTHUR F. BENNETT 1964

LIAM T. MAHER 1963

SEAN CARROLL 1962

JAMES ADAM 1961

HARRY C. DELAHUNT............................ 1960

ALPHONSUS J. SWEENEY. 1959

ANTHONY M. SHERRY 1958

DANIEL F. STEPHENSON............................1957

WILLIAM BRENDAN SMITH 1956

NOEL JUDD 1955

HUBERT L. CORRIGAN 1954

FREDERICK J. HOLDEN............................1953

DANIEL MORRISSEY 1952

THOMAS F. HARVEY JACOB 1951

JOHN H. TRAYNOR.................................. 1950

LOUIS DE COURCY................................... 1949

ARTHUR GANLY 1948

PETER J. MCNULTY..................................1948

FRANCIS E. O'CONNOR 1947

REGINALD N. MACARTHUR......................1946

ARTHUR W. BENNETT 1945

WILLIAM S. CORRY 1944

ALEXANDER HASSETT...............................1943

WILLIAM P. SMITH 1942

CAPT. WILLINGTON MOLONY................. 1941

EDWARD ARCHBOLD............................... 1940

WILLIAM J. HERON 1939

DENIS P. HOEY 1938

HENRY CONNOLLY........................ 1936/1937

T. MORGAN GOOD................................. 1935

LAURENCE C. CUFFE............................... 1934

ALBERT MACARTHUR.............................. 1933

RAYMOND JUDD 1932

LIONEL V. BENNETT 1928/32

GEORGE W. GREENE 1927

JAMES S. MCMAHON........................ 1925/26

LAURENCE C. CUFFE........................ 1923/24

GEORGE H. LENNON 1922

ABOUT THE AUTHOR

Con Power has been a journalist for the past thirty years. He read history and took a double first-class honours at University College Dublin before completing his MA degree.

Originally a financial reporter, he became Property Editor of The Irish Press Group in 1980 and has chronicled the vicissitudes of Irish property ever since — through the doldrums after the Gallagher Group collapse to the various peaks along the way.

He has contributed to many international publications and gained first-hand experience of the building industry when he worked outside newspapers for a period as Editor, Overseas Information, with the Industrial Development Authority and as Publications Officer with An Foras Forbartha (The National Institute for Physical Planning and Construction Research).

Power is the author of the highly successful *Maxwell House Guide To Housebuyers* which has now run to several editions.

From a horseracing background, he has written extensively on the bloodstock industry and compiled a Manual of Horsemanship for the Racing Apprentice Centre for Education. He also edited *The Irish Horse*, the official journal of The Irish Thoroughbred Breeders' Association and co-edited a Centenary History of Leopardstown Racecourse.

Since the closure of The Irish Press Group in 1995, the author has established a weekly property section in *Business & Finance* magazine and is now the editor of *Plan* magazine.

Apart from writing, he has recently begun to paint and has exhibited in a number of exhibitions. He lives in Leixlip, County Kildare with his wife Arlene and family.

INDEX

100 Years and More A-Growing, 13, 32

Abbey Street, 11, 13, 18
Abercorn, the Duke of, 206
    Basin, Belfast, 206
Aberdeen Angus & Hereford
    Breeders' Association, 19
Adam & Sons, James, 8
Adare Manor, 119
Adelaide Road, 99
Addison Lodge, 13
Adelphi Cinema & Café, 14
advertising, 23, 32–4, 42, 48, 71, 79,
    95, 117, 133–4, 180, 190
aerodromes, 13–4
Agricultural Credit Corporation, the, 4
agriculture, 3–4, 35, 49, 58–9, 79, 98,
    159, 195–6, 204, 229
Agriculture House, 118, 143
Ailesbury Road, 191
Allen, L., 123
Allied Irish Bank Group, 99, 163, 172
AMEC, 190
America, 11, 140, 155, 159, 190–1
American Society of Appraisers, 140
Anglo-Irish Trade Agreement, 35
    Treaty, the, 1
apartments, 81, 145, 147, 158, 161,
    179, 191, 197–8, 200
apprenticeship, 18, 24–5, 113
architects, 153, 200, 209
    and valuation, 91
Architects' Council of Europe (ACE),
    209
Architects' Journal, The, 103
architecture, 36–7, 39–40, 52, 60–1,
    76, 82, 81, 87, 100–1, 143, 146, 179–
    81, 200, 209
Ardee, 50

Argos, 208
Arklow, 120
Arks Ltd., 13
Armstrong, G., Kells, 8, 5
Arnott & Co., 165
Artane Castle, 202
Arthur's Quay, Limerick, 203, 205
Ashbourne, 204
Ashford Castle, 73, 196
Aspro (Ireland) Ltd., 76
Associated Properties, 102
Association of Combined Residents'
    Associations (ACRA), 106
Aston Deller, 189
Athgarvan Stud, 196
Attorney General, 21
auctioneering
    as a profession, definition of, 16–8,
        110
    profession,
        registration of the, 153–4
        rules and regulations for the,
            92–3, 154
    rules, fines for breaches of, 27–8
auctioneering,
    case law on, 41
Auctioneers and House Agents Acts
    1947–73, 64, 110–4, 126–7, 134, 137,
    174
    Valuers, House & Estate Agents
        Bill, 46–8, 63–4
Auctioneers' & Estate Agents'
    Association of Ireland, 4
        Association America, 74
        Institute of the United Kingdom, 24
Aungier Street, 40, 197
Australia, 140, 181, 192

Baardon, J., 96
Babylonians, the, 9
back to the future — the fifties, 79–96
Bailey, D., 119
Bailly, J., 108
Baily, 195
Ballsbridge, 51, 82, 118, 120, 150, 166, 189
Ballybofey, 81
Ballyfermot, 38, 83, 101
Ballymena, 8
Ballymore Eustace, 11
Ballymun, 105, 120, 185
Banagher Distillery, 14
Banbridge, 83
Bank of Ireland, 4, 102, 212
banks, 41, 64, 101–2, 119, 188, 216–7
Bannon, M., 103
Barna, 43
Barrett, S., 123
Barry, R., 123
Bateman's *Law of Actions*, 74
Bath Avenue, 3
Battersby & Co., 8, 1, 13–15, 18, 29, 32–4, 42, 52, 56, 118, 223
Bauhaus, 39
Beckett, Samuel, 195
Belfast, 8, 13–4, 83, 96, 117, 143–5, 176–7, 205–7
Belgrave Square, 80
Benburb Street, 3
Bennett, L.V., 9
Bennett, A.W., 70–1, 84, 113
Bennett & Son, 30
Beresford Place, 11
Bergin, D., 118, 166
Bergin's, 191
Bewley & Draper's, 14
Birr Castle, 118
Blackrock, 3, 12, 40, 76, 81, 119, 202
    Shopping Centre, 202
Blanchardstown, 104
    Town Centre, 181, 202
Blandford Arms, 81
bloodstock, 159, 178, 192

Bloody Sunday, 149
Blowick, J., 83
Bluebell, 101
Board of Works (Office of Public Works), 40, 173, 180–1
Bohan, Fr. H., 144
Bohemian Picture Theatre, 14
Bolton Street, 65, 150, 168, 219
Bord na Móna, 83
Bord Pleanála, An, 152, 170
Bowie, N., 119
Boyd Barrett, J.R., 36
Bradley, A., 225
brave new world — the seventies, 123–60
Bray, 2, 13, 38, 108, 137, 159
Brazen Head, the, 14
Brent Walker, 191
breweries, 13–4
Brewery Road, 230
Bridge End, Belfast, 206
Brighton Road, 195
Britain, 3–5, 24, 35, 82, 117, 127, 132, 138, 146, 188, 190
British
    Chancellor of the Exchequer, 234
    Embassy, 88, 149
    forces, withdrawal of, 2
    Government, 14
    Land Corporation, 180
    Monopolies Commission, 133
Broadhead, J., 72
Brooks Thomas, 144
Brown Thomas (BT), 36, 38, 165
Browne, W., 96
Buckley, C., 118, 154, 166
builders and valuation, 91
builders' direct house sales, 42–3
Builders' Federation, the, (*see also* Construction Industry Federation (CIF), 80
building
    contracts, 37, 61, 82
    leases, 106

building (cont'd)
  materials, wartime shortages of,
    59
  slump, 175
  societies, 34, 82, 103, 169, 186,
    188, 194, 208–9, 218
    Acts, 185–6
Bunclody, 120
Burton, P., 123
Busáras, 61
Business & Finance, 225
business parks, 201
Buswell's Hotel, 14
Butler, J., 50

Cabra, 38
Café Kylemore, 208
Campbell, J. and G., 13
Canada, 155, 181
candlestick biddings, 9
capital
  acquisitions tax, 146
  gains tax, 146
Capitol Theatre, the, 14
Cara Data Processing, 170
Carlisle Buildings, 13
Carrickfergus, 206
Carrickmacross, 165
Carrisbrook House, 117
Castle Court, Belfast, 207
  Publications, 155
Castlepark Road, 76
castles, 13, 118–9
Castletown House, 196
Cavan, 8
Census of 1926, 2
Central Statistics Office Statistical
  Abstracts, 224
Centre for Urban & Retail Studies,
  TCD, 200
Chambers of Commerce, 12, 23, 34–5,
  37, 72, 154, 214–5
Charleville estate, Enniskerry, 118
Chartered Surveyors' Institution, 50, 68
Chelmsford Avenue, 120

Christchurch, 197
Churchtown, 230
cinemas. 13–4
City Square, Waterford, 202
Civil Service Bridge Club, 155
Civil War, the, 1, 31
Clare Street, 163
Clarence Hotel, 92
Clark, H., 37
Clarke & Son, Wm., 14
Clarke, K., 234
Cleere, W.K., 80
Cleland family, the, 13
Clery & Company, 13, 36, 165
Clonard Estate, Sandyford, 142, 190,
  198
Clondalkin, 104
Clones, 8, 81
Clonliffe Road, 3
Clonmel, 8
Clonmel, Lord, 13
Clonshaugh, 101
Clontarf, 2, 38, 76, 120
Cloughran, 81
Clover Meats, 166
coin auctions, 120
Cole, J.J., 48
Coliemore Road, 195
Collector of Customs and excise, 135
College Green, 15, 163, 189
College of Commerce, Rathmines,
  111, 157, 168
  Estate Management, 65, 111, 150
  Technology, Bolton Street, 150, 168
Collins, Michael, 1
commission, 92
Commission on Ground Rents, 109
Communique, 155
Companies' Acts 1908–17, 5
  Office, 217
comparative
  costs, 2
  house values, 2
Competition Act 1991, 226
computerisation, 169–70, 212, 217

Conlon, M., 48, 50
Connacht, 55
　committee, 149
Connacht Tribune, 43
Connaughton, P., 172
Connemara Marble Quarries, 14
Connolly, H., 50
Conroy, Judge J., 84
conservation, 81
Constitution Review Group, 230
construction, house, 31, 37, 60, 67,
　76–7, 80, 82, 104, 119, 146–7, 158,
　162, 167, 175–7, 180, 185, 190–1,
　195, 197–8, 208, 208
Construction Industry Federation
　(CIF), 36, 82, 159, 173
Consumer Credit Act 1995, 210
Consumer Price Index, 213
Control of Building Order
Control of Manufacturers Act, 82
Convention for the Protection of the
　Architectural Heritage of Europe,
　181
Cooke, A., 175, 183, 216, 219–20
Coolatin House, 118
Coolock, 101
Coonan, Kildare, 8
Coopers & Lybrand, 126
Córas Iompair Éireann (CIE), 61
Corballis, R., 118
Cordier, E., 108
Corish, R.E., Wexford, 108, 124, 150
Cork, 3, 8, 102, 118, 123, 132–3, 137,
　142, 143, 167, 175, 179, 189, 198,
　202, 205
　branch, 21, 24, 30
　City and County committee, 149
　Marts, 159
Corrigan, H.L., 84
Corry, W.S., 66, 84
Costigan & Co., 11
costs, comparative, 2
Council of Agriculture, 52
Cowan, J., 206
Cowper, James, 9

Craigie and Ganly, 8
Crampton, G & T, 76
Crawley, 169
Crosse & Blackwell, 14
Crossmaglen, 176
Crosthwaite Park, 51
Crowley, L., 163
Cruise's Street, Limerick, 203, 205
Crumlin, 3, 83
Cuffe & Sons, L., 52
Cuffe, L.C., 15, 23, 47, 52
Cumann na nGaedheal, 31, 52
Cumisky & Cooke, 216
　Cooke Scales, 216
Cummins, Dr. D.J., 87
Currency Commission (1927), 23
Custom House, the, 1, 143, 145, 181
　Docks Development Authority,
　178–80, 199

Dáil Éireann, 51
Dalkey, 35, 80, 195
Dalton's London Weekly, 79
Daly, Judge O., 80
Dame Street Picture House, 14
D'Arcy's Brewery, 14
Dardis, P.G., 60
Daresbury, Lord, 73
DART, 185
Dartry, 204
databank, 169–70, 203
Dawson Street, 64, 117–8
Deauville, 159
de Courcy, L., Limerick, 72, 150
Deller, P., 189
Denmark, 61
Dennehy's Motor Works, 13
Department of Agriculture, 20, 48,
　143, 172
Department of Civil Defence, 105
Department of Defence, 68
Department of the Environment, 105,
　147, 198, 204
　(Northern Ireland), 206
Department of Finance, 97

Department of Industry and
Commerce, 36, 69
Department of Industry, Commerce
& Tourism, 174
Department of Justice, 174, 233
Department of Supplies, 59
deposits, law on, 41, 94
depression, global, 35
Derry, 146, 207–8
Destruction of Dublin, The, 101
de Valera, Eamon, 13, 79, 82, 124
Deutsches Kulturinstitut, 88
development,
    ribbon, 38, 80
    suburban, 83
Devlin, F., 223
Diamond, the, Derry, 207
distilleries, 13–4
Dixon's, 208
Dockrell & Son, Ltd., Thomas, 15, 52,
58
Dockrell, H., 58
    family, the, 23
Doherty, S., 174
D'Olier Street, 13, 74
Donabate, 195
Donegal, 208
Donegall Quay, Belfast, 206
Donnybrook, 3, 13
Donnycarney, 38
Donohoe, B., 216
Doris, M., 118
Dorset Street, 189
Douglas Court, Cork, 202
Douglas Newman Good, 225
Doyle, J., 215
Drimnagh, 38
Drogheda, 24
    Meat Factory, 15
Druker Fanning, 118
Druker, I., 118
Drumcondra, 3, 51, 167, 230
Drumcree Orange Parade, 207
Dublin, 2–5, 7–9, 11–5, 18–9, 23–4,
30–40, 42–3, 47, 49, 52, 57–61, 65–6,

70, 72–4, 76, 80–3, 85–87, 92–3, 95–
102, 104, 108–111, 116–7, 124–5,
128–34, 136–7, 141–5, 148–50, 154–
5, 157–9, 162–3, 165–8, 170, 178–82,
184, 188–90, 193, 195, 197–205, 210–
3, 215–9, 223, 225, 228
    European City of Culture, 200,
    210
Dublin
    Airport, 36, 61, 143
    Artisan Dwelling Company, 3,
    102
    Building Operatives' Public
    Utility Building Society, 34
    Cattle Market, 15, 19, 52
    Castle, 1, 124
    Chamber of Commerce, 12, 23,
    34–5, 37, 72, 154
    Corporation, 31, 36, 40, 73, 82,
    141
        Civic Offices, 143
    Distillery Company, 14
    Flat Dwellers' Association, 124
    Housing Inquiry 1939, 37
    Institute of Technology (DIT),
    219, 232
    Model Building Society, 34
    Newspaper Committee, 93
    Port Tunnel, 197
    Reconstruction (Emergency
    Provisions) Act 1924, 3
    Stock Exchange, 13
    Vocational Education Committee,
    City of, 65
    Workingmen's Benefit Building
    Society, 34
Dukes, A., 177
Duleek, 81
Dundalk, 165
    Shopping Centre, 203
Dundrum, 76, 167, 189
Dungarvan, 50
Dun Laoghaire, 13, 51, 76, 80, 143,
167, 189
Dunloe Castle, 13

Dunnes Stores, 191, 208
Durrow Brick & Tile Works, 13
Dutch auctions, 9
Dwyer, A., 223
Dylan, Bob, 105

Earlsfort Developments, 118
Earlsfort Terrace, 36, 60, 163
Eastern Europe, 234
Economic & Public Utility Building
  Society, 34
Economic Commission for Europe
  Committee of Housing, Building
  and Planning, 107
Economic War, the, 35, 79
Edenderry, 5
Éire, 52, 65
Elcock, L., 24
electricity, 31, 97
Electricity Supply Board (ESB), 97,
  101, 150, 170, 182
Elvery's, 13
Emergency Powers Orders, 59
employment, 98, 143, 164, 177, 208
England, 180
  the North of, 133
Ennis, 8, 108, 123
Enniscorthy, 81, 120
Enniskerry, 118, 195
Enniskillen, 207
Ennistymon, 108
Estate Agents Co-Operative Ltd., 134
Etchingham, J., 42
Eucharistic Congress, the, 39
Europa Nostra, 181
European
  City of Culture, 200, 210
  Community (EC), 146, 164, 191
  Economic Community, 115
  Group of Valuers of Fixed Assets
    (TEGOVOFA), 193, 212
  Monetary System, 157
  Property Agents Group (EPAG),
    193, 212

Secretariat for the Liberal
  Professions (SEPLIS), 173
Structural Funds, 201
Union, 193, 200, 219, 227, 233–4
Eustace Street, 86
Evening Mail, 93
Evered & Co., 14
Expo 70, 143
Eyre Square Centre, 202

Fairview, 36, 38, 120
Fairyhouse Racecourse, 192
Famine, the Great, 3
Fanning, P., 118
Farmar, T., 104
Farrelly, D.P., 123
Feakle, 144
Federation of Building Trades
  Employers, 36
fees, 19, 25, 40–1, 74, 95, 108–9, 115,
  126–40, 226–8
  Land Commission and, 84
  solicitors and, 67–8
Fenian Street, 104
Ferrier Pollock, 142
FIABCI, *see* International Real Estate
  Federation
Fianna Fáil, 31, 35
fin de siècle — the nineties, 193–221
Finance Acts, 127, 159
fine art, 178, 191–2, 204
fines for breaches of auctioneering
  rules, 27–8
FINEX Europe, 200
Finglas, 83, 185, 202
Finnegan Menton, 216
FitzGerald, A., 118, 166, 171
FitzGerald, A., Snr., 169
FitzGerald, D., 36, 61
FitzGerald, M., 166
Fitzpatrick, H.J., 87–8, 155
Fitzwilliam, Countess of, 118
Fitzwilliam Estates, 90
Fitzwilliam Lawn Tennis Club, 143
Fitzwilliam Square, 86

Fitzwilliam Street, 101
Flack, R., 118
Flanagan, O.J., 93, 116, 123
Flynn, P., 185
Fottrell, F., 5
Four Courts, the, 1
Foxrock, 38, 104, 195
Foyleside Centre, 208
France, 132, 140, 169, 227
Francis Street, 197
Franks & Franks, 72
Frascati Centre, 202
Frederick Street, South, 99
Freeman, D., 3
French, I., 189–90, 217
Friends' Provident Buildings, 15
Fulton & Company, John, 13

Gallagher Group, 162–4
Gallagher, M., 162
Gallagher, P., 162–4
Gallaher's Buildings, 13
Galway, 3, 49, 101, 118, 137, 167, 198, 203, 205
    Regional Technical College (RTC), 168, 219, 232
Gandon, James, 1, 14, 181
Ganly & Sons, 8
Ganly, J, 4
Ganly, A., 84
Gardiner Street, 197
Garvey, G.B., 4
Gavigan, T., 172–3
gazumping, 185
General Council of County Councils, 52
General Council of Registered Auctioneers, House & Estate Agents, 46
Geneva, 107
George III, King, 25
George's Avenue, Blackrock, 81
George's Quay, 81, 145
Georgian Dublin, 39, 100–1, 210–1, 215

German Minister, 13
Germany, 55
Glasnevin Cemetery, 15
Glenageary, 35
Glencairn estate, 57
Glendalough, 13, 40
glimmer man, 59
globalisation, 223
Goff's Bloodstock Sales, 159, 178, 192
Gogarty, O., 37
going, going, gone — the thirties, 29–53
Good, T. Morgan, 37–8
Gorey, 123
Gormanstown Aerodrome, 14
Gosford Castle, 13
Gosford, the Earls of, 13
Goulding, W., 42
Governor-General, 13
Grafton Arcade, 95
Grafton Street, 66, 179
Grangegorman Mental Hospital, 15
Grant's, Cork, 102
Gray & McDowell, W.P., 8
Gray, W.P., 8
GRE Properties, 202
Great Famine, the, 3
Great War, the, 1, 26
Greece, 234
Green Property, 102, 181, 202
Greene & Sons, Roger, 43, 74–5
Greene Brothers, Mageney, 50
Greene, G.W., 4, 15
Greene, J.N., 50
Greene, M., 196
Gresham Hotel, the, 4, 14, 49, 60
Grey, M., 48, 84, 116, 155, 192
Greystones, 108, 120
Griffin, R., 8
Griffith, R., 44
Gropius, W., 39
Grosvenor Estate, 202
ground rents, 18, 50, 56, 106–7, 109
Group 91 Architects, 200
Guardian, The, 146

Guinness & Mahon, 99
Guinness, J.H., 99
Gulf War, the, 199
Gunne, 225
Gunne, F., 166
Gunne, P.B., 165

Hall, J.B., 12
Hamilton & Hamilton, 64, 72–3, 109,
    112, 118, 142, 189
Hamilton, B., 73
Hamilton, Chief Justice L., 175
Hamilton, H., 73, 189
Hamilton, W., 73
Hamilton Osborne King (HOK), 118,
    189–90, 200, 217, 225
Hammam & Edinburgh Hotel, the,
    14
Hammond, E., 118
Harcourt Street, 86
Hardwicke Ltd., 99, 180
Harkin, F.J., 8
Harte, P., 123
Harold's Cross, 96
Harrington, H., 13
Harrington, R., 127, 130
Hassett, A., 48
Haslett, A., 50
Haslett & Son., Alex, Monaghan, 50
Haughey, Charles, 113, 159
Hawkins House, 99
Hayes, F., 105
Headfort estate, 196
Healy & Co. Ltd., G.F., 5
Healy, J.J., 116, 149, 173, 210, 215
Healy, Mrs. N., 215
Heather, J., 83
Henry, G., 118
Henry Street, 202
Herkner, Friedrich, 53
Herodotus, 9
Hibernian Insurance Company, 15
Hicks, F.E., 36
Hicks, F.G., 3

highs and lows — the eighties, 161–
    92
High Street, 12
Hill, F., 118
Hillier Parker, 190
hire purchase, 93–4
Hire Purchase Information Ltd., 94
history of auctioneering, 10–12
HM Disposals Board, 14
Hibernian Insurance Company, 15
Hoey, D.P., 48, 52
Hogan, B., 100
Holden, F.J., 84
Holles Street, 87
    Hospital, 101
Hollybank Avenue, Ranelagh, 230
HomeBond warranty scheme, 194,
    196
Hone, D., 155
Hooke & McDonald, 197–8
Hoover Ltd., 13
Hope, A., 76
hospitals, 15
hotels, 14, 39, 141, 143, 205–
house
    construction, 31, 34–5, 38, 58, 60,
        67, 76–7, 80, 82, 104, 119, 146–7,
        158, 162, 167, 175–7, 180, 185,
        190–1, 195, 197–8, 208
    design, 3, 148
    improvement grants, 3
    prices, 35–6, 51, 55, 57, 80–2, 96,
        120–1, 125–6, 141–2, 158, 167,
        175–7, 180, 185, 190–1, 194–5,
        198
houses, country, 34, 81, 118–9
housing,
    social, 194
Housing Act 1925
Housing (Building Facilities) Act
    1924, 2
Housing (Private Rented Dwellings)
    Acts, 168
Howard Street, Belfast, 14
Howlin, Brendan, 216

Howth, 38, 80, 195
Howth Road, 120
Hughes, H., 25
Hungary, 234

IBM, 99
Iceland, 208
ICS Building Society, 34, 216
Ilac Centre, 202
Inchicore, 38, 101
Incorporated Law Society, 19–20, 67–
8, 89–92, 109, 113, 153–6, 169, 173,
217
Incorporated Society of Auctioneers
and Landed Property Agents, 74
Incorporated Society of Valuers and
Auctioneers (ISVA), 150
Increase of Rent Acts, 26, 43–4
Independent Newspapers, 13
Industrial Development Authority
(IDA), 148, 164, 201
industrial estates, 95, 101
information superhighway, 234
inner city development
Institute of Professional Auctioneers
and Valuers (IPAV), 123–4, 127–8,
139, 146, 174, 224
insurance companies, 15, 52, 58, 119,
143
Insurance Amalgamation Agreement
1938, 52
Intercontinental Hotel, 124
International Financial Services
Centre (IFSC), 178–80, 199–200
International Fund for Ireland (IFI),
208
International Real Estate Federation
(FIABCI), 107–8, 124, 181–2, 212–3,
227
European Study Days, 125, 182–3
World Congress in Ireland, 117,
124, 212–3
Internet, 212, 217, 234
Inter-Professional Group, 173

Investment Property Databank (IPD),
203
Ireland Pavilion, 143
Iris Oifigiúil, 46
Irish Assurance Company, 52
Irish Auctioneers' and Estate Agents'
Association (IAA) (renamed Irish
Auctioneers and Valuers Institute),
5, 7–10, 15, 17–25, 30, 35, 37–8, 40–
1, 43, 45–50, 52, 55, 59–73, 75, 77,
85–96, 107–17, 123
benevolent fund, 71
code of conduct, 68–9
educational activities, 65, 111
library, 50
new headquarters, 86–8, 149, 156
objects of, 5–7
reorganisation of, 49
yearbook, diary and calendar, 7–
8, 19, 24, 35, 64, 72, 75, 79
Irish Auctioneers and Valuers
Institute (IAVI), 123–7, 139–40, 151–
7, 159, 168–77, 181–3, 187–8, 192–3,
195, 210–21, 223–4, 226, 229, 232–4
educational
committee, 157
qualifications, 150–1, 218–9
headquarters, 142, 210–1
journal, 187
Practice Handbook, 216, 220
regional committees, 149
training and education, 149, 157,
168, 218–20
yearbook, 146
Irish Builders and Decorators Review, 37
Irish Cement Building, 166
Irish Civil Service Building Society, *see*
ICS Building Society
Irish Co-operative Organisation
Society, 172
Irish Dairy Shorthorn Breeders'
Society, 23
Irish Dunlop Company, 99
Irish Estates (Management), 61, 201
Irish Farmers Association, 172, 215

Irish Free State, the, 1, 8, 12, 24–5, 35, 43, 58
Irish Georgian Society, 100–1
Irish Government,
    the first, 1
    the Provisional, 3
Irish Independent, 12, 23, 93, 95, 125, 171
Irish Industrial Benefit Building Society, 34
Irish Intercontinental Bank, 202
Irish Leaseholders' Association, 50
Irish Life Assurance Company, 81, 99, 144–5
Irish Museum of Modern Art, 180
Irish National Insurance Company, 15, 88
Irish Pedigree Sheep Breeders' Association, 19
Irish Pension Fund Property Unit Trust (IPFPUT), 102
Irish Permanent Building Society (IP), 103, 162
Irish Press, 52, 93, 95
Irish Red Cross Society, 60
Irish soldiers, deaths of, in World War II, 2
Irish Times, 23, 39, 56, 59, 61, 93, 95, 97, 100–1, 141, 158, 195, 225
Irish Tourist Association, 39
Islandbridge Munitions, 14
Italy, 227
Iveagh, the Earl of, 13
Iveagh Trust, the, 34, 73

Jackson-Stops & McCabe, 57, 73, 109, 195, 225
Jackson-Stops, H., 57
Janelle Shopping Centre, 202
Japan, 143
Jervis Centre, 202
Johnson, Dr. Samuel, 3
Johnston, F., 87
Johnston Mooney & O'Brien, 189

Joint Oireachtas Committee on Building Land, 148
Jones Lang Wootton (JLW), 119, 225
Jordan, K., 116, 148
Jordanstown, 168, 219
Joyce, James, 40, 87
Joyce, Mr., 57
Judd, R., 10–11, 10–1, 29, 42, 47–8, 56, 84
Judd, C., 85
Jury's Hotel, 21, 85, 163, 200

K Club, 118
Kanturk, 123
Keane, D., 118
Keane Mahony Smith (KMS), 118, 169
Keating & Sons, J.F., 210
Keating, Seán, 53
Keeneland, 159
Kelleher, T., 36
Kells, 8, 50, 52, 123
Kennedy Industrial Estate, John F., 95, 101
Kenny Report, the, 148
Keogh, T., 118
Kerry, 170
Kieran & McGee, Ardee, 50
Kildare, 8, 90
    County Gaol, 15
    Sales Paddocks, 178
Kildare Street, 36, 62, 72, 81, 99, 118, 143
Kilcullen, 11
Kilfenora, 13
Kilkenny, 170, 203
    Castle, 13
Killarney, 13
Kill, 178
Killeen Road, 101
Killiney, 80, 195
    Castle Hotel, 169
Killyhevlin Hotel, Enniskillen, 207
Kilmainham, 180
Kimmage, 35, 42
King, J., 73

King, J.O., 73
Kingstown (Dún Laoghaire), 2
Knight, G.A., 8
Knowles's of Grafton Street, 95
Korea, 227

Lagan Weir project, Belfast, 206
Laganbank, Belfast, 206

Laganside Corporation, 206
    project, Belfast, 205–6
Laing Developments, 143
Lambert Smith Hampton, 118, 223
land
    leasing, 172
    policy, white paper on, 170
    prices, 37, 55, 57, 81, 141, 148,
        204, 234
    tenure, 25
land,
    building, 56, 204
Land Acts, 25, 39, 84, 94, 114–5, 172
Land Acts 1923–7, 26
Land Commission, 83–4, 94, 109, 114
Land (Finance) Rules 1925, 25
Land Purchase Acts, 39
Land Registry, 107, 217
    Rules 1926, 25
landlord and tenant
    Commission, 156
    legislation, 26, 39, 43–4, 104, 106–
        7, 134, 156
Lansdowne House, 99
Lantern Theatre, 155
Laughlin, J.J., 39
law
    agents, 43
    on auctioneering, 41, 45–8
    on valuation, 45
    rating and valuation, 43, 51
    rent restriction, 26, 43–4
Law Society Gazette, 67, 90
Law Union and Rock Insurance
    Company, 15
LAWLINK, 217

Lawrence's, 13
Le Corbusier, 52
Lee, H. and C., 141
Leeson Street, Lower, 101
legislation, 2, 3, 25–8, 39, 44–8, 51,
    62–4, 110–4
Leigh, Vivien, 204
Leinster Club, the, 14
Leinster committees, 149
Leinster House, 1, 181
Leinster Place, 81
Leixlip, 77
Lemass, Seán, 97, 103
Lenihan, B., 113
Lennon, G.H., snr., 4, 15
Lennon, G.H., jnr., 15
Leon, A., 154
Leonard, P., 4
Leonard, T., 202
Leopardstown Park, 51
letting of lands, agreement for, 20
Lewis, C., 181
liability for injuries, law on, 41, 49, 108
licensing, 8, 25–7, 60, 110–4, 128–9,
    134–5, 153–4, 174–5, 224, 232, 234
Liffey, River, 31, 73
Lillingstone, L., 73
Limerick, 3, 72–3, 137, 146, 150, 167,
    179, 198, 203, 205
    civic offices, 205
    Junction, 49
    Regional Technical College, 168,
        219, 232
LINK, 170
Lisney, H., 72
Lisney's, 51, 118, 143, 166, 190, 225
    Research Association, 184
Local Government
    (Building Land) Bill, 170
    (Financial Provisions) Acts, 167
    (Planning and Development)
        Acts, 152, 170
    (Rates on Small Dwellings) Act
        1928, 43
London, 100, 119, 130

London Provident Association, 34
Londonderry, 8
Long, J., 178
Longford, 83
Low, G., 4
Low Ltd., Gavin, 19
Lucan, 120, 137, 189
Luttrelstown Castle, 118
Lutyens, Sir E., 40
Lynch, Jack, 115, 124
Lyons Estate, 195
Lyons, E., 118

MacArthur, A., 24, 47, 58, 73, 95
MacArthur family, the, 74, 95
MacArthur, Mrs. A., 24, 73
MacArthur, Mrs D., 94–5
MacArthur, P., 4
MacArthur, R.N., 84, 94–5
MacArthur Ltd., Albert, 74
MacCartney, F.J., 8
MacEntee, S., 47
MacGonigal, Maurice, 53
Mac Thomáis, É., 66
Mackey Ltd., Sir James W., 13
Mackie, S.W., 4
Madden & Son, D.J., Rathkeale, 66
Madden, D.J., 66
Magilligan Prison, 164
Magnier, M., 196
Maher, L., 60, 108, 157
Maher & Sons, W., Roscrea, 157
Mahers, Tipperary Town, 234
Mahon, A.P., 110
Mahony, D., 118
Malahide, 120, 137, 195
Malone, Prof. P., 98
Marino, 38
Market Cross, Kilkenny, 203
    Parade, Cork, 102
market tolls and rentals, 93
Marks & Spencer, 191, 208
Marlboro Street, 11
Marlborough Developments, 143
Marrowbone Lane Munitions, 14

Marsh, Cork, 8
Mason Owens & Lyons, 118
Masonic Girls' School, 189
Masterpiece Theatre, 14
May, Roberts & Co., 14
Mayo, 73
McArdle, M., 176
McCabe, L.J., 57–8, 108, 124
McCaffrey, P., 225
McCarron, T., 118, 142
McCarthy, J., 175, 212
McDonald, F., 101
McDonald, K., 198
McFarlane, J., 117, 189
McGee, J.T., 50, 66
McGuinness, T., 8
McGuire, E.A., 36, 119
McGuire, James, 36
McGuire, John, 36
McInerney Properties, 180
McKenna, D., 223–8
McKenna, T.P., 52
McMahon & Probert, 72
McMahon, Ennis, 8
McMahon, D., 170
McMahon, J.S., 4, 15, 17–9, 21
Meath, 52
Mecklenburgh Lane, 11
Meehan, C., 232–3
Megran, J., 73
membership
    certificate, 24
    corporate, 220
    fees, 5
    listings, 8, 215, 218
    numbers, 22, 30, 77, 96, 123, 159,
        168, 218
    qualifications (*see also* licensing),
        123
MEPC (Ireland), 102
Merchant Banking Ltd., 164
Merchant's Quay, 148, 162
    Centre, Cork, 191, 202
Merlin Estate, 82
Merrion Road, 149

Merrion Square, 85–7, 142, 149, 198, 210, 216
Mespil Estate, 81
Mespil Road, 144
Metropole Cinema, 14
Metropole Hotel, the, 14
Mexico, 227
Mexico City, 107–8
MIAA, 7, 50
MIAVI, 182
militaria, auction of, 148
Minister for Agriculture, 93
Minister for Defence, 21, 68
Minister for Finance, 23, 47, 51, 64, 71, 109, 159, 177, 213
Minister for Home Affairs, 20
Minister for Industry & Commerce, 52
Minister for Justice, 21, 48, 50, 62–3, 70, 111, 113, 174–5, 232
Minister for Labour, 154
Minister for Lands, 83
Minister for Local Government, 34–5, 103
Minister for Supplies, 62, 64
Minister for the Environment, 167, 185–6, 216
Ministers for State, 172, 174, 178
Mitchell, J., 174
Mitchell Ltd., George, 13
misdescription, law on, 41–2
mock auctions, 20–1
modern times — the sixties, 97–121
Molesworth Street, 99, 117, 169
Monaduff, 81
Monaghan, 165
Monarch Properties, 202
Monkstown, 2, 80, 217
Montreal, 108
Montreux, 212
Morehampton Mews, 179
Morgan Scales & Co., 150
Morrissey, A., 150
Morrissey, D., 48, 61
Morrissey, T., 118

Morrissey & Sons, Daniel, 109, 118, 150
mortgage
    interest relief, 152
    subsidy schemes, 152
Moss Street, 145
Mount Coote estate, 73
Mount Kennedy estate, 118
Mount Merrion, 35, 40, 51
Mount Street, 87
Mountmellick, 123
Mulcahy, J., 225
multiple-listing system (MLS), 212
Municipal Art Gallery, 13
Municipal Offices, Dublin, 36
Munster, 55, 213
    committee, 149
Munster and Leinster Assurance Company, 15
Murphy, Buckley & Keogh, 109, 166
Murray, S., 225
Myrtle Park, Dun Laoghaire, 80

Naas, 15
Naas Road, 95, 101
na gCopaleen, M., 61
Napier, R.P., 83
Nassau Street, 99
National Association of Realtors (NAR), 155, 181, 213
National Botanical Gardens, 15
National Building Regulations, 194
National College of Art & Design, 53
National Economic & Social Council (NESC) Review of Housing Policy, 183–4
National House Building Guarantee Company, 157
    Scheme (NHBGS), 157–8, 196
National Housing Conference, 105
National Prices Commission (NPC), 117, 126–40
National Shell Factory, 14
National University, 52

Navan, 8, 73
    Shopping Centre, 203
Neutrality (War Damage to
    Property) Bill, 61
new beginnings — the twenties, 1–2
New Ireland Assurance Company, 99
New South Wales, 134, 140
New York, 107
    Cotton Exchange, 200
    World's Fair, 52
Newlands Cross, 120
Newmarket, 159
Newport, 123
Newry, 81
Newspaper Managers' Committee,
    109
Newtownpark House, 119
Nolan, M., 184
Noonan, M., 174
North & Co., James H., 8, 18, 52, 94–
    5, 109, 141, 155, 216
North, F., 52
North British and Mercantile
    Insurance Co., 15
North Quays, 197
North Strand, 120
Northern Bank, 217
Northern Ireland, 8, 66, 132, 138,
    205–8, 232
    Government of, 123
    house construction in, 6
    troubles in, 145–6, 205, 207
    war damage in, 58
Northern Ireland
    Committee, 83, 176
    Department of the Environment,
        206
    Housing Executive, 145, 176, 206
    practice, 216
    Property Market Analysis
        Project, 176
Northside Shopping Centre, 102
Norwich Union Building, 117–8
nuclear war, 105–6
Nutgrove Shopping Centre, 202

Oak Apple Green, 179
Oakwood Avenue, 120
objects of the Association, 5–7
O'Brien of Kilfenora, Lord, 13
O'Callaghan Properties, 202
Ó Cofaigh, E., 209–10
O'Connell, J., 42
O'Connell Bridge House, 95, 99
O'Connell Street, 11, 13
O'Donnell, R., 169
O'Donoghue, C., 171
Offaly, 170
Office of Public Works (Board of
    Works), 40, 173, 180–1
office property, 97–100, 104, 117–9,
    129–30, 141, 144, 146, 179, 184, 199–
    201, 207
O'Hara, R., 153
O'Hogan, A., 118, 190
oil shortages, 125, 142
Oireachtas, an t-, 21
Old Leighlin, 81
Olivier, Laurence, 204
O'Loughlin, A., 225
Ombudsman, Office of the, 118
Omni Park, 202
Ormond Quay, Lower, 5
O'Reilly, A.J.F., 195
O'Reilly, P.F., 67
O'Reilly's Auction Rooms, 116, 119–
    20, 148, 162, 178
O'Riordan, J., 118
Ormeau Bridge, Belfast, 206
Orthopaedic Hospital, the, 15
Orwell Road, 96
Osaka, 143
Osborne King & Megran (OKM), 73,
    117–8, 143–4, 189
Ossory, the Earl of, 13
O'Toole, D., 118
Ove Arup, 61
Owen, N., 232
Owens Advertising & Marketing,
    Peter, 190

Palmer, J.D., Waterford, 8, 73
Palmerston Road, 51, 120
Paris, 107–8
Park Drive, 80
Parkway Centre, Limerick, 203
Parnell Square, 85
Parnell Street, 145
partnerships, 28
Patrick Street, Cork, 102
Pavilion Cinema Theatre, Sligo, 14
pawnbroking, 148–9
Pawnbroking Act 1965, 116
Peamount Sanatorium, 15
Pembroke, 3
Pembroke Estate, the, 86
Pembroke Street, 166
Pepys, Samuel, 9
Peterson and Son, N., 4
petrol rationing, 59–60, 69–70
Phibsboro, 1
Phoenix Brewery, 14
Phoenix Park, 104, 120
    Distillery, 14
    Racecourse, 163
Pierce, D., 118
Pigeon House Power Station, 31
Planning Advisory Board, 67
Planning and Development Act 1963,
    103, 152
Player & Sons, John, 14
Plaza Ballroom and Restaurant, 14
Plunkett, E., 89, 91
Poland, 234
Portrane Mental Hospital, 15
Potterton, T.E., 52
poverty, 31, 37–8, 104
Power, R., 202
Power Corporation, 191, 202
Power Securities, 118, 142, 179
Powerscourt estate, 118
Powerscourt House, 142
Powerscourt Townhouse Centre, 179
President of Ireland, 124
Price Waterhouse, 180
Prices Acts, 126

Probate Office, 50
Probert & Franks, 72
Programmes for Economic
    Expansion, 97–8
property management industry, 146
property services industry (PSI),
economic analysis of, 223–8
Property Valuer, The, 171, 175, 177,
    186, 220, 227, 229
Protection of Auctioneers, Valuers,
    House & Estate Agents Bill, 21–2
Prussia Street, 15, 19
public houses, 81
publicity, 22
Publicity Club of Ireland, 24

Quarryvale, 202
Queen's Quay, Belfast, 206
Queen's Theatre, Dublin, 14
Queensland, 140

Radcliff Hall, 204
Raheny, 11, 76, 185
Raleigh Cycle Company, 13
Ranelagh, 76, 120, 230
rates, 43, 71, 167
Rathborne's Candle Factory, 15
Rathfarnham, 51, 80
Rathgar, 3, 96, 104, 162
Rathmines, 2, 51, 80, 96, 150, 166,
    168, 202, 216
rationing, wartime, 59–60, 69–70
Ravenhill Reach, Belfast, 206
Reading University, 150
Real Estate Studies Unit, University
    of Ulster, 205
Redcross, 81
registration, 153–4, 174–5, 218–9
rent restrictions, 26, 34, 70, 168
Rent Restriction Acts, 26, 43–4, 70–1
Rent Tribunal, the, 168
residential property tax (RPT), 152,
    170–1, 213
Restrictive Practices Commission,
    175

Re-Valuation Bill, 51
Reynolds, T., 159
Richmond Shopping Centre, Derry,
   207
Ringrose, D., 223
Ringsend, 14
Rinn Cinema, Ringsend, 14
Robertson, M., 40
Robinson, H., 118
Roman auctioneering, 10
Romania, 234
Roscrea, 60, 108
Rotary Club, 159
Rowan Hamilton, Col., 13
Royal City of Dublin Hospital, 15
Royal Dublin Society (RDS), 1, 20, 124
Royal Exchange Coffee Room, the, 11
Royal Hibernian Academy, the, 13
Royal Hibernian Hotel, 118
Royal Hospital, Kilmainham, 180
Royal Institute of Architects of
   Ireland (RIAI), 36
Royal Institution of Chartered
   Surveyors, 150, 153
Royal Liver Friendly Society, 34
Rural Housing Organisation (RHO),
   143–4
Russborough House, 196
Russia, 146, 234
Ryan, P., 123
Ryan, T., 195
Ryan's Tourist (Holdings), 99

Sadlier, J., 23
St. Stephen's Green, 13, 72, 86, 118,
   143, 162–3
      Shopping Centre, 202
St. Thomas's Church, 36
St. Vincent's Hospital, 162
Salix Trust, 102
Sandford Cinema, Dublin, 14
Sandycove, 40, 73, 76
Sandyford, 57, 142, 190, 198
Sandymount, 76, 204
Saorstát Éireann, 1, 21, 25, 36

Saratoga, 159
Savoy Cinema, Dublin, 14
Scales, D., 150, 173, 216
School of Professional Studies,
   Rathmines, 150
Schweppes, Ltd., 14
Scott & Co., R.W., 14
Scott, M., 40, 52, 61
Seanad Éireann (Irish Senate), 66, 84–5,
   156, 171
Seán Lemass House, 162
Second Co-operative Benefit
   Building Society, 34
Second Dublin Mutual Benefit
   Building Society, 34
Second Equitable Benefit Building
   Society, 34
Second Victoria Mutual Building
   Society, 34
Section 23 tax incentives, 162, 164,
   167, 171, 179, 190
Section 29 tax incentive, 164
Selfridge jnr., H., 36
Senate (*see* Seanad Éireann)
SEPLIS, (Secretariat for the Liberal
   Professions), 173
Shamrock Cycle factory, 13
Shannon Free Airport, 101, 144
Shannon, River, 31
Shaw, G.B., 80
Shelbourne Hotel, 7
Sherry, A.M., 89, 108, 155
Sherry FitzGerald, 142, 166–7, 190–1,
   198, 225
Shield Insurance Company, 89
shipping, 15
shopping centres, 102, 104, 144, 179,
   181, 191, 201–3, 206–8
Shrewsbury Road, 167, 195
Siemens-Schuckert, 31
Simon Community, 169
Single European Market, 193
Skibbereen, 116
Slane, 81
Slazenger Company, 163

Slovakia, 234
slums, 34, 38, 97
Smith & Son, Patrick, Navan, 8, 30
Smith, D., 118
Smith Griffin & Company, 117
Smith, W., 73
Smithfield, 12
Smurfit, M., 195
Smyth, B., 166
Society of Chartered Surveyors, 173,
   223, 226
sole agency, law on, 42
solicitors, role of, 19–20, 40, 67–8, 89–
   90, 109, 134, 188–9, 192
Solicitors Property Service (SPS), 188
South Quays, 197
Spain, 227
Sproule, S., 87
Square, The, Tallaght, 202
stamp duty, 71, 151–2, 172, 213–4
Stamshaw Ltd., 202
Stapleton, M., 211
Stephenson, D.F., 94–5, 109, 156
Stephenson, D., Jr., 156
Stephenson, M., 156
Stephenson, P., 141, 156, 175, 216
Stephenson, S., 143
Stephenson Gibney & Associates, 143
Stillorgan, 104
   Shopping Centre, 102, 107
Stormont Castle, 13
Straffan House, 118, 163
Strathmore Road, 195
Stynes, S., 190
Sunday viewing, 71–2, 83, 109
Supreme Court, the, 167
Sutton, 167
Swan Centre, 202
Sweepstakes site, Irish, 189
Swift, Dean J., 30
Switzer's, 66, 165

Taisce, An, 100
Tallaght, 104, 147, 190, 202
   Aerodrome, 14

Tallon, R., 143
Taoiseach, An, 82, 115–6, 124, 174
Tattersalls Ireland, 192
Technical Schools, Bolton Street, 65
TEGOVOFA (European Group of
   Valuers of Fixed Assets), 193
Telecom Éireann, 189
Telefís Éireann, 115
telephones, 39
Temple Bar, 179, 200
   Area Renewal and Development
      Act 1991, 200
   Properties, 200
Temple Hill, 40
tenements, 39–40
Terenure, 36, 51, 143, 167
theatres, 13–14
Thomas & Bryan, 155
Thomas Street, 11
Tiernan Homes, 196
Tipperary branch, 7
Tipperary Town, 234
Tivoli Theatre, the, 14
Tokyo, 107
Toole, T.F., 4
Torca Cottage, 80
Tóstal, An, 85
tourism, 39
towards the millennium, 223–34
town planning, 37, 38, 103
Town Planning Acts, 37, 51
Town Tenants Act 1906, 26
Townsend Street, 145
trade, international, 3, 35, 82, 119
Treacy, J., 169
Treasury Holdings/Jermyn
   Investments, 102
Trinity College (TCD), 66, 200
Trinity Group, 212, 217
Trinity Street, 15
Trocadero Centre, 192
Trump, D., 202
Tubbercurry, 162
Tuite, W., 225
Tuohy, B., 149

Twain, Mark, 231
Tynan, T., 118
Tyndall, Hogan & Hurley, 100

Ulster, 8
    committee, 149
Ulsterville Avenue, Belfast, 206

United Nations, 182
    Conference on Human
        Settlements, 204
    Economic and Social Council, 107
United States, 147, 155, 181, 202, 227,
    231
University Club, the, 14
University College Dublin, 36
University of Ulster, 168, 176, 205,
    219
urban renewal, 205–8
Urban Development Areas Bill 1982,
    170
Urban Development Renewal Act
    1986, 178–9

valuation, 18, 44–5
Valuation Office, the, 20
valuer, role of the, 18
Valuers' institution, 74
Varming, J., 61
Victoria Street, Belfast, 14
Viney, M., 97
Vocational Education Commission,
    50
Voluntary Health Insurance Board,
    88

wages, 36, 82, 124, 177
Wales, 180

Walker, G., 202
Walkinstown, 189
war and peace — the forties, 55–77
War, the Civil 2
War of Independence, the, 1
Warner, F., 4, 192
Washington, 181
Waterford, 3, 8, 73, 81, 101, 137, 147,
    167, 179, 198, 202, 205
Watling Street, 11
wealth tax, 146
Webb & Co., James H., 42
Weekly Realtor, The, 134
Weir, Miss A.,
Weston, G. and H., 165
Westmeath branch, 24
Westminster, Duke of, 202
Wexford, 59, 124, 150, 170
Whitaker, T.K., 97, 231
Wilkinson, W.H., 4
Williams & Woods, 145
Williams, C., 118
Williams & Co., H., 163
Wills, W.D. & H.O., 14
Willow Park Estate, 185
Wilton Place, 85
Windsor Terrace, 80
Winstanley, R., 119
Woodbine Estate, Raheny, 185
Woodford Estate, Stillorgan, 230
World War II, 2, 58, 79
World Wide Web, 217

yearbook, diary and calendar, 7–8,
    19, 24, 35, 64, 72, 75, 146
Yeats, J.B., 192, 204
Yom Kippur War, 125
Young Members' Association, 216